Closet Italians

*To Helen:
Hang in there dear!
[signature]*

Closet Italians

❖

*A Dazzling Collection of Illustrious Italians
with Non-Italian Names*

Nick J. Mileti

Library of Congress: 2004094843

ISBN: Hardcover   1-4134-6145-X
        Softcover   1-4134-6144-1

Copyright © 2004 by Nick J. Mileti.

All rights reserved. No part of this book may be reproduced or transmitted in any form or by any means, electronic or mechanical, including photocopying, recording, or by any information storage and retrieval system, without permission in writing from the copyright owner.

This book was printed in the United States of America.

For more information visit
www.closetitalians.com

Or contact
closetitalians@aol.com

To order additional copies of this book, contact:
Xlibris Corporation
1-888-795-4274
www.Xlibris.com
Orders@Xlibris.com

25307

Contents

PROLOGUE 23

Chapter I
ILLUSTRIOUS ITALIANS WITH NON-ITALIAN NAMES BORN PRIOR TO 1400

VITRUVIUS (90 B.C.-20 B.C.) Roman architect and engineer. Wrote the most important treatise on architecture and engineering in history. 36

VIRGIL (70 B.C.-19 B.C.) Greatest Roman poet. Famous for epic poem 'The Aeneid.' 38

    OVID (43 B.C.-18 A.D.) Most popular poet of his day. Famous for 'Metamorphoses,' the best-known classical source of over 250 myths 38

PLINY THE ELDER (23 A.D.-79 A.D.) Historian. Wrote first encyclopedia. 40

    PLINY THE YOUNGER (61 A.D.-113 A.D.) Famous for letter to Emperor describing his first encounter with Christians as governor, and for letters to historian regarding his uncle Pliny the Elder's death at eruption of Mount Vesuvius in 79 A.D. 40

PETER LOMBARD (1100-1160) Scholastic and theologian of Middle Ages. Major influence on Thomas Aquinas. 42

SAINT THOMAS AQUINAS (1225-1274) Principal Saint of Catholic Church. Writings form basis for philosophy of today's Church. 44

PETRARCH (1304-1374) Humanist and scholar. Father of Renaissance. 46

Chapter II
ILLUSTRIOUS ITALIANS WITH NON-ITALIAN NAMES BORN IN THE 1400'S

JOHN CABOT (1450-1498) Explorer. Discovered Newfoundland. 50

    SEBASTIAN CABOT (1476-1557) Mariner and mapmaker 51

ALDUS MANUTIUS (1450-1515) Greatest editor, printer and publisher of the Renaissance. Invented octavo-sized books. 52

CHRISTOPHER COLUMBUS (1451-1506) One of history's most important mariners. Completed four trips across the Atlantic in a ten-year period. 54

POLITIAN (1454-1494) Most outstanding poet and humanist of 15th Century. 56

HIERONYMUS ALEANDER (1480-1542) One of the most learned men of his time. Famous for drafting Bull of Excommunication of Martin Luther. 58

RAPHAEL (1483-1520) Third towering artist of High Renaissance along with Leonardo and Michelangelo. His work changed the direction of painting. 60

JULIUS CAESAR SCALIGER (1484-1558) Humanist. Wrote first systematic treatise on poetry. Nostradamus studied philosophy under him. 62

    JOSEPH JUSTUS SCALIGER (1540-1609) Founder of modern historical criticism. 63

TITIAN (1485-1576) Leading painter of 'Venetian School.' Initiated unique use of color and bold sweeping strokes that revolutionized painting. 64

Chapter III
ILLUSTRIOUS ITALIANS WITH NON-ITALIAN NAMES BORN IN THE 1500'S

JEROME CARDAN (1501-1576) Writings helped create modern algebra. Wrote first practical gambler's manual on laws of probability. Many inventions, including the universal joint, which is named in his honor. 68

BALTHAZAR BEAUJOYEULX (1502-1587) Inventor of modern ballet. 70

GABRIEL FALLOPIUS (1523-1562) Anatomist, physician and surgeon. Most famous for discovering the tubes leading from the ovary to the uterus, which are named in his honor. 72

HIERONYMUS FABRICIUS (1537-1619) Pupil of Fallopius. Founder of embryology. Discovered the valves in the veins. Teacher of Englishman William Harvey 74

MARQUIS (MARECHAL) D'ANCRE (1580-1617) Confidant of Maria de Medici. Despised by the French court. 76

L'ALBANE (1578-1660) One of the finest painters to come out of Carracci's Bologna School. Style called 'idyllic classicism'. 78

Chapter IV
ILLUSTRIOUS ITALIANS WITH NON-ITALIAN NAMES BORN IN THE 1600'S

JULES MAZARIN (1602-1661) Father of King Louis XIV and Prime Minister of France. Shaper of present day France, along with Richelieu and Louis XIV. 82

JEAN-BAPTISTE LULLY (1632-1687) Most important composer of what is called 'French' ballet and opera. 84

LE PROCOPE (1686) Located in Paris. The first literary coffee shop and the oldest continuously operating restaurant in the world. 86

Chapter V
ILLUSTRIOUS ITALIANS WITH NON-ITALIAN NAMES BORN IN THE 1700'S

ROGER JOSEPH BOSCOVICH (RUDJER BOSCOVIC) (1711-1787) Croatian mathematician and astronomer. Developed the first coherent description of atomic theory. 90

CAESAR RODNEY (1728-1784) Legend in Delaware history. Held largest number of public positions in history of the state. Made courageous dash to sign the Declaration of Independence. 92

NAPOLEON BONAPARTE (1769-1821)
Military genius. Emperor of France. 94

BONAPARTE FAMILY (Four brothers and
three sisters, from 1768-1860) Given royal titles and
positions by Napoleon 96

BARTHOLOMEW BERTHOLD (1780-1831) Prominent
fur trader. Forts, towns and colleges have been named in
his honor. 98

Chapter VI
ILLUSTRIOUS ITALIANS WITH NON-ITALIAN NAMES BORN IN THE 1800'S

COUNT JOSEPH TELFENER (1836-1898) Italian
nobleman and financier. Built railroads. 102

SIR ARTHUR SULLIVAN (1842-1900) Composer of
comic operas. Famous as the music-writing partner of
team known as 'Gilbert & Sullivan.' 104

CHARLES JOSEPH BONAPARTE (1851-1921)
Grandson of Napolean's youngest brother,
Jerome. Creator of F.B.I. 106

PIERRE PAUL FRANCOIS CAMILLE SAVORGNAN
(COUNT DE BRAZZA) (1852-1905) Only peaceful
explorer in Africa's history. Colonized Equatorial Africa
for the French. Brazzaville in the Congo Republic is
named in his honor. 108

ELEANORA DUSE (1858-1924) Most famous
stage actress of her time. Inventor of new, natural,
style of acting followed to this day 110

BUTTERCUP DICKERSON (1858-1920) First Italian-American to play in Major League Baseball. 112

PING BODIE (1887-1961) Excellent outfielder. Inspiration for future baseball stars including Joe DiMaggio. Bestowed nickname 'Bambino' on roommate Babe Ruth. 112

FEDERIGO ENRIQUES (1871-1946) Mathematician. Helped found the Italian school of algebraic geometry. Most famous for publishing a classification of algebraic surfaces. 114

ALFRED E. SMITH (1873-1944) Politician and statesman. Liberal Governor of New York for four terms. First Roman Catholic to run for President of the United States. 116

GEORGIA O' KEEFFE (1887-1986) Shaper of modern art in America. 118

GENEROSO POPE, SENIOR (1891-1950) Businessman and publisher. 120

GENE POPE (1927-1988) Founder of 'The National Enquirer,' the most influential tabloid in American history. 120

CHARLES ATLAS (1893-1972) Inventor of isometrics. Father of physical culture industry. 122

JOHNNY DUNDEE (1893-1965) Featherweight and junior-lightweight world boxing champion. 124

LOU AMBERS (Born 1913) Two time lightweight champion of the world. 124

WILLIE PEP (Born 1922) Lifetime record of
230 wins, 11 losses and one draw.
Two-time world featherweight champion. 125

LOU LITTLE (1893-1979) One of the greatest college
football coaches of all time. 126

HARRY WARREN (1893-1981) Most successful
composer of American popular music in history.
Famous for writing '42nd Street.' 128

WALTER PISTON (1894-1976) Renowned music educator
and classical 'American' music composer. 130

Chapter VII
ILLUSTRIOUS ITALIANS WITH NON-ITALIAN NAMES BORN BETWEEN 1900-1909

FRANCES WINWAR (1900-1985) One of the
greatest biographers in American history. 134

WALTER LANTZ (1900-1994)
Created cartoon character Woody Woodpecker. 136

GENE SARAZEN (1902-1999) One of the
greatest golfers of all time. Hit the most famous shot in
golfing history. 138

EDDIE LANG (1902-1933) Father of the jazz guitar. 140

JOHN SCARNE (1903-1985) Gambling expert and
author. Best-ever sleight-of-hand card performer. 142

GIORGIO CAVALLON (1904-1989) Painter.
One of America's first 'Abstract Impressionists.' 144

IRON EYES CODY (1904-1999) 'American Indian' actor.
Became celebrity from TV anti-litter campaign
of seventies. 146

EMILIO GINO SEGRE (1905-1989) Received Nobel Prize
for work in nuclear and high-energy physics. 148

TONY PASTOR (1907-1969) Band leader.
Discovered Rosemary Clooney. 150

JOHNNY DESMOND (Born in 1922) Pop singer. 151

GIULIO RACAH (1909-1965) Physicist.
Considered second only to Enrico Fermi. 152

DOLORES READE HOPE (Born in 1909)
Singer and philanthropist. Wife of
legendary comedian Bob Hope. 154

Chapter VIII
ILLUSTRIOUS ITALIANS WITH NON-ITALIAN NAMES BORN BETWEEN 1910-1919

FRANKIE LAINE (Born in 1913) Singer of pop, blues,
jazz and country. Best known for singing movie and
TV title songs, including 'Rawhide.' 158

ALFRED DRAKE (1914-1992)
Star of Broadway musical comedies. 160

ERNEST BORGNINE (Born in 1915) TV and
movie actor. Best known for TV show, McHale's Navy 162

R. S. LOUIGUY (1916-1991) Songwriter.
Wrote song 'La Vie En Rose.' 164

EDITH PIAF (1915-1963) Cabaret singer. 164

DEAN MARTIN (1917-1995) Singer and actor.
Star of stage, movies and TV. 166

JOSE GRECO (1918-2001) Greatest 'Spanish'
dancer of all time. 168

ROBERT STACK (1919-2003) Movie and TV actor.
Most famous for role as crime-fighter Eliot Ness. 170

HARRY CARAY (1919-1998)
Colorful Chicago baseball play-by-play announcer. 172

Chapter IX
ILLUSTRIOUS ITALIANS WITH NON-ITALIAN NAMES BORN BETWEEN 1920-1929

YVES MONTAND (1921-1991) Actor, singer and
political activist. 176

ANGELO DUNDEE (Born in 1921)
Greatest fight trainer of all time. 178

RAY ANTHONY (Born in 1922) Dance band leader.
Big Band activist 180

JOEY MAXIM (1922-2001) Light-heavyweight boxing
champion. Famous for defeating legendary
Sugar Ray Robinson. 182

VITTORIO GASSMAN (1922-2000)
International stage and screen actor. 184

EARL HAMNER (Born in 1923) Writer.
Most famous for creating TV show 'The Waltons.' 186

GUY WILLIAMS (1924-1989) Actor.
Played 'Zorro' on TV. 188

MARCELLA HAZEN (Born in 1924) Author of
Italian cookbooks. Helped make Italian food
popular all over the world. 190

FELICE BRYANT (1925-2003) Country and
pop songwriter (with husband). Famous for
University of Tennessee fight song. 192

TONY BENNETT (Born in 1926) Pop and jazz singer. 194

ED MC BAIN (Born in 1926) Fiction writer.
Most known for '87th Precinct' novels. 196

KAYE BALLARD (Born in 1926)
Cabaret singer, actor and comedienne. 198

HUGO PRATT (1927-1995) Illustrator and writer.
Most famous for comic book character 'Corto Maltese.' 200

CARDINAL JOSEPH LOUIS BERNARDIN (1928-1996)
First Italian-American Cardinal in the Catholic Church. 202

BRUCE KIRBY (Born in 1928) Character actor in
movies and on TV. 204

    BRUNO KIRBY (Born in 1949) Movie actor. 205

BILLY MARTIN (1928-1989) Major league
baseball player and manager. 206

VIC DAMONE (Born in 1928) Pop singer. 208

    BOBBY DARIN (1936-1973)
    Songwriter, actor and singer. 209

VINCE EDWARDS (1928-1996) Actor.
Famous as doctor 'Ben Casey' on TV. 210

JOE PASS (1929-1994) One of greatest jazz guitarists
of all time 212

PAT COOPER (Born in 1929) Comedian. 214

DON CORNELL (1919-2004) Pop singer. 215

Chapter X
ILLUSTRIOUS ITALIANS WITH NON-ITALIAN NAMES BORN BETWEEN 1930-1939

JERRY VALE (Born in 1930)
Pop singer specializing in Italian songs. 218

ERIK AMFITHEATROF (Born in 1931)
International journalist. 220

ANNE BANCROFT (Born in 1931)
Distinguished stage and screen actor. 222

GAY TALESE (Born 1932) Renowned
non-fiction writer. Creator of 'new journalism.' 224

CAROL LAWRENCE (Born in 1933)
Singer, dancer and actor. 226

REGIS PHILBIN (Born in 1933) TV personality. 228

SOPHIA LOREN (Born in 1934)
International movie star. 230

GARRY MARSHALL (Born in 1934) Producer, director, writer and actor. Most famous as creator of TV sitcoms 'Happy Days,' 'Laverne and Shirley,' and a dozen others. 232

FREDERIC TUTEN (Born in 1935)
Versatile writer and educator. 234

JOSEPH CERRELL (Born in 1935)
Political consultant and community leader. 236

RENATA TREITEL (Born in1935) Teacher and poet. Most famous as a translator. 238

NEIL LEON RUDENSTINE (Born in 1935) Educator. Twenty-sixth president of Harvard University. 240

JAMES DARREN (Born in 1936) Actor, singer, TV director. Known for roles in 'Gidget' movies. 242

    MARIA MULDAUR (Born in 1943) Versatile singer. Most famous for pop hit 'Midnight at the Oasis.' 243

RICHARD CELESTE (Born in 1937) Politician and Educator. Past Governor of Ohio, Head of Peace Corps and U. S. Ambassador to India. 244

MARLO THOMAS (Born in 1937) Actor and writer. Most famous for TV show 'That Girl.' 246

CONNIE STEVENS (Born in 1938)
Singer, movie star and businesswoman. 248

CONNIE FRANCIS (Born 1938) Pop singer.
Most famous in Europe. 250

    JONI JAMES (Born in 1930) Pop singer. 251

PATRICIA DE STACY HARRISON (Born in 1939)
Politician and activist for women in business.
First Italian-American to head the
Republican National Committee. 252

DION (Born in 1939) Versatile singer.
Most famous for 'doo-wop' hits. 254

    HENRY FIOL (Born in 1947)
    International salsero (Latin singer)......................... 254

ELEANOR SMEAL (Born in 1939) Feminist activist
and leader. 256

FRANKIE AVALON (Born in 1939) Actor and singer.
Most known for 'Beach' films.' 258

    BOBBY RYDELL (Born in 1942) Pop singer. 258

    FABIAN (Born in 1943) Pop singer. 258

Chapter XI
ILLUSTRIOUS ITALIANS WITH NON-ITALIAN NAMES BORN BETWEEN 1940-1949

PATRICK J. LEAHY (Born in 1940)
U.S. Senator from Vermont. 262

    MARY LANDRIEU (Born in 1955)
    U. S. Senator from Louisiana. 262

BILL PARCELLS (Born in 1941)
Professional football coach. 264

FEDERICO FAGGIN (Born in 1941)
One of the inventors of the first microprocessor. 266

DONNA LEON (Born in 1942)
International writer of crime novels. Famous for
'Commissario Guido Brunetti' series. 268

MICHAEL BENNETT (1943-1987) Broadway director and
choreographer. Most famous for conceiving,
choreographing and directing 'A Chorus Line.' 270

PENNY MARSHALL (Born in 1943) Actor and director.
Best known for role as Laverne DeFazio in sitcom
'Laverne and Shirley.' 272

    CINDY WILLIAMS (Born in 1947) Actor and
    producer. Shirley in 'Laverne and Shirley.' 273

MICHAEL CRISTOFER (Born in 1945) Actor, director and
writer. Wrote 'The Shadow Box' for Broadway. 274

MICKEY DOLENZ (Born in 1945) Actor, director and
'voice' of cartoon characters. Member of
'Beatles' copycat group 'The Monkees.' 276

DAVID CHASE (Born in 1945) Writer and producer.
Most famous for creating TV show 'The Sopranos.' 278

LIDIA BASTIANICH (Born in 1946)
Owner of 'Felidia' Italian restaurant in NYC. 280

    JOSEPH BASTIANICH (Born in 1968)
    Wine merchant and restaurant owner. 281

SUSAN SARANDON (Born in 1946)
Actor and social activist. 282

SONIA GANDHI (born in 1946)
Important and revered political figure in India 284

MARISA BERENSON (Born in 1947)
Fashion model and actor. 286

PETER CRISS (Born in 1947)
Rock and Roll star. Member of rock group 'Kiss.' 288

BERNADETTE PETERS (Born in 1948)
Singing and dancing Broadway star. 290

    PAULA PRENTISS (Born in 1939) Movie actor. 291

STEVEN TYLER (Born in 1948) Rock and Roll star.
Lead singer of rock group 'Aerosmith.' 292

    LIV TYLER (Born in 1977) Model and actor. 293

MIKE MARAN (Born in 1949) Writer, storyteller,
producer and director of live theatre. 294

BRUCE SPRINGSTEEN (Born in 1949)
One of the most famous Rock and
Roll stars in history. Known as 'The Boss.' 296

NICK TOSCHES (Born in 1949)
Journalist, biographer and novelist. 298

Chapter XII
ILLUSTRIOUS ITALIANS WITH NON-ITALIAN NAMES BORN BETWEEN 1950-1959

LOUIS J. FREEH (Born in 1950) Career in
law enforcement. Headed F.B.I. for eight years. 302

DINO MENEGHIN (Born in 1950) One of the
best international basketball players of all time. 304

FRANCO HARRIS (Born in 1950) One of the
greatest running backs in NFL history. 306

    TED HENDRICKS (Born in 1947)
    One of the best linebackers in NFL history. 307

STEVEN VAN ZANDT (Born in 1950)
Rock star, television star, radio personality and
freedom fighter. 308

ANJELICA HUSTON (Born in 1951)
Distinguished motion picture actor. 310

MORGAN BRITTANY (Born in 1951)
Actor. Famous as Pamela Ewing on 'Dallas.' 312

    KAYE STEVENS (Born in 1935)
    Cabaret singer and actor. Famous as
    Jeri Clayton in 'Days of our Lives.' 313

FRED GARDAPHÉ (Born in 1953)
Literary scholar. Most known for his service to
Italian-American writers and poets. 314

ANNA QUINDLEN (Born in 1953)
Journalist, novelist and active feminist. 316

LINDA STRACHAN (Born in 1953) Writer of
children's books. Activist for children's reading. 318

HULK HOGAN (Born in 1953)
Professional 'wrestling' star. 320

GIORGIO DUBOIN (Born in 1959)
One of the best bridge players in the world. 322

Chapter XIII
ILLUSTRIOUS ITALIANS WITH NON-ITALIAN NAMES BORN BETWEEN 1960 AND 1969

STEVE VAI (Born in 1960) Guitar playing rock star, songwriter, orchestrater and record producer. 326

DANA REEVE (Born in 1961)
Actor and singer. Wife of Christopher Reeve. 328

NICOLAS CAGE (Born in 1964) Movie star. 330

    TALIA SHIRE (Born in 1946)
    Actor and producer. 331

BROOKE SHIELDS (Born in 1965)
Model and actor. 332

VIN DIESEL (Born in 1967)
Actor. Known for playing 'action heroes.' 334

MATT LE BLANC (Born in 1967) TV actor. Known for role as Joey Tribbiani on TV sitcom 'Friends.' 336

JOELY FISHER (Born in 1967) Singer and actor. Known for role as Paige Clark on TV show 'Ellen.' 338

    TRICIA LEIGH FISHER (Born in 1968)
    Singer and actor. 339

MARY LOU RETTON (Born in 1968)
Champion Olimpic gymnast. 340

ASHLEY JUDD (Born in 1968)
Movie and TV actor. 342

Chapter XIV
ILLUSTRIOUS ITALIANS WITH NON-ITALIAN NAMES BORN BETWEEN 1970 AND 1979

LIZA HUBER (Born in 1975) Model and actor.
Cast of soap 'Passions.' 346

    LINDSAY KORMAN (Born in 1978)
    Singer and actor. Cast of 'Passions.' 346

    JESSE EDEN METCALFE (Born in 1978)
    Actor. Cast of 'Passions.' 346

Chapter XV
ILLUSTRIOUS ITALIANS WITH NON-ITALIAN NAMES BORN BETWEEN 1980 AND 1989

MYA (Born in 1980) R & B singer. 350

    FRANKIE MUNIZ (Born in 1985) Movie actor.
    Known for 'Agent Cody Banks' roles. 350

ALICIA KEYS (Born in 1981) Singing star who
combines classical and modern influences. 352

READING GROUP GUIDE 355

Prologue

In the course of researching the 17th Century for my book "BEYOND MICHELANGELO: The Deadly Rivalry between Francesco Borromini and GianLorenzo Bernini," I discovered a startling fact: A pivotal man in French history, whom everyone in the world thinks was French, was, in fact, Italian. What is even more amazing, due to the efforts of the French, the entire world has harbored this fantasy for over three hundred and fifty years.

—

One night at a fancy dinner party in Palm Beach, honoring an ex-ambassador to France, I thought I'd have some fun. I steered the conversation so that I could (casually) mention that the great Jules Mazarin was actually Italian and had been co-opted by the French.

CO-OPT: To take into a group (for a faction, movement or culture). To absorb, assimilate, take over, appropriate.

When my tablemates heard that the legendary 'French' statesman, Jules Mazarin, was Italian, they were incredulous. These were learned, cosmopolitan people, including a doctor, a college president, an attorney, and even a historian. They were all connected to France in some way—but not one of them knew that Jules Mazarin was Italian.

The shocked group finally quieted down and asked me to prove it.

I explained that I learned a great deal about Jules Mazarin during the years and years of research for my Bernini/Borromini book (including living in Rome for three years) and gave them a condensed biography:

"Giulio Mazzarini was born in Italy, of Italian parents. He was one of Bernini's best friends. Mazzarini initially went to France as nuncio (papal ambassador), and while in Paris, the legendary Cardinal Richelieu took him under his wing.

"When Richelieu died in 1642, Mazzarini replaced his mentor as Prime Minister and virtual ruler of France. In fact, Giulio Mazzarini is considered one of three people in all of history—along with Richelieu and King Louis XIV—who sculpted the structure of present day France.

"Giulio Mazzarini served France as Jules Mazarin. The reason Mazzarini changed his name was pure politics. The shrewd statesman knew the French—especially the notoriously xenophobic French court—would resent an Italian of less than noble birth running their country."

Silence.

Then, much to my surprise, everyone (even the wives) got indignant. They acted as if it was my fault that one of their country's most revered and famous statesmen of all time was Italian, not French.

My little fun idea had obviously hit a nerve. I decided not to tell the highly charged group that Jules Mazarin was also the father of King Louis XIV. I mean, how much can a person handle, in one night, in Palm Beach?

—

The explosive situation got me thinking. I concluded that since this issue stirred such emotion, it must be important. How many other famous people in history are Italian but have Non-Italian Names? I wondered.

The more I thought about the matter, the more intrigued I became so I decided to research the question.

—

In my research, I quickly found innumerable books extolling the many virtues and deeds of Italians (and Italian-Americans) over the centuries. But I could not find even one book dedicated to Illustrious Italians with Non-Italian Names. I knew I was on to something, and pressed on.

I uncovered numerous interesting matters—in

addition to the fact that the French are expert at the fine art of co-opting.

For example, I was surprised to discover that there were Italian individuals who changed their Italian names from Italian to . . . Italian (of course, with Italian Names they could not be included in this book). Here are just three from long ago:

Donato di Betto Bardi became Donatello, the sculptor;

Jacopo Robusti became Tintoretto, the painter; and

Andrea di Pietro della Gondola became Palladio, the architect.

Here are three examples from modern times:

Alphonso Giuseppe Giovanni Roberto D'Abruzzo became Robert Alda, the actor (note that he used the first two letters from his first name [Al] and the first two letters from his last name [da]). Alan Alda, the actor, is his son;

Alfred Arnold Cocozza became Mario Lanza, the singer; and

Rodolpho Rafaelo Pierre Filibert Guglielmi di Valentina d' Antonguolla became Rudolph Valentino, the heartthrob.

—

Besides finding Italians who changed their Italian name to a different Italian name, I found numerous

Closet Italians

Illustrious Italians with Italian Names whose accomplishments surprised me and may also surprise you (their Italian Names also preclude inclusion in this book).

Most people know that Marconi invented the radio, Giannini founded The Bank of America, Monteverdi invented the Opera and Joe Barbera created Yogi Bear and the Flintstones. Here are a few Illustrious Italians (and their accomplishments) that most people may not know:

The Anemometer (which measures the speed of wind) was invented by Leon Battista Alberti;

The Mercury Barometer was invented by Evangelista Torricelli;

The Effects of Electricity on Animal Nerves and Muscles was discovered by Luigi Galvani—hence the word 'galvanize';

Methane Gas was discovered and isolated by Count Alessandro Giuseppe Antonio Anastasio Volta, and, the Electrophorus (the basis of the electrical condensers still in use today) was also invented by Count Volta, as was the First Electric Battery (The Voltaic Pile). The unit of electromotive force that moves the electric current is now called the 'volt' in Count Volta's honor;

The Thermometer, the Rings of Saturn and the Four Major Moons of Jupiter were all discovered by Galileo;

Comparative Physiology was founded by Marcello Malpighi;

The Piano was invented by Bartolomeo Cristofori;

Violins were invented in Italy in the early 1500's (by an unknown party), and the Violin (as we know it today) was invented by Antonio Stradivari, the Guarneri and Amati families;

Ballet was invented by Bergonzio di Botta of Tortona;

The Telephone was invented by Antonio Meucci, sixteen years before Alexander Graham Bell made his fraudulent claim;

The modern Typewriter was invented by Pellegrini Turri;

The Blimpie chain was founded by Tony Conza, and the Subway chain was founded by Fred DeLuca;

Chef Boyardee was founded by Hector Boiardi; Chun King and Jeno's Pizza Rolls were founded by Jeno Paulucci; Conair was founded by Lee Rizzuto, and Planters Peanuts was founded by Amadeo Obici;

Bechamel Sauce was introduced to the French court by the chef's of Catherine de Medici. The French strongly dispute this and have co-opted the sauce;

And, happily . . .

The Ice Cream Cone was invented by Italo Marcioni.

In my research, I also uncovered a number of other fascinating Italians but, alas, they had Italian Names and could not be included in this book. Some of them are:

Sister Blandina (Rosa Maria Segale): She brought education to the Rockies and health care to New Mexico. Fearless, she faced down a lynch mob and once saved the life of a member of Billy the Kid's gang;

Bernard Castro: He invented the 'Castro Convertible,' the easy-open sofa bed. This Castro is not to be confused with Fidel Castro of Cuba;

Lorenzo Da Ponte: In Vienna, this multi-talented man was Mozart's librettist on 'The Marriage of Figero,' 'Don Giovanni' and 'Cossi fan tutti,' and in America, he was Columbia University's first professor of Italian language and literature;

Guido d'Arezzo: Over a thousand years ago, this Benedictine Monk invented the system of musical staff notation still in use today, and gave the world the musical syllables do, re me fa, so la (which he took from a hymn). The French also claim him;

Lawrence Ferlinghetti: His father changed his name from Charles Ferlinghetti to Charles Ferling in 1919, but in 1954 his son, Lawrence Ferling, changed his name back to Lawrence Ferlinghetti. A poet and publisher of renown, he is outspoken and a defender of human rights. He published beat poet Allen Ginsberg, and his City Lights Bookstore became the San Francisco hangout of the beat generation in the fifties and sixties;

Dario Fo: This actor/Director/Writer won the Nobel Prize for Literature in 1997 for "emulating the jesters of the Middle Ages in scourging authority and upholding the dignity of the downtrodden." Do not confuse this Fo with Orientals, who have similar names;

Filippo Mazzei: Who wouldn't love the man who originally wrote the words that his friend Thomas Jefferson famously paraphrased in the Declaration of Independence: "We hold these truths to be self-evident. That all men are created equal, that they are endowed by their Creator with certain inalienable Rights;"

Amedeo Modigliani: He was a Sephardic Jew who was born in Italy and painted in Paris. Not surprisingly, the French try to co-opt him;

Sir Moses Montefiore: He was also Jewish, born in Livorno, Italy and raised in London, England. He was one of the greatest philanthropists the world has ever known, and lived to be one hundred. The English have co-opted him (notice the title);

Maria Montessori: She was the first female physician in Italy. Working with poor children, she believed that intelligence was common but only uncommonly tapped in children. Her once revolutionary teaching methods are now accepted and followed worldwide;

William Paca: He was descended from the family that emigrated from Italy to America in 1640. He voted for the adoption of the Declaration of Independence and was one of Maryland's four signers on August 2, 1776;

Salvatore Quasimodo: A Sicilian poet who won the Nobel Prize for Literature in 1959—not to be confused with Victor Hugo's bell-ringer in 'The Hunchback of Notre-Dame," and

Charles Angelo Siringo: He was a real cowboy who chased Billy the Kid, worked for Pinkertons, infiltrated

Butch Cassidy's gang (working undercover), and wrote the first autobiography of a working cowboy.

—

Finally, I discovered Illustrious Individuals with Non-Italian Names who were born in Italy and therefore are technically Italian. I have not included them in the book, because I felt including them would not be honest since they do not have Italian blood flowing through their veins. Just five examples:

Archimedes: The father of calculus was born in Syracuse, Sicily, but Sicily had been Greek for some five hundred years when he was born there;

Florence Nightingale: She was born in Florence, Italy (hence the first name), but her parents were English, visiting Italy when she was born;

El Greco, whose real name is Domenikos Theotokopoulos: The painter was born on the island of Crete, when Crete was a Venetian possession. His parents, however, were Greek;

John Singer Sargent: Born in Florence in 1856, the painter lived and returned to Italy all of his life, but his parents were expatriate Americans; and

Giuseppe Valadier: The architect and urban planner who designed the Piazza del Popolo in Rome was born in Rome, but his parents were French.

—

When I started my research, I feared that I would end up with the world's thinnest volume. I was wrong. How did I find all of these Italians with Non-Italian Names?

Simple. The stars were there; it was merely a case of locating them in the vast universe.

A politician once said, "A billion here and a billion there, and pretty soon you're talking about real money." Well, a clue here and a clue there—and a lot of luck—and pretty soon a simple case of curiosity evolved into this eye-popping book of hundreds of Illustrious Individuals most people don't know are Italian.

Actually, I'm convinced that I will continue to discover additional surprises in the future. I'm also confident that most readers will personally know someone who should have been included in the book. To you, I apologize, and promise to consider any name forwarded to me for any revised edition.

To say that the three-year research process was exciting would be the understatement of the century. Imagine what a thrill it was to discover—to use only one example—that the quintessential 'French' song (La Vie En Rose) was written by an Italian, R. S. Louiguy (Luigi Gugliemi), and sung by the quintessential 'French' chanteuse Edith Piaf (Edith Giovanna Gassion, whose mother was Italian), who once had as a prodigy and lover the quintessential 'French' actor, Yves Montand (an Italian named Ivo Livi).

—

Needless to say, since beginning to research this book, I've given considerable thought to names, and why the individuals featured in this book have Non-Italian Names, even though they are Italian. There are a number of explanations, and I give you several:

Individuals, whose mother's are Italian, have their father's Non-Italian surname (for example, Bruce Springsteen);

Italian women married, and took their husband's surname (Dana Morosini became Dana Reeve/Mrs. Christopher Reeve);

Mistakes were made at Ellis Island (Lanza became Lantz);

Names were changed for show biz, or other career purposes (Anna Maria Italiano became Anne Bancroft);

Names were changed to avoid discrimination (Salvatore Guaragna became Harry Warren);

Hard to pronounce or long names were shortened (Francesca Vinciguerra became Frances Winwar);

Names were changed for social acceptance purposes (Giulio Bordone became Julius Caesar Scaligero [and then Scaliger]);

Individuals were known by their Latin names (Girolamo Fabrizio became Hieronymus Fabricius), and

Names were changed by co-opting countries, to suit their own agenda (Giovanni Caboto became John Cabot).

Nick J. Mileti

"**CLOSET ITALIANS:** *A Dazzling Collection of Illustrious Italians with Non-Italian Names*" has two basic goals.

Primarily, I want the book to be fun to read. Obviously, if its not interesting, and you're not entertained, you'll never finish it. (After reading the book, I think you'll agree that part of the fun is that it helps us understand the real meaning of the French expression 'corriger la fortuna'— which I have been informed means, more or less, 'to correct one's circumstances through denial of the past').

Equally important, I hope that you emerge with a deeper understanding of the contributions Italians have made to every aspect of civilization over the centuries. After all, as the brilliant writer, Erik Amfitheatrof (an Illustrious Italian with a Non-Italian Name) has said, "The aim of any social history is to instruct as well as entertain."

—

A final point. You will notice the book contains no entries of Emperors who ruled the Roman Empire over a period of some five hundred years—from about 23 B.C. to 476 A.D.—even though most of them were Italians with Non-Italian Names. I didn't include any of the fifty-plus Emperors because there are innumerable writings on those individuals. Besides, most of them were not very Illustrious.

NJM

CHAPTER I

Illustrious Italians With Non-Italian Names
Born Prior To 1400

Nick J. Mileti

VITRUVIUS

(Born c. 90 B.C; Died in 20 B.C.)
REAL ITALIAN NAME: MARCUS VITRUVIUS POLLIO

Vitruvius was a Roman architect and engineer who wrote—and thankfully left for the Western World—the single most important book in the history of architecture and engineering.

John Lienhard, of the University of Houston College of Engineering, colorfully described Vitruvius as the "chief engineer of the civilized world in the years just before Christ was born." Vitruvius served under Emperors Julius Caesar and Augustus, and under Octavius wrote the now famous 'De Architecture libri decem.' Considered the most comprehensive architectural book ever written, the 'Ten Books on Architecture' (its English title) is the only treatise on architecture and engineering to have survived from antiquity. The books talk mostly about buildings, but also deal with what are today called engineering disciplines: Design of roads, bridges and towns (civil engineering); pumps of all kinds, including machines used to heat water in public baths (chemical engineering); amplification in theaters (acoustics); and even building materials such as bricks, stone, timber, sand and lime (material science). Astronomy, timekeeping, medicine, sundials, water clocks, music, and even the arts are also discussed.

Written about 27 B.C. 'De Architecture' was read in manuscript form until 1486, when, after being rediscovered, it was first printed (in octavo size) by the great editor, printer and publisher Aldus Manutius. 'De

Architecture' fueled the revival of classicism because a good deal of the work looks back to classical Greece. Because the treatise was printed and was therefore readily available (and because of its classical Greek foundation) the treatise helped spur the Renaissance, and has been an inspiration and influence on architects to this day.

Vitruvius' theory of proportion has become the most studied section of his books. He wrote "In the human body, the natural center is the navel. If a man lies on his back with his hands and feet outstretched and a pair of compasses are centered on his navel, his fingers and toes will touch the circumference of the circle: In the same way, it is possible to fit the human figure into a square, since the height from the top of the head to the sole of the foot is the same as the width of the outstreached arms."

Leone Battista Alberti, the Renaissance architect and writer, used Vitruvius' ideas in his buildings and wrote that mathematical laws and proportions govern architecture. The idea spread like wildfire, but the most noteworthy disciples of Vitruvius were Bramante, Leonardo and Palladio. Obviously, the most famous illustration of these mathematical rules is Leonardo's drawing of what is known as the 'Vitruvian Man.' In the 17th Century, the great Baroque architecture Francesco Borromini took Vitruvius' and Alberti's principals of mathematics(as they relate to architecture) to their logical conclusions in his two classic Roman churches: petite 'San Carlino,' and his masterpiece 'Sant' Ivo.'

VIRGIL

(Born October 15, 70 B.C. near Mantua, Italy; Died 19 B.C.)
REAL ITALIAN NAME: PUBLIUS VERGILIUS MARO

Virgil (or Vergil) is the greatest Roman poet in history, and is most famous for his epic poem 'The Aeneid.'

Virgil lived through the civil wars that marked the violent end of the Roman Republic. During the reign of the Emperor Augustus, Virgil became a member of his court. In 31 B.C. Augustus defeated his ex-ally Mark Antony, and ordered his poet to write about the glory of his (Augustus's) Rome. For the rest of his life, from 30 to 19 B.C., when he died, Virgil worked on his epic 'The Aeneid,' which he never finished. Its literary models are Homer's epic poems 'Iliad' and 'Odyssey.'

Alfred Lord Tennyson called Virgil "wielder of the stateliest measure ever moulded by the lips of man."

OVID

(Born c. 43 B.C. in Sulmona, Italy; Died c. 18 A.D.)
REAL ITALIAN NAME: PUBLIUS OVIDIUS NASO

Ovid, Rome's most popular poet in his day, is important to the art, music and literature of western civilization.

Ovid was a sensual man who defied his parent's wishes and shunned his legal education and government positions. He turned to literature, and his talent was such that in his teens he was reading his works to audiences who appreciated his word play, internal narrative structure and gender play. Especially gender play. Ovid's poems fall into three categories: erotic poems in his early period (most popular at the time), mythological poems in his middle period (most lasting), and poems of exile in his later years (most melancholy and filled with despair).

Among the erotic poems, 'Ars Amatoria' (Art of Love) was a study of finding and enjoying love. It contained instructions on how to acquire and keep a lover, and, not surprisingly, became an instant best seller. Also, not surprisingly, it was censored. 'Metamorphoses,' in the mythological category, is Ovid's greatest and most well known work. It has been an inspiration for writers for two thousand years, and is the best-known classical source for over 250 myths. Chaucer and Shakespeare are but two examples of great writers who were influenced by Ovid. A serious ladies man, legend has it that in 8 A.D., Ovid was banished from Rome and exiled to Romania by the Emperor Augustus for compromising one of the Emperor's favorite female relatives.

Nick J. Mileti

PLINY THE ELDER

(Born 23 A.D. in Como, Italy;
Died in 79 A.D. in the shadow of Mt. Vesuvius)
REAL ITALIAN NAME: GAIUS PLINIUS SECUNDUS

Pliny the Elder was a Roman nobleman, scientist and historian who made detailed notes on almost everything he observed during his lifetime.

Today, scientists use the scientific, testing method, but 2,000 years ago, scientists used the direct observation method. This is why Pliny the Elder took so many detailed notes. He was the author of some 75 books, and left behind an additional 160 volumes of unpublished materials on scientific and antiquarian subjects.

Moreover, Pliny the Elder wrote a thirty-seven volume manuscript entitled 'Natural History.' The work is considered the world's first encyclopedia and is the most famous of Pliny the Elder's works. His plan in writing 'Natural History,' Pliny the Elder explained, was to "set forth in detail all the contents of the entire world." This sounds suspiciously like where Joe Gould got the inspiration for his now famous non-existent book. Pliny the Elder's book does exist, however, although it is quite fanciful.

PLINY THE YOUNGER

(Born in 61 A.D.; Died in 113 A.D.)
REAL ITALIAN NAME: GAIUS PLINIUS
CAECILIUS SECUNDUS

Pliny the Younger was Pliny the Elder's nephew. He

was a writer, administrator and confidant of Emperor Trajan, who appointed him to several important positions.

While a governor of Pontus/Bithynia from about 111 to 113 AD, Pliny the Younger encountered Christianity for the first time. Following his usual custom, the cautious administrator wrote the Emperor, asking him what to do. The letter and Emperor Trajan's reply are as intriguing as they are famous.

Pliny the Younger is most famous, however, for his eyewitness, detailed, and chilling account of the eruption of Italy's Mount Vesuvius, in 79 A.D (the eruption that buried the city of Pompeii). The reason he wrote his observations is a sad one. Pliny the Younger was eighteen years of age when the tragedy occurred, and he personally observed it. Tacitus, the most important historian of the time, asked Pliny the Younger to document his recollections of the eruption because, tragically, he observed his uncle, Pliny the Elder, die in the calamitous event.

Pliny the Younger's two celebrated letters to Tacitus put the reader right in the middle of one of the most well-known, and unusual, natural disasters in the history of man.

PETER LOMBARD

(Born c. 1100 in Novara, Italy;
Died c. 1160 in Paris, France)
REAL ITALIAN NAME: PETRI LOMBARDI

Peter Lombard, was the most important theologian of the Middle Ages. An early Scholastic, Lombard was (along with Albert the Great) the most important influence on Saint Thomas Aquinas, one of the greatest intellectual figures of the Middle Ages.

Lombard gained fame in his time as a teacher (he taught theology in the School of Notre Dame in Paris from 1136 to 1150—in 1144 he became canon) rising to the position of archbishop of Paris shortly before his death. It is as a writer, however, that Lombard is best remembered and how he made his mark on history.

As a writer, his major contribution was 'Sententiarum Libri Quatuor,' today usually called 'The Book of Sentences' or 'Sentences.' The theological handbook was a clever way for Lombard to teach. He posed questions, which he answered with quotes he had compiled from the assertions and arguments of ancient philosophers and earlier theologians—the fathers—and then wrote his own conclusions. The sentences are arranged into four books, which cover the gauntlet of religious subjects, including God and The Trinity, angels and demons, incarnation, and the virtues and redemption. It is on the subject of the Sacraments, however, that the writing had its greatest impact. The book redefined the Sacrament from being merely a symbol ('the sign of a sacred thing') to something that was a means of grace on its own right ('capable of conveying the grace for which it is the sign').

In addition, Lombard's writing crystallized the doctrine that seven Sacraments fulfilled the required conditions. These views were accepted as official dogma of the Catholic Church at the Council of Trent, which was convened in 1545 in reaction to Martin Luther's attack on the Church.

Almost immediately (relatively speaking) 'Sentences' became the principle theological textbook for the Middle Ages and was the subject of thousands of commentaries. The most important, and famous, of these commentaries was written by Thomas Aquinas one hundred years later. Called 'Scriptum Super Libros Sententiarum' ('Writings on the Book of Sentences'), it was Aquinas' first major work.

In fact, Peter Lombard's writings were so important, during the period Thomas Aquinas was held in captivity by his family, his sister smuggled three writings to him: The Holy Scriptures, Aristotle's 'Metaphysics' and 'Sentences' by Peter Lombard. When Thomas Aquinas was sent to Paris in 1252 to teach in the Dominican's school, his duties consisted primarily of explaining 'Sentences' to his students. Even more important, when Aquinas left Paris for Rome in 1259, after seven years of teaching Peter Lombard, not surprisingly Lombard's 'Sentences' furnished materials and the basic plan for his (Thomas Aquinas') monumental work, the 'Summa Theologica.'

The French have co-opted Petri Lombardi, calling him Pierre Lombard.

Nick J. Mileti

SAINT THOMAS AQUINAS

(Born c. 1225 in Roccasecca, Italy;
Died in 1274 at Fossanova, Italy)
REAL ITALIAN NAME: THOMAS D'AQUINO

Saint Thomas Aquinas, philosopher and theologian, is one of the principal Saints of the Catholic Church whose writings form the basis of the teachings of today's Catholic Church.

While still in his teens, after the death of his father, the Count of Aquino, Thomas stole away from his noble family and began the short journey to Rome to join the Dominican friars. The youth's mother, a Countess, shocked that her noble son would join a mendicant Order, had her other sons intercept Aquinas and return him to the family. He was imprisoned in the family castle for over a year, during which time every sort of de-programming imaginable was attempted—including prayers and sex—but to no avail. In 1245, the Countess—awed by the depth of her son's commitment to God—relented.

The Dominican's recognized Aquinas's extraordinary intellect and dispatched him to study with the scholar Albertus Magnus (Albert the Great). The seven-year association with Magnus in Germany and France shaped Aquinas's entire life. In 1250, Aquinas was ordained a priest. Shortly thereafter, he began to teach at the University of Paris, concentrating on explaining Peter Lombard's 'Sentences' to his students. He eventually received his doctorate in theology and became a professor of philosophy. In 1259, after teaching for seven years, Pope Alexander IV summoned Aquinas to Rome, where he remained for a decade as an advisor and lecturer to the papal court. While in the Eternal City, Aquinas began writing his greatest work, 'The Summa Theologica,' which is a comprehensive analysis of theology based on the teachings of Magnus and Lombard. In 1268, Aquinas returned to Paris and engaged in philosophical debates with several French theologians. Two years later, he wrote the compelling 'De Unitate Intellectus Contra Averroistas,' which cemented his position and was pivotal in the history of the Catholic Church. Actually, what Thomas Aquinas accomplished almost eight hundred years ago cannot be overstated: His greatest triumph was convincing the Church that Aristotelian philosophy could be reconciled with Christian theology. This was extremely significant because the Church's acceptance that there is no quarrel between reason and revelation led to an awakening of interest in Greek classics and science. This, in turn, laid the foundation in Italy for the most important movement in the history of mankind—the Renaissance. Pope John XXII canonized (made a saint) Thomas Aquinas in 1323. In 1567, Pope Pius V proclaimed Saint Thomas Aquinas a Doctor of the Church. Saint Thomas Aquinas's writings form the basis of today's official Catholic philosophy—he left the Church over eighty writings on philosophical and theological issues. Saint Thomas Aquinas has been co-opted by the French—figuratively and literally. Although he died near his birthplace in Italy, the remains of Aquinas were moved to the Basilica of Saint Sernin at Toulouse, France on the order of Pope Urban V (1362-1370) a Frenchman and one of the seven Popes who made Avignon, France, the seat of the Roman Catholic Church from 1305 to 1378.

Nick J. Mileti

PETRARCH

(Born in 1304 in Arezzo, Italy; Died in 1374)
REAL ITALIAN NAME: FRANCESCO PETRACCOLO
(OR PETRACCO)

Petrarch was a poet, the greatest scholar of his age and a major force in the development of the intellectual movement called the Renaissance.

He maintains that lofty distinction for two reasons. First of all, Petrarch was the first known philologist. Petrarch began the unprecedented movement to collect and re-evaluate the literature of ancient Rome and Greece. Throughout his life, Petrarch traveled throughout Italy—as well as to Germany, France, and Spain—searching for old Latin and Greek manuscripts. In the course of his research, Petrarch unearthed numerous priceless literary works of antiquity, including works of Cicero. Incidentally, these were some of the manuscripts the great printer Aldus Manutius published in book form over 100 years later.

Secondly, Petrarch was a major force in the development of the Renaissance because he possessed a spirited and analytical mind, which was always probing. These are traits that every scholar in the Renaissance would come to demonstrate.

Equally important, Petrarch was the founder of what we today call 'Humanism.' He believed that the Latin and Greek classics contained the wisdom of the ages, and therefore, by studying them, one could gain confidence in his own ability to make moral judgments and lead a full life, with dignity.

In his early twenties, Petrarch began writing sonnets (love poems), and the ones inspired by Laura became popular with the public. In fact, his 'Sonnets For Laura' is considered one of the greatest books of love poems of all time—yet, amazingly, there is a question as to whether Petrarch ever even met Laura.

Petrarch did not invent sonnets—the poetic form had been invented in the 13th Century in Sicily—but he was the first to make them popular. Sonnets returned the favor and made Petrarch famous. In 1341, at the young age of thirty-seven, he was crowned as a Poet Laureate in Rome. A good part of Petrarch's fame today is based on two compilations—the 'Trionfi' (allegorical and moral in nature), and the 'Canzoniere' (where the subject of love prevails). A prolific letter writer, Petrarch sometimes even wrote to famous dead figures. He wrote of poetry and literature, of life, of fame, and of every other human condition.

Petrarch was a close personal friend of another great writer, Giovanni Boccaccio, the author of 'Decameron,' who was also interested in humanistic studies and research.

To help understand Petrarch's importance in history, consider this: At various times over the centuries, scholars have averred that Petrarch eclipsed the legendary Dante.

CHAPTER II

Illustrious Italians With Non-Italian Names
Born In The 1400's

Nick J. Mileti

JOHN CABOT

(Born in 1450 in Genoa [or Gaeta], Italy; Died 1498)
REAL ITALIAN NAME: GIOVANNI CABOTO

John Cabot, merchant, navigator and seaman, laid the basis for the English colonization of America, and was one of a handful of adventurers whose discoveries changed the map of the world.

After reading the writings of Marco Polo, Cabot wanted to see the fabulous Chinese cities of the Far East described by Polo—plus, he wanted to engage in trade for their gold and spices. To finance his projected voyage of discovery, he tried his hometown of Venice first. When those efforts failed, he solicited various monarchs in Europe—including Portugal and Spain—who all turned him down.

Realizing that all of the discovery money on the continent was committed, Cabot tried a new tack. For 'political' reasons, John Cabot moved to England with his family in 1484. Eventually Cabot convinced Henry VII, King of England, to finance a trip of discovery. In return for the financing, whatever Cabot discovered would inure to the English King.

Like Magellan and Columbus, Cabot was a highly capable seaman who also thought the best route to the Orient's riches was west, not east. In 1496, Cabot sailed west with one ship, had a disagreement with the crew, ran into bad weather, and turned back. The next year, on May 2, 1497, he set sail from Bristol, England with eighteen men in a seventy-foot boat, and had considerably better luck. Five weeks after setting out, on June 24, sailing a shorter, more northerly route than Columbus, instead of finding the Northwest Passage to the Orient, Cabot discovered what he called 'new found land'—today's Newfoundland. Cabot was convinced he'd found an island off the coast of Asia and so reported to the King when he arrived back in Bristol on August 6, 1497. The entire trip (called his first voyage) took almost exactly three months. King Henry was impressed with Cabot's reports of his trip and his maps, (the first) of what was actually the North American coast, so the following year the King approved a second voyage (this time to look for what is today named Japan) and financed one ship. English merchants, anxious to exploit the Orient, financed four more ships for the voyage. In 1498, the five ships set sail, but unfortunately, John Cabot's second voyage of discovery ended in tragedy. One ship was spared—it returned for repairs early in the trip—but John Cabot's ship (and three others) disappeared without a trace.

SEBASTIAN CABOT

(Born 1476; Died 1557)

John Cabot's son, Sebastian, was also an accomplished mariner, but without his father's successes. Fortunately he had other talents: Sebastian achieved his own fame as a mapmaker.

Giovanni Caboto, and his son, Sebastian, have been co-opted by the English. Perhaps this is where the French learned the maneuver.

Nick J. Mileti

ALDUS MANUTIUS

(Born in 1450 at Bassiano, Italy; Died in 1515)
REAL ITALIAN NAME: ALDO MANUZIO

Aldus Manutius was the greatest editor, printer and publisher of the Renaissance, and perhaps of all time.

After studying Latin and Greek at the Universities of Rome and Ferrara respectively, Manutius developed a passion for the Classics. Following his studies, Manutius became a tutor to children of noble families. In the course of his teaching, he saw a need for books by classical authors, and in true entrepreneurial fashion, Manutius decided to leave teaching and try to fill the need. In 1490, Manutius acted. He quit teaching and moved to Venice, Italy, which was the center of the European printing industry. To fund his dream, Manutius borrowed money from a former pupil. He named his new enterprise the Aldine Press, and his concept was simple—he wanted to publish the best possible books at the lowest possible prices. In this case, 'best possible books' meant concentrating on the classical Greek and Latin scholars.

Manutius knew those works were not only needed in everyday life, they were critical tools for the humanists of the Renaissance. Not surprisingly, the Aldine Press was wildly successful from the onset. Between 1494 and 1515 (when Manutius died), the Aldine Press produced some 134 editions—a typical edition running between 1,000 and 2,000 copies. Included therein were 30 first printed editions of the most significant Greek authors. The works of Homer, Plato, Sophocles, Demosthenes and Euripides are a few of the notable Greeks he published. Manutius also printed most of Aristotle's works. Latin authors published include Cicero,

Pliny, Virgil and Horace. Although he emphasized Greek and Latin scholars, Mautius also published others, including the Italian scholar Petrach and the Dutch scholar, Erasmus. His efforts insured the future of a considerable number of rare manuscripts. Aldus Manutius was responsible for many innovations in printing—for example, he invented the style of type known today as Italics. The octavo-sized book, however, is undoubtedly Manutius' most significant innovation. Ralph Stanton of Simon Fraser University described its importance as follows, "Guttenberg's invention of the typographical book in about 1450 created a product which was designed to be used in an institutional setting, mainly in churches and monasteries. Aldus completed the transformation of the book into an object for personal use. The change to personal computers from mainframes is the post-modern equivalent of that earlier transformation."

Actually, the Renaissance—that period of unparalleled cultural achievement and recovery of values that occurred in Italy and replaced the Dark Ages—should be labeled the 'Rinascita,' which means 'rebirth' in Italian. The French, however, affixed their own label (Renaissance) to the movement, and, for unknown reasons, the French word has stuck. Egregious French co-opting is successful once again.

Nick J. Mileti

CHRISTOPHER COLUMBUS

(Born 1451 in Genoa, Italy; Died in 1506)
REAL ITALIAN NAME: CRISTOFORO COLOMBO

Christopher Columbus is one of the most well-know people in history because most people believe he discovered America. While this is what children in the United States are taught in school, it is not true. In fact, Columbus never reached the American mainland.

America was discovered by a different Italian. His name was Giovanni Da Verrazzano.

Sailing under the French flag, in March 1524, Verrazzano landed at Cape Fear in North Carolina. He continued northward, exploring America's eastern seaboard, discovering, among other places, New York Bay, Block Island and Narragansett Bay. Interesting note: Giovanni Da Verrazzano entered New York Bay eighty-five years before Henry Hudson, the man generally credited with the discovery.

Columbus spent his childhood in Genoa, Italy, and as a young man, lived on the sea, as did most young men who lived in Genoa at the time. All of the talk of the time was that land lay beyond Madeira and the Azores, and could be discovered by sailing west from Europe into the Atlantic Ocean. Not surprisingly, Columbus became interested in westward voyages and began studying maps and books. He accepted Marco Polo's assumptions (many of which were erroneous) and dreamt of finding a shortcut to India to exploit the spice trade. Columbus first sought support from the Italians, but was rebuffed. Next he promoted John II, King of Portugal, for an exploratory trip but was turned down. Apparently the King feared that existing ships did not have the range to reach the Orient.

In 1485, a determined Columbus moved to Spain looking for money to support his dream. After seven years of badgering, he convinced Queen Isabella of Spain—King Ferdinand II went along with the Queen's wishes—to finance his voyage.

In 1492, after a journey of over two months, Columbus landed at what he called Guanahani (San Salvador), Hispaniola (Haiti and the Dominican Republic), Cuba and many smaller islands. He thought he'd reached islands off the coast of Asia and named the natives 'Indians'. Columbus made three more trips across the Atlantic Ocean between 1493 and 1502, landing in, among other places, Trinidad, Venezuela (including the mouth of the Orinoco River), Mexico, Honduras, Panama and Jamaica.

To this day, Christopher Columbus, like Napoleon, is an extremely controversial historical figure. Most of the moral indignation centers on Columbus's treatment of the natives on the lands he discovered. Whatever the truth of that accusation, there can be no dispute that Christopher Columbus was a courageous adventurer and one of the greatest mariners of all time, completing four successful voyages across the Atlantic in a period of ten years, from 1492 to 1502.

Nick J. Mileti

POLITIAN

(Born July 14, 1454 at Montepulciano, Italy;
Died Sept. 28. 1494 in Florence, Italy)
REAL ITALIAN NAME: ANGIOLO DE'AMBROGINI
DA MONTE PULCIANO OR ANGELO POLIZIANO

Politian is considered the outstanding poet and humanist of the 15th Century.

A precocious youth, in 1464, when he was only ten years old, Politian was sent to Florence where he studied Latin, Greek and philosophy. While still a teen—to the amazement and joy of the nobles and scholars of Florence and Tuscany—he wrote, translated, and published numerous Latin and Greek works.

In his early twenties, Politian's extraordinary talent was recognized by Lorenzo de' Medici (Lorenzo the Magnificent), who was the power, and chief patron of the arts in Florence at the time. Medici took Politian into his household, where he became Lorenzo's companion. Politian's first assignment for his patron was to tutor his eldest son, Piero (age three).

From 1480, at the tender age of twenty-six, Politian taught Greek and Latin literature at the University of Florence. Within a short time, because of his extraordinary intellectual and literary abilities, Politian was attracting students and scholars from all over Europe.

Following the lead of Petrarch, who began the movement over 100 years earlier, Politian was a philologist—he also made a large part of his life's work the recovery of the best Greek and Latin manuscripts.

Politian worked closely with his contemporary, the great Renaissance publisher based in Venice, Aldus Manutius (the Aldine Press), to insure publication of these and other works.

Politian was also a prolific author and writer throughout his lifetime. On the scholarly front, he wrote many literary works and translations of Greek texts. For example, he translated much of 'The Iliad' from Greek into Latin, and, in 1489, wrote the 'Miscellanea,' which laid the groundwork for future scholarly studies in philology.

His Latin and Italian verses were unusual and precedent setting—he wrote and defended vernacular poetry. His two most famous works are 'Stanze per la Giostra' written in 1478, and the verse-play 'Orfeo,' written around 1480, which was one of the earliest plays written in Italian rather than Latin. Both masterpieces are inspired by Politian's love of beauty, and both reveal his poetic genius.

A true Renaissance man—in the present usage of the term—his range of interests and talents included history, architecture, botany and jurisprudence. For this reason, Politian's writings and ideas had substantial influence on the leading Florentines of his time, including Leonardo, Botticelli, Michelangelo, Ghirlandaio and Machiavelli.

Nick J. Mileti

HIERONYMUS ALEANDER

(Born in Motta di Treviso, Italy February 13, 1480;
Died in Rome, February 1, 1542)
REAL ITALIAN NAME: GIROLAMO ALEANDRO

Humanist Aleander was considered one of the most learned men of his time. Today, he is most known for drafting and obtaining the Bull of Excommunication of Martin Luther at the Diet (Conference) of Worms in 1521 that outlawed Luther and his followers.

A zealot, Aleander advocated extreme measures to repress Luther's doctrines, thereby incurring the wrath of his friend Erasmus and other moderate thinkers who wanted the Church to reform.

Aleander's more positive and significant religious accomplishment was drafting the outline for the Catholic Church's policy to fight Luther's claims. Aleander's ideas were incorporated into the directives of the Council of Trent, now known as the Counter Reformation.

As a youth, Aleander studied at the University of Padua and then went to Venice where he met and befriended the great Renaissance book publisher, Aldus Manutius, and the distinguished Dutch humanist and theologian, Erasmus. Both men had an enormous impact on Aleander's life. Manutius exposed Aleander to the classics (especially Greek), and Erasmus gave Aleander a philosophical outlook on life. Consequently, Aleander became one of the most respected teachers and scholars of classical languages, lecturing in Venice and other nearby towns.

Closet Italians

Called to France at the invitation of King Louis II as professor of belles lettres, Aleander introduced Greek studies to Paris. The most popular teacher at the university, Aleander's lectures often attracted a thousand or more students. He also taught Latin and Hebrew at the university and became rector. Ill health forced Aleander to retire from these strenuous positions.

In 1519, Aleander went to Rome where Pope Leo X appointed him librarian of the Vatican. His health improved, so the following year Aleander accepted the papal appointment as papal nuncio (ambassador). In that capacity, he represented the Pope, at the coronation in Germany of Charles V as Holy Roman Emperor, and at the infamous Diet of Worms. In 1536, Pope Paul III made Aleander a Cardinal.

Aleander must be distinguished from his grandnephew, who is known by his Italian name Girolamo Aleandro. 'Aleandro the Younger' lived from 1574 to 1629 and was also a distinguished scholar and writer.

Girolamo Aleandro has been co-opted by the Dutch.

Nick J. Mileti

RAPHAEL

(Born April 6, 1483 in Urbino, Italy;
Died April 6, 1520 in Rome)
REAL ITALIAN NAME: RAFFAELLO SANZIO

Raphael was the third towering artist of the High Renaissance, along with Leonardo da Vinci and Michelangelo.

What Leonardo achieved by the force of his intellect, and Michelangelo achieved by the force of his passion, Raphael achieved by the force of persistent study. Moreover, Raphael was like a sponge. With ordinary mortals, this talent would merely produce a good copyist. In Raphael's case, however, after absorbing new techniques and ideas, he had the extraordinary capacity to grow by what was taught to him.

For example, his father taught him to paint when he was old enough to hold a brush, and Raphael quickly surpassed him. Then, when his father sent him to study under the master artist Pietro Perugino, the precocious Raphael quickly absorbed the master's style. Art experts and historians have confused the works of the two artists over the years—they have repeatedly called early Raphael paintings Perugino paintings.

In 1504, when Raphael was twenty-one years old, he went to Florence, one of the cultural centers of Italy at that time. In that artistically charged city, Raphael met Leonardo and Michelangelo, among others. His work immediately reflected the influence of the two artistic giants—particularly Leonardo. Raphael's paintings became less gentle, and more forceful and energetic.

In 1509, Pope Julius II summoned Raphael to Rome. An accomplished architect—as were many artists in the Renaissance and Baroque periods—Raphael was commissioned to redesign Saint Peter's basilica for the ambitious Pope. In addition to his architectural work on Saint Peter's, Raphael painted several murals in the Vatican. Today, the Raphael stanze (rooms), particularly 'The School of Athens,' which immortalizes the classical philosophers, are almost as famous as Michelangelo's Sistine Chapel.

A modest, kind, and well-mannered gentleman, Raphael was a serious 'ladies man,' whose conquests produced awe. Giorgio Vasari, writing at the time, said he "pursued his amorous pleasures beyond all moderation," and claimed that this caused Raphael's untimely death (probably indicating syphilis).

Leonardo (1452-1519) died at sixty-seven, and Michelangelo (1475-1564) lived eighty-nine years—obviously, longevity, combined with massive talent, contributed to their ability to influence other artists. When one considers the fact that Raphael died when he was only thirty-seven years old, his influence on artists over the ages borders on the unbelievable. Raphael's work changed the direction of painting well into the Baroque, and is still admired for its clarity of form, harmonious rhythm and coloring. Raphael is buried among royalty in the Pantheon in Rome.

Nick J. Mileti

JULIUS CAESAR SCALIGER

(Born in 1484 in Riga, Italy; Died 1558 in Agen, France)
REAL ITALIAN NAME: GIULIO BORDONE

Julius Caesar Scaliger was a writer, humanist, philosopher and physician.

As a youth, the ambitious Bordone claimed he was descended from the noble della Scala family of Verona. Consequently, as he later bragged, "(I) settled myself into the names of this family." He had changed his name to Scaligeri &/or Scaligero—which the French later changed to Scaliger. Incidentally, today, some five hundred years later, no one believes Bordone's claim that he was related to the della Scala clan.

In his youth, Scaliger served in the military, studied art under Dürer, and became a doctor. In 1526, at the age of 42, Scaliger went to France as physician to the Bishop of Agen. After turning to humanism, he wrote learned works on philosophy, grammar, botany and zoology. Nostradamus journeyed to Agen and, along with other scholars, studied under Scaliger. In 1561, Scaliger wrote the first attempt at a systematic treatise on poetry, which was a key text in Renaissance literary theory. In his time, the philosopher Julius Caesar Scaliger was considered the equal of, or second to, Erasmus. Scaliger's fame is much less than that of Erasmus, however, for an unusual reason. His personality. Julius Caesar Scaliger was vain, arrogant, and contentious, or colorful and controversial, depending on your point of view. One thing is certain: When Scaliger defended Cicero's style and claimed Erasmus was a mere parasite, the great man made many enemies.

Closet Italians

JOSEPH JUSTUS SCALIGER

(Born Aug. 5, 1540 in Agen, France;
Died Jan. 21, 1609 in Holland)

Joseph Justus Scaliger, son of Julius Caesar Scaliger, was a scholar and humanist, but is mostly known for his groundbreaking work in chronology (the science that deals with measuring time by regular divisions and that assigns to events their proper dates) and epigraphy (the deciphering of ancient inscriptions).

Young Scaliger became the founder of modern historical criticism by establishing a chronological foundation for the modern study of ancient history. In 1583, young Scaliger surveyed all the ways then known of measuring time and placed the study of ancient calendars and dates on a scientific basis. Like his father, Joseph Justus Scaliger was also a great humanist—he was learned in philosophy, mathematics and languages.

In the words of George W. Robinson, "Whether Joseph Scaliger should be reckoned the greatest scholar of all time, or share that palm with Aristotle, is, perhaps, an open question. Of his primacy among scholars of modern times there can be no doubt." The French have co-opted father and son.

Nick J. Mileti

TITIAN

(Born c.1485 in Pieve di Cadore, Italy;
Died c. 1576 in Venice)
REAL ITALIAN NAME: TIZIANO VECELLIO

Titian, like Raphael, is one of the key figures in western art. He was the leading painter of what is known today as 'The Venetian School,' and he initiated the unique use of color that has become a Venetian tradition over the centuries.

Titian received his most important early training in the studio of Giovanni Bellini, who had a profound effect on him. Titian's earliest work is also highly influenced by his subsequent teacher, the artist Giorgione. When Giorgione died prematurely in 1510, Titian completed a number of his unfinished paintings, causing confusion about attribution that exists to this day. In 1516, Bellini died and Titian became official painter to the Republic of Venice. In other words, Titian was now recognized as the Number One painter in the Republic. This vote of confidence seemed to inspire a brilliant period in Titian's career. He produced numerous masterpieces, vivid with colors, deep and intense, but always harmonious.

From roughly 1530 to 1550, during what are called his middle years, Titian turned to portraiture and revolutionized the art. Breaking precedent, Titian observed his famous and powerful sitters with amused detachment and objectivity. This allowed the master to penetrate the façade and portray the real character—the inner man or woman—of his subjects.

A perfect example of this distinctive ability is Titian's remarkable painting of Pope Paul III (Farnese). The painting is considered the greatest portrait ever painted—rivaled only by Velazquez's painting of Innocent X (Pamphili) executed some hundred years later. Studying the two portraits, Titian's influence on Velazquez is obvious. Both stunning portraits present viewers an almost eerie journey into the inner lives of the two extremely complex men of intrigue.

In another break from tradition, Titian often added stylistic elements to the backgrounds of his portraits—such as a column or a curtain—which replaced neutral backgrounds of previous artists. Items such as these have become a staple of formal portraiture. In 1545, Titian traveled to Rome for his first and only visit. While in the papal city he met Michelangelo and studied his 'modern' works—including the ceiling of the Sistine Chapel and 'The Last Supper'—which had a profound effect on him. Titian was also greatly impressed and influenced by Raphael's rooms in the Vatican. In the later years of his long life, Titian took the style of Michelangelo and Raphael several steps further by adding startling color to bold, sweeping strokes. When he added these newer traits to the unprecedented movement that always characterized his works, its easy to see how Titian revolutionized painting of the late Renaissance, and permanently affected future artists, from the Carracci, through the Baroque, to the Impressionists, and even to today's 'modern' school.

CHAPTER III

Illustrious Italians With Non-Italian Names
Born In The 1500's

Nick J. Mileti

JEROME CARDAN

(Born September 24, 1501 in Pavia, Italy;
Died September 21, 1576 in Rome)
REAL ITALIAN NAME: GEROLAMO CARDANO

Jerome Cardan was an extremely complex and highly controversial man whose life fluctuated wildly. He was a mathematical genius (who helped create modern algebra), a physician of great renown, an inventor, a prolific author, a scholar and a professional gambler (who wrote the first book on how to beat the odds in dice and cards). Oh yes, he was also a renowned astrologer who believed in the occult.

Cardan's mother was a peasant. His father was a mathematician and lawyer who inspired Cardan to strive for greatness. Cardan studied at the Universities of Pavia and Padua, receiving a Doctorate in Medicine in 1525. Teaching and writing followed. Because of his contentious personality, Cardan moved from position to position. Between assignments, Cardan gambled to put food on the table. He became expert at chess, dice and card games. Inspired by his intense interest in games of chance, Cardan wrote the first study on the theory of probability—'Liber de ludo aleae'—which was not published until more than one hundred years later in a collection of his works published in 1663. The short treatise, which calculated odds for gambling, is considered the first practical gambler's manual. In 1545, Cardan wrote 'Ars Magna' (Great Art), his greatest mathematical work, and one of the cornerstones of the science of algebra. Cardan's manuscript included his invention of the algebraic formula for finding square roots. In fact, his treatise was the first publication of the idea of a complex number. The scholarly Cardan also wrote the first clinical description of Typhoid Fever, made the discovery that links electricity to magnetism (by determining that white amber attracts light objects, while a magnetic black rock [a loadstone] attracts only iron), and invented the universal joint (today called the 'Cardan Driveshaft').

Alongside his many accomplishments, the complex Cardan fervently believed in the occult. Cardan practiced the art of astrology and physiognomy—he would predict a person's future by the wrinkles and lines on his face. He also believed in palmistry, and even predicted the date of his own death (legend says he committed suicide on September 21, 1576, in order to fulfill his morbid prophesy). Always anxious to promote himself, in one of history's earliest—and boldest—promotional stunts, in 1570, Jerome Cardan cast the horoscope of Jesus Christ. To no one's surprise but Cardan's, this act led to his arrest by the Inquisition. After a short period of unpleasant incarceration, Cardan moved to Rome, was forgiven by Pope Pius V, granted a pension, and wrote what is considered the first modern psychological autobiography, 'De Vita propria liber.'

Like his contemporary Julius Caesar Scaliger, Jerome Cardan was a difficult man—aggressive, tactless, uncompromising and supremely confident in his views. Not surprisingly, these two giants of the Renaissance were, to put it kindly, not friends.

Nick J. Mileti

BALTHAZAR BEAUJOYEULX

(Born c. 1502 in Savoy, Italy; Died in 1587)
REAL ITALIAN NAME: BALTAZARINI DI BELGIOIOSO

Balthazar is considered the inventor of the modern ballet, as we know it today. He was the first to combine poetry, scenery, costumes, dance, singing and music into one cohesive whole.

An accomplished musician—he was considered the best violinist in the world (read Europe, the only place it mattered)—Balthazar went from Italy to France in his fifties. He immediately became a prodigy of Catherine de Medici, who clung to, and loved all things Italian. Balthazar became her valet de chamber, and undoubtedly, her lover. He also served under several other monarchs.

In any case, in 1573, for Catherine de Medici, Balthazar choreographed the ballet 'Balet des Polonais,' to celebrate the arrival of the Polish ambassador in Paris.

While this was successful, it was in 1581/82 that Balthazar became world-famous. He staged and choreographed 'Le Balet Comique de la Reine,' again for Catherine de Medici.

Balthazar served as stage manager, choreographer and inventor of the ballet's plot. For the first time, dances were woven into the plot, instead of standing alone, like peaches ripe to be picked. Using geometric formations for dances, Balthazar integrated the dances as a part of the action, and designed the dances so that they provided continuity between the verse, the singing, and the music.

The ballet, which lasted over five hours, told the story of the ancient Greek myth of Circe, who had the magical power to turn men into beasts. In this 'ballet de cour,' Balthazar cleverly glorified the absolute monarchy of France, which remained in place until the revolution. Balthazar—presaging the librettos supplied to opera fans in America—shrewdly supplied copies of the verses to the audience, so they would understand his story.

This ballet, 'Le Balet Comique de la Reine,' was important to France for two reasons: First, it established Paris as the ballet capital of the world (it was imitated in most every other court in Europe), and secondly, it single-handedly displayed the splendor of late Renaissance culture in France.

Baltazarini di Belgiosioso was, not surprisingly, co-opted by the French.

Nick J. Mileti

GABRIEL FALLOPIUS

(Born in 1523 in Modena, Italy;
Died Oct. 9, 1562 in Padua, Italy)
REAL ITALIAN NAME: GABRIELLO FALLOPIO

Gabriel Fallopius, esteemed anatomist, was also a physician and surgeon. He is most famous for discovering the tubes leading from the ovary to the uterus. The tubes were subsequently named 'Fallopian Tubes' in his honor.

Fallopius studied medicine at the University of Ferrara, one of the best medical schools in Europe at the time. Fallopius also studied at Padua—another of the world's most famous centers for medical training—under the renowned Andreas Vesalius (Vesalius helped establish surgery as a separate medical profession and also proved many existing medical theories wrong). Ironically, in subsequent years, Fallopius accurately corrected much of his teacher Vesalius's work, to the consternation of many conservative medical men of the time. To discredit Fallopius, the critics claimed he was jealous of the great Vesalius.

After traveling in Europe, Fallopius became a professor of anatomy at Ferrara. In 1549, he was named professor of anatomy at the University of Pisa, Italy's best University. Three years later, in 1551, Cosmo I, Grand Duke of Tuscany, lured Fallopius back to the University of Padua. He was granted the prestigious chair, Professor of Anatomy and Surgery. Fallopius was also appointed Professor of Botany and Superintendent of the botanical gardens.

Fallopius studied the human skeletal system, especially the anatomy of the head. He was the first to give an accurate description of the inner ear, the lachrymal passages to the eye, and the ethmoid bone and its cells in the nose. Fallopius also discovered the little canal that the facial nerve passes through after leaving the auditory—it is named for him. A relentless researcher, Fallopius also studied the human reproductive system. He named the vagina and placenta, and was the first to describe the clitoris. His description of the canal, which leads from the ovary to the uterus, is named the 'Fallopian Tube' in his honor.

Fallopius also invented what was later named the condom. His earliest version was a sheath of linen, which he medicated. It was designed to fit over the tip of the penis and under the foreskin. The purpose of the device was to prevent disease, but since it was thick and killed all sensation, it quickly fell out of favor.

Try as he might, Fallopius was unable to find valves in the veins of the body. That discovery was left for his pupil, Hieronymus Fabricius, the revered anatomist and embryologist, who became famous for being the teacher of William Harvey.

'Opera genuinaomnia,' Gabriel Fallopius's collected works, was published in Venice in 1584, twenty-two years after his death. In it, Fallopius described tumors under 38 headings and pronounced cancer incurable.

Nick J. Mileti

HIERONYMUS FABRICIUS

(Born in 1537 in Aquapendente, Italy;
Died May 21, 1619 in Padua, Italy)
REAL ITALIAN NAME: GIROLAMO FABRIZIO

In addition to being the foremost anatomist of the day, Hieronymus Fabricius is considered the founder of embryology.

Hieronymus was the favorite pupil of Gabriel Fallopius at the University of Padua, and was his assistant in anatomy. When Fallopius died in 1562 at the age of thirty-nine, Hieronymus was named his successor as Professor of Anatomy, in spite of his tender age of twenty-five. Three years later, he was also named Professor of Surgery. Hieronymus remained at the University of Padua for the remainder of his career, and held both posts until he retired some fifty years later.

Among his many accomplishments, Hieronymus Fabricius achieved one of the goals that had eluded his teacher. Hieronymus discovered the valves in the veins of the human body. In 1579 he publicly demonstrated the valves, and in 1603, he published—with detailed illustrations—the first accurate description of them. Hieronymus was a prolific writer, and his publications were widely read. They helped him build an international reputation that attracted pupils from all over Europe. In fact, when William Harvey learned of the valve discoveries, he went from England to Padua to study under Hieronymus, graduating with honors in 1602.

Harvey eventually uncovered a major problem. His teacher had misinterpreted the purpose of the valves in the veins (Hieronymus maintained that the valves acted to retard the flow of blood as it comes *from* the heart, thus preventing the blood from being distributed too rapidly throughout the body). Harvey eventually determined the correct purpose of the valves in the veins, which is that they control the flow of blood one-way, *toward* the heart. This discovery led Harvey to develop an accurate theory of how the heart and circulatory system operate. Incidentally, Harvey was always quick to acknowledge how much Hieronymus's discovery of the valves in the veins meant for his own discovery of the circulation of the blood.

Fabricus' treatise in 1600, 'On the Formation of the Fetus,' was the first work of its kind. In it, he compared the late fetal stages of different animals. Hieronymus also studied the anatomy of the larynx and the eye. He was the first to give a full description of the larynx, the first to describe the location of the lens in the eye, and the first to demonstrate that the pupil in the eye changes size.

After Hieronymus Fabricius died in 1619, a statue was erected in Padua to honor him. The Senate of Venice also recognized his many incredible contributions to mankind by giving him a generous pension and several important titles.

Nick J. Mileti

MARQUIS (MARECHAL) D'ANCRE

(Born c. 1580 in Florence, Italy;
Died April 24, 1617 in Paris, France)
REAL ITALIAN NAME: CONCINO CONCINI

This Italian (and his Italian wife, Leonora Dori Galligai) thoroughly dominated the French government from 1610 to 1617, the first seven years of young King Louis XIII's reign.

Galligai was a childhood friend of Maria de Medici, and she went with the entourage when Maria went from Italy to France to marry Henry IV in 1600. Also in the entourage was an adventurer named Concino Concini, whom Galligai married the next year. The couple led a relatively quiet life in France, enjoying all of the privileges of their relationship with the Queen, influencing her as subtly as they knew how—not subtly enough, however, because King Henry IV threatened to banish them from the court several times (but did not because he didn't want to upset his wife).

A drastic change occurred when Maria's husband, King Henry IV, was assassinated in 1610. Maria de Medici became Regent (because her son, Louis XIII was only nine years old), and she replaced her husband's chief advisor, the duc de Sully, with Concino Concini.

Concini and his wife treated the King and his court with contempt, concentrating all of their efforts and schemes on the Queen, who appeared intoxicated with her long-time friend and her husband. To the French court, it seemed like the Italian Queen bowed to the Italian's every wish, which was more or less true. The

French nobility suspected that Concini instituted an elaborate spy system and raided the treasury, which was also more or less true. It's not that these actions were unusual, the problem was that a foreigner was guilty of them. Bottom line, the Italian couple's biggest problem was that the French nobility resented their power.

The nobility bided their time. Their chance came in 1613, when Maria appointed Concini Marquis d'Ancre and Marechal (Marshall) of France (the country's highest honor, even though d'Ancre had never seen combat). The nobles made their move and rebelled. D'Ancre repulsed the attempted coup and the couple continued to influence the Queen.

Their victory was short-lived, however. In 1617, Louis XIII, now sixteen years old, decided he was ready to assert his authority. The young King knew that to be an effective ruler he had to neutralize the Queen, d'Ancre and Galligai. No problem. He exiled his mother to Chateau Blois, and ordered the assassination of her chief advisor and his wife.

On April 24, 1617, the Royal Guards shot d'Ancre outside the palace and a xenophobic mob chopped up his body. Less than three months later, d'Ancre's wife, Leonora Dori Galligai, was beheaded and burned.

Nick J. Mileti

L'ALBANE

(Born in 1578 in Bologna, Italy; Died in 1660 in Bologna)
REAL ITALIAN NAME: FRANCESCO ALBANI

Art experts call l'Albane's painting style 'idyllic classicism.' He is considered one of the finest painters, along with Guido Reni and Domenichino, to come out of the Bologna School, and his style was copied—especially by French artists—for over one hundred years.

Studying and working in Bologna under master teacher and painter, Annibale Carracci, one of the precursors of the Baroque, l'Albane perfected Carracci's new classicism into a distinctive style of his own. When Carracci moved to Rome in 1601, l'Albane followed Carracci and became his principal assistant. While in Rome, l'Albane perfected his technique.

In 1635, the Frenchman, the Comte de Carrouges, commissioned l'Albane to paint a sereies of mythological subjects—and the floodgates opened. L'Albane's paintings were eagerly sought-after in France, and all of the major French collectors of the time, including Mazarin, featured his works in their collections.

In 1658, l'Albane was hailed in France as "one of the four evangelists of modern painting." His best works are landscapes, where people are depicted in harmony with nature—soft, atmospheric renderings in a delicate style, later developed by Claude Lorrain.

Since the French co-opted him, it's not surprising that King Louis XIV himself owned thirty-one l'Albane paintings, and even today, the Louvre, and other French museums, hold over thirty important l'Albane's.

In the year 2000, the official catalogue for an exhibit of l'Albane's paintings in the Louvre museum in Paris stated:

"The translation into French of the surname of a seventeenth-century Italian artist is always a sign of great favour and the work of l'Albane did not escape this rule."

Without a doubt, that statement is the absolute most clever justification for French co-opting Italians anyone will ever see.

Ever.

CHAPTER IV

Illustrious Italians With Non-Italian Names
Born In The 1600's

Nick J. Mileti

JULES MAZARIN

(Born July 14, 1602 in Piscina, Italy; Died March 9, 1661)
REAL ITALIAN NAME: GIULIO MAZZARINI

Jules Mazarin is one of the most important men in the history of France. As Prime Minister, he pursued an 'absolutist' policy, which strengthened the crown, and paved the way for the epochal reign of King Louis XIV (The Sun King).

In Italy, his native country, the ambitious, talented Mazarin rose from officer in the Pope's Guard to papal ambassador to France. In France, he became Assistant to Cardinal Richelieu, the Prime Minister of France. In 1641, Mazarin was named a Cardinal in the Catholic Church, and became Prime Minister of France when Richelieu died in 1642. Mazarin was a handsome, soft-spoken man whose gentle manner belied his cunning. These traits allowed Mazarin's personal accomplishments to rival his historically important professional accomplishments. Consider: Mazarin is the real father of Louis XIV (which means that the most important King in French history is half-Italian). Here's how this extraordinary fact came about.

Anne of Austria (daughter of the King of Spain) was the wife of King Louis XIII of France. This was an arranged marriage in 1615, when they were both fourteen years old. The marriage was never consummated.

Queen Anne was totally frustrated with her husband. He liked boys and so did she—so they lived apart throughout their marriage. The King flirted with his preferences, and the Queen flirted with an Englishman, the Duke of Buckingham.

The ensuing scandal was taken advantage of by Mazarin, who comforted the vulnerable Queen Anne and became her lover.

Jules Mazarin and Queen Anne had two children during their affair. The first, born in 1638, was named Louis. This child became Louis XIV, King of France.

Following the death of her husband (King Louis XIII) in 1643, Anne became Queen Regent because her son Louis was only four years old. With the King out of the way, Mazarin and Queen Anne were then secretly married.

Over the centuries, the official French explanation of Louis' birth range from the sublime ("The Queen's pregnancy was widely considered miraculous"), to the ridiculous ("While hunting in December of 1637 and caught in a storm, the King found shelter in his wife's residence. Here they slept together [for the first time] and exactly nine months later, Louis was born.").

As pointed out in the prologue, the French have co-opted Giulio Mazzarini.

Nick J. Mileti

JEAN-BAPTISTE LULLY

(Born in 1632 in Florence, Italy;
Died March 22, 1687 in Paris)
REAL ITALIAN NAME: GIOVANNI BATTISTA
LULLI

The Italian Giovanni Battista Lulli became Jean-Baptiste Lully, the most important composer of 'French' ballets and operas in the Baroque period (1600 to 1750). Lully's music produced a radical change in the style of dance—he replaced traditional slow movements with lively ballets and rapid rhythms—which greatly influenced western music down to the present day.

The fourteen-year old Lully went to France in 1646, to tutor Mlle de Montpensier in Italian. Fortunately, the position in her court allowed the young prodigy to greatly expand his musical knowledge. Seven years later, in 1653, a key event occurred in Lully's life. What happened was, he danced in the same ballet—'Ballet de la nuit'—as the fourteen-year old King Louis XIV. (This is the ballet, by the way, that gained Louis XIV the nickname 'Sun King' because he danced the role of the same name). From this date forward, a life-long association with King Louis XIV began for Lully.

In order to achieve higher and higher positions and powers in the notoriously xenophobic French court, in December 1661, following the lead of his fellow Italian, patron, and friend, Cardinal Jules Mazarin (who had died earlier in the year), the ambitious Lully became a naturalized French citizen and Gallicized his name. Lully's tactic worked, because shortly thereafter, he was appointed Master of Music to the royal family, responsible for all music in the court. Over the years, Lully was appointed to numerous key positions in the court. A dedicated and tireless artist, Lully wrote thirty 'French' ballets between 1658 and 1671. Lully incorporated dances in his ballets—two examples are today called the minuet and the gavotte. In fact, today's music for dance and ballet is mostly derived directly from Lully. Lully wrote thirteen 'French' operas between 1673 and 1687. His style of opera grew out of his popular ballets. He carried over such items as the overture, and because of the King's fondness for dance, Lully put a substantial amount of ballet music in his operas. He also introduced the principle that operas, as well as ballets, should have substantial orchestral presence. His ballet/opera 'Persee' is considered his crowning achievement. Lully also, for the first time—Praise God—had women perform women's parts, instead of using males in wigs and masks. Lully also wrote incidental music for many of his friend Moliere's plays.

It is only fitting that an Italian, should have this critical role in the development of ballet—after all, another Italian, Bergonzio di Botta, staged the first ballet ever; in Italy, in 1448. Moreover, the word ballet comes from the Italian word 'ballare' (to dance). For almost 350 years, the musical genius, Giovanni Battista Lulli, has been co-opted by the French.

Nick J. Mileti

LE PROCOPE

ESTABLISHED IN 1686 BY FRANCESCO PROCOPIO DEI COLTELLI

Le Procope is a 300 + year old 'French' bistro/restaurant/café located in Paris.

Francesco Procopio moved from Palermo, Sicily to Paris, France in 1686 and immediately looked for a café like the ones he patronized at home.

Francesco combed the city, and was appalled by what he saw. He found what we would today call taverns. They were unattractive places with low ceilings that resembled stables rather than places to eat and drink. Not only that, the taverns all had earthen floors. Worse, there wasn't a cafe (coffee-shop) to be found anywhere in Paris.

Inspired by the attractive establishments he'd left behind in Italy, Francesco went to work. In the Latin Quarter he found a storefront building that resembled an apartment rather than a barracks. He tiled the floor with tiles imported from Italy. He hung paintings on the walls and chandeliers on the ceilings.

Francesco created something unique—there was no other establishment like it in Paris, or France for that matter. He decided to name his establishment after himself. He called it Procopio.

The French didn't know what to make of Procopio. Even though the food and beverages were excellent, business was slow in the beginning. But Francesco didn't travel all the way to Paris to fail. Fortunately, he not only had taste, he was resourceful. To attract thinking men, he made the city's only newspaper available for his clientele—free. To attract writers, he made paper, pens and ink available—also free.

Francesco's ideas worked. Procopio became a meeting place for intellectuals and creative people, and the very first literary coffee shop was born. For over three hundred years, everyone of any stature—and, of course, a few wannabees—in the arts, letters and politics has frequented Le Procope, including Voltaire, Balzac, Victor Hugo, Anatole France, Diderot and even Benjamin Franklin and Napoleon.

The French Revolution was hatched at Le Procope—Robespierre, Danton and Marat gathered in the café to plot and write while they ate and drank. Today, the restaurant, with its original décor, still attracts local politicians, but added to the mix are curious tourists who want great French food and authentic 'French' atmosphere.

At some point, the French co-opted Procopio and christened it 'Le Procope.'

Francesco Procopio would no doubt choke on his morning cappuccino if he knew the French changed the name of his cafe, which is acknowledged to be the oldest continuously operating restaurant in the world.

CHAPTER V

Illustrious Italians With Non-Italian Names Born In The 1700's

Nick J. Mileti

ROGER JOSEPH BOSCOVICH
(RUDJER BOSCOVIC)

(Born May 18, 1711 in Dubrovnik [then Ragusa];
Died February 13, 1787 in Milan)

Roger Boscovich, a mathematician, physicist, and astronomer was a precursor of modern scientific thought—developing the first coherent description of atomic theory. He is equally famous for persuading Pope Benedict XIV to remove Copernicus from the Index of Forbidden Books in 1758.

Boscovich's father was Croatian and his mother, Paula Bettera, was Italian, of a noble family. The polymath traveled extensively in his long and notable career, but spent most of his time in Italy—once stating he considered Italy his "only real sweet mother."

At the age of fifteen, Boscovich joined the Jesuits and went to Rome to complete his novitiate at Bernini's magnificent Sant' Andrea al Quirinale. Following his 'graduation,' the still youthful Boscovich studied physics and mathematics at the Collegium Romanum. In unprecedented recognition of his brilliant mind, Boscovich was appointed professor of mathematics at the prestigious Jesuit college at the tender age of twenty-nine, where he taught for twenty years. Living when the Jesuits were under fire (and eventually suppressed), Boscovich, like Galileo before him, was a highly controversial scientific genius because, unlike most of the other scientists and scholars of the day, Boscovich preferred direct observation and measurements to abstract theories. In fact, his practical approach allowed him to correct numerous mistakes in the astronomy writings of the time; Pope Benedict XIV commissioned him to correct the maps of the Papal States. A student of Isaac Newton's 'new, natural philosophy,' Boscovich promoted international cooperation in large-scale earth measurements (allowing for the earth's curvature, the exact positions of the points on its surface, and the description of the variations of its gravity field). He also gave the world the first geometric procedure for determining the equator of a rotating planet from three observations of a surface feature, and for computing the orbit of a planet from three observations of its position.

A prolific writer, Boscovich wrote more then 150 books, treatises and dissertations. His most famous work, 'Theory of Natural philosophy derived to the single law of forces, which exist in nature,' contains his atomic theory and his theory of forces. It was originally published in 1758 in Vienna, and was subsequently published in Venice (1763), London (1922), the United States (1966) and Zagreb (1974). In it, the brilliant scholar writes that the ultimate elements of matter are indivisible points (later called atoms) which are centers of force, and this force varies in proportion to distance. He wrote this over one hundred years before the birth of the present atomic theory.

Roger Boscovich was made a Fellow of the Royal Society of London and was a member of the Russian Academy of Sciences. Today, the Institute of Theoretical Physics in Zagreb is named in his honor, as is the Astronomical Society of Belgrade. The 'Boscovich Archives' exist in the Rare Books library of the University of California at Berkeley, his face appears on a series of Croatian monetary notes and stamps, and even a crater on the moon is named in his honor.

Nick J. Mileti

CAESAR RODNEY

(Born October 7, 1728 in Kent County, Delaware; Died June 26, 1784)

Caesar Rodney was a soldier, Judge, Governor, and patriot, but is most well-known for his courageous dash to sign the Declaration Of Independence.

"Caesar Rodney's lineage shows both English and Italian heritage." So begins the Official State of Delaware biography of Caesar Rodney, entitled "Delaware's Hero for all Times." The biography goes on to say: "Caesar Rodney rides through history as not only Delaware's Hero but a Hero of America and its War of Independence. He held more public offices than any other Delawarean before or since. He was a soldier, judge, a delegate to the American Continental Congress, speaker of Delaware's Assembly, President (Governor) of Delaware, a justice of the state's Supreme Court, and held many other local offices."

Of those many, prestigious offices, speaker of Delaware's Assembly was, perhaps, most interesting. Here's why. In 1769, as speaker, Caesar Rodney tried to have a law passed prohibiting the importation of slaves into Delaware. Even though the effort was unsuccessful, the effort gives a major insight into the morals of this principled gentleman. Rodney was also speaker when Delaware declared its independence from England on June 15, 1776. Rodney's position as a Delaware delegate to the Continental Congress was even more significant, because, when the official history mentions "riding through history," here's what they are talking about. The

English had made serious mistakes in their relations with their American colony, and in the early summer of 1776, the Continental Congress was meeting in Philadelphia to contemplate declaring its independence from the British Crown. Two of Delaware's delegates split their vote—Thomas McKean voted for independence and George Read voted against it—creating a tie in Delaware's vote. This would not normally be important, but the Continental Congress wanted a unanimous vote before declaring America's independence from the Crown. Knowing Rodney's feelings about the delicate matter, on July 1, 1776, McKean summoned Caesar—who had returned to Kent County to put down a Loyalist uprising—urging him to return to Philadelphia immediately to cast his vote. McKean's urgent message made it clear that the entire question of Independence From England rode on his (Rodney's) shoulders.

The eighty mile ride took the ill statesman all night and most of the next day. Rodney rode, through a violent thunderstorm and torrential rain, on muddy roads, crossing fifteen streams by ford, bridge, or ferry, and finally arrived at the State House in Philadelphia covered in mud. He was so exhausted, two men had to carry him into the chamber—still in his boots and spurs—just in time to give (in Rodney's modest words) "My Voice in the matter of Independence."

In 1999, the first state quarter, minted by the United States in honor of Delaware's history, depicts Caesar Rodney's dazzling ride to vote for freedom.

Nick J. Mileti

NAPOLEON BONAPARTE

(Born August 15, 1769 in Corsica;
Died 1821 on Saint Helena)
REAL ITALIAN NAME: NAPOLEONE BUONAPARTE

One of the most well known and colorful figures in all of history, Napoleon was a brilliant military man and reformer who was crowned Emperor of France.

Like many others before and after him—Napoleon down played his favored birth and created the myth of humble beginnings in order to make himself look better. In fact, Napoleon's parents were both Italian and nobility—not wealthy, but nobility nevertheless. His mother and father were descended from an Italian family that had emigrated from Tuscany to Corsica in the 16th Century, when it was still ruled by the Italian Republic of Genoa. The island was sold to the French shortly before Napoleon's birth in 1769, which is the basis for the French claim that Napoleon was French.

Napoleon's father, Carlo-Maria Buonaparte, married Laetizia Ramolino in 1764. Carlo was a student at Pisa, but quit college to support his growing family (which eventually numbered eight surviving children). Napoleon attended a school for nobles and then moved on to cadet school in Paris. The French military would never be the same.

Napoleon was a twenty-year-old Lieutenant when the French Revolution broke out in 1789, and rose quickly through the ranks of the military. By 1793, he was appointed Brigadier General, at which point he was still using his Real Italian Name—which is spelled with a 'U'— Buonaparte. In 1796, following the example of one of his idols, Jules Mazarin, Napoleon changed his name from Buonaparte (pronounced Boo-oh-nah-par-tay) to Bonaparte (Bone-a-part). Consequently, in 1804, in France it was not generally known that an Italian was crowned Emperor of France.

The French had co-opted Napoleon.

A military genius, who thought big and had an ego to match, Napoleon's numerous victories and defeats are well known and extremely well documented in literature and motion pictures. What is less known are Napoleon's other accomplishments and legacies, which are significant. For example, his legal and administrative reforms—particularly the Civic Code of 1804 [usually called the Napoleonic Code and still used in Louisiana], and his tax system which removed the allowances for wealth and nobility—installed real equality in the French government and were eventually copied in various forms all over Europe.

Napoleon was ignominiously exiled not once but twice—first to Elba, an island off of Italy, after a resounding military defeat in 1814, and then, in 1815, to Saint Helena, an island in the Atlantic, after yet another bitter defeat (this time at Waterloo) while trying to make a comeback. Napoleon's incredible success and absolute power lasted less than twenty years, but this fascinating Italian's imprint on history will last forever.

Nick J. Mileti

BONAPARTE FAMILY: BROTHERS AND SISTERS OF NAPOLEON BONAPARTE

REAL ITALIAN NAME: BUONAPARTE

When Napoleon Bonaparte became Emperor of France and controlled a substantial portion of Europe, like most nice Italian boys, he remained close to his family. He not only didn't forget his four brothers and three sisters, he became their protector and took very good care of them. He granted them titles and arranged marriages for what he considered their (and his) advantage. In fact, Napoleon even gave his mother a title—Madame Mere.

Like Napoleon, all of his brothers and sisters were born in Ajaccio, Corsica, of Italian parents—so naturally they were all Italians with Non-Italian names. Here's the list:

JOSEPH BONAPARTE (Born in 1768; Died 1844 in Florence): Was made King of Naples, then King of Spain. Spanish rebels forced him to abdicate in 1813, following which he moved to America where he lived for over twenty-five years;

LUCIEN BONAPARTE (Born in 1775; Died 1840 in Rome): A passionate republican, he was made Prince of Canino by Pope Pius VII;

ELISA BONAPARTE (Born in 1777; Died 1820 in Trieste): Admired for her intelligence, she was made Princess of Lucca and Piombino, and then Grand Duchess of Tuscany;

LOUIS BONAPARTE (Born in 1778; Died 1846 in Livorno): Was made King of Holland;

PAULINE BONAPARTE (Born in 1780; Died 1825 in Florence): The prettiest and most loyal of Napoleon's siblings, she was made Princess of Guastalla. She married into the noble Borghese family;

CAROLINE BONAPARTE (Born in 1782; Died 1839 in Trieste): The most ambitious of the sisters, she was made Grand Duchess of Cleves and Berg. She married Joachim Murat, who Napoleon made a general and then King of Naples, making Caroline Queen of Naples;

JEROME BONAPARTE (Born in 1784; Died 1860 near Paris): Lived for a time in America where he married Elizabeth Patterson. The marriage was annulled and he was made King of Westphalia.

In his short-lived, but incredibly significant dynastic period, Napoleon also took care of his in-laws and made his son, born Napoleon Francois-Joseph Charles in 1811—called Napoleon II—King of Rome.

Nick J. Mileti

BARTHOLOMEW BERTHOLD

(Born December 31, 1780 in Italy;
Died April 20, 1831 in St. Louis MO)
REAL ITALIAN NAME: BERTHELEMI ANTOINE
MATHIAS BERTOLLA DE MOCENIGO

Bartholomew Berthold was one of the most prominent and successful fur traders in history.

At seventeen years of age, in 1798, Berthold immigrated to America from Italy to represent his brother, who manufactured glass beads in Venice. At that time, the white men (most of whom were French) were using beads, and other trinkets, to trade for furs with the Indians. It was at this time that he changed his name. In 1809, Berthold moved to Saint Louis where he formed a partnership with his wife's brother Pierre Chouteau, Jr. The pair initially opened a store, which sold dry goods, hardware, groceries and (of course) glass beads. Berthold was soon one of the fledgling city's most successful and distinguished citizens. In 1813, Berthold was one of the founders of the Bank of Saint Louis, and in 1817, the Bank of Missouri.

In 1834, lightning struck. Probably in reaction to the disastrous smallpox epidemic of 1832, America's richest man, John Jacob Astor, decided to retire from the fur business. Berthold joined three others and purchased the western department of Astor's American Fur Company. In 1846, the partnership acquired the fur trading post on the Missouri River named Fort James and changed the name to Fort Berthold, in honor of its most renowned partner. Several years later, business was booming, and a second post was built nearby, and was also named for Bartholomew Berthold.

The owners and suppliers of the upper Missouri trade received their furs from two sources: Mountain men and Indians. The colorful mountain men were a hardy breed. They rendezvoused in the city once a year to deliver their pelts. Not surprisingly, they then spent the money (and then some) on the usual suspects—wine, women and song. Actually, the trappers always seemed to be in debt to the company owners, including Berthold, who became wealthy and lived the good life in Saint Louis, where there is a Berthold Avenue.

As for the Indians—there were three Indian tribes in this area that brought their buffalo skins to the fur trading posts; the Mandan, the Hidatsa and the Arikara, now known as the Three Affiliated Tribes. In 1851, the Treaty of Fort Laramie with the Federal Government granted the three tribes over twelve million acres in west central North Dakota. Today, the Reservation consists of less than 450,000 acres and is known as the 'Fort Berthold Reservation.' It is the home of the Three Affiliated Tribes. In 1900, when the nearest railway point forty miles away from Fort Berthold began turning into a village, it was named Berthold (North Dakota) in honor of Bartholomew Berthold. In 1973, Fort Berthold Community College was founded—it is responsible for the higher education of the Fort Berthold Reservation tribes.

CHAPTER VI

Illustrious Italians With Non-Italian Names
Born In The 1800's

Nick J. Mileti

COUNT JOSEPH TELFENER

(Born in 1836 in Naples, Italy;
Died Jan. 1, 1898 in Rome, Italy)

In 1880, Count Joseph Telfener created a company—'The New York, Texas and Mexican Railway Company'—to build a railroad that would link, are you ready for this, New York City with Mexico City. How's that for thinking big?

One year earlier, in 1879, the dashing Italian nobleman, who was living in Rome at the time, had married an American girl named Ada Hungerford. Shortly after their Roman wedding, Telfener's new father-in-law, Daniel Hungerford, a promoter from California (who had fostered the marriage for social purposes) convinced Telfener that America was the real land of opportunity. Previously, Telfener, a successful financier and sportsman, had worked in other parts of the world. In fact, in 1877, in Rome, Victor Emmanuel II, King of Italy, bestowed the title of Count on Joseph Telfener, to honor him for his numerous achievements in engineering, including the successful construction of a railroad in Argentina. After establishing the company in Paris, Telfener, and his associates, chose Texas as the starting point for his American venture, because of the liberal land grants the state offered to encourage rail construction.

To construct the railway, Telfener imported 1,200 Italian laborers, engineers and skilled craftsmen—mostly from Lombardy—and paid for their passage from Italy to America. Telfener promised the workers, upon completion of the job, he'd pay a portion of the

Closet Italians

costs to relocate their families from Italy to America. This was not as altruistic as it appears. The company would secure from the State of Texas, 10,240 acres for each mile of track completed. Telfener figured that if the workers were united with their families, they would remain in America and buy land from him along the tracks. Construction got underway in September 1881, with two crews laying track simultaneously, one crew starting from west of Rosenberg Junction, Texas, and the other starting from east of Victoria, Texas. Nine months later, July 4, 1882, the last spike was driven amid celebratory fireworks and parties. Although only 91 miles were completed, the railroad, popularly known as 'The Macaroni Line,' aided growth in coastal Texas.

For their efforts, Telfener and his group had earned a staggering 940,000 acres of Texas land. But, there was a problem. Hard as it may be to believe, the State of Texas had committed more acreage than actually existed. Consequently, but not surprisingly, in 1882 the legislature voided the railroad land grants. Without the land certificates, the banks pulled back, wounding all railroad developers in the state of Texas. In 1885, Telfener sold the line to his brother-in-law, J. W. Mackay, a wealthy mining engineer from Nevada (MacKay's wife, Louise, won later fame as the grandmother of Irving Berlin's wife). Later that same year, Mackey sold the railroad to the Southern Pacific.

Today, a portion of Villa Ada—Count Joseph Telfener's magnificent, wooded, sprawling estate on Via Salaria, near Rome's center—is a sumptuous, popular public park, second only to Rome's incomparable Villa Borghese.

Nick J. Mileti

SIR ARTHUR SULLIVAN

(Born May 13, 1842 in South London;
Died November 22, 1900 in London)

Arthur Sullivan was one of the greatest musical composers of comic opera in history, and the words 'Gilbert and Sullivan' will always stand for the best in that genre.

Sullivan's father was Irish, and his mother was Italian—from an old Italian family. One biographer said, "Sullivan's Italian blood gave him a vivacity of manner."

A true child prodigy, by the age of eight Sullivan was able to play every instrument in his father's band. For the next twenty years, Sullivan studied, wrote and conducted serious music. In 1871, when Sullivan was twenty-nine years of age, lightning struck. Arthur Sullivan met W. S. Gilbert, and almost immediately the world of comic opera took on a dimension never seen before or since.

In the next twenty years, Gilbert, writing the words, and Sullivan, writing the music, created a series of box-office and critical hits that may never be surpassed: 'Trial by Jury' (1875), 'The Sorcerer' (1877), 'H.M.S. Pinafore' (1878), 'Pirates of Penzance' (1880), 'Patience' (1881), 'Iolanthe' (1882), 'Princess Ida' (1884), 'The Mikado' (1885), 'Ruddigore' (1887), 'Yeoman of the Guard' (1888), and 'The Gondoliers' (1889).

The fact that Gilbert and Sullivan were able to collaborate so successfully over the years is all the more amazing when one considers how totally different in nature and personality the two men were. The amiable and generous Sullivan lived large—women and gambling were an important part of his life—while Gilbert was abrasive, confrontational and frugal. In 1890, in all-too-typical Hollywood fashion, an inconsequential matter triggered a rupture in one of the world's most beloved musical marriages. Even though the rift was repaired three years later—and two more G & S operas were created—the damage had been done. The Gilbert and Sullivan miracle ended in a whimper.

Everyone loves Sullivan's unfailing melodious music. In addition to recognizing his genius for good melodies, the writer T.F. Dunhill lauded Sullivan's music for its unpretentiousness, unaffected simplicity, striking lucidity, and pungent sense of humor and satire ("which almost invariable are coexistent with a sense of beauty"). The brilliant French composer and avid historian Camille Saint-Saens once said, "Sullivan was as much a satirist in musical notes as Gilbert in the verbal test. Their repartees in collaboration often reminded of the sarcasms of Voltaire." An important English observer added that Sullivan recognized "it was not only necessary to set his text to music which was pleasing in itself, but to invent melodies in such close alliance with the words that the two things become indistinguishable . . . In this respect, Sullivan did more for the English stage than any musician of his time."

In 1881 Arthur Sullivan was knighted by Queen Victoria.

Nick J. Mileti

CHARLES JOSEPH BONAPARTE

(Born 1851 in Baltimore, Maryland; Died 1921)
REAL ITALIAN NAME:
CHARLES JOSEPH BUONAPARTE

Charles Joseph Bonaparte (the grandson of French Emperor Napoleon Bonaparte's youngest brother, Jerome) was an attorney, political leader, and member of President Theodore Roosevelt's cabinet. He created the F.B.I. in America in 1908.

First, a word about Napoleon's youngest brother, Jerome. Jerome Bonaparte visited America in 1803 when he was nineteen years old. He met, fell in love, and within two months, married Elizabeth (Betsy) Patterson, the daughter of one of the richest men in Maryland. Before the marriage could be broken-up (Napoleon and Betsy's father both objected), in 1805 Jerome Bonaparte and Betsy Patterson had a child, whom they named Jerome Napoleon Bonaparte. The next year, in 1806, Napoleon I issued a decree annulling the marriage. He then appointed his brother, Jerome, King of Westphalia.

Now, a word about the above mentioned child. A Harvard University graduate, Jerome Napoleon Bonaparte married Susan May Williams in 1829. The couple settled in Baltimore and twenty-two years later, in 1851, Charles Joseph Bonaparte was born.

Finally, our subject, Charles Joseph Bonaparte (who is Napoleon's brother's grandson).

Like his father, Charles studied at Harvard (undergraduate and Law). He became a political leader in Baltimore, serving as a member of the Board of Indian Commissioners, chairman of the National Civil Service Reform League, and trustee of The Catholic University. Charles was also one of the founders of the prestigious National Municipal League. In 1905, President Theodore Roosevelt appointed Charles Joseph Bonaparte Secretary of the Navy of the United States. The next year, the President moved Charles into the more important position of Attorney General of the United States, in which office he served for the remainder of Roosevelt's term.

In 1908, Charles Joseph Bonaparte, on his own initiative (but, of course, with the encouragement and approval of the President) issued an order that created a permanent national investigative force that was answerable only to him as Attorney General. The 'force' was eventually called the 'Bureau of Investigation', then the 'United States Bureau of Investigation' (1932), and finally the "Federal Bureau of Investigation' (1935).

The F.B.I has had a colorful, but checkered history, due in large part to the forty-eight year reign—1924 to 1972—of J (John) Edgar Hoover, one of the most powerful and controversial men in the history of the United States of America.

Nick J. Mileti

PIERRE PAUL FRANCOIS CAMILLE SAVORGNAN (COUNT DE BRAZZA)

(Born in Italy in 1852; Died in 1905 in Dakar)
REAL ITALIAN NAME: PIETRO PAOLO
DI BRAZZA SAVORGNANI

The gentle explorer, Pierre Savorgnan, colonized French Equatorial Africa, and founded the city of Brazzaville, the capital of the independent Congo Republic.

Born in Italy, Savorgnan grew up in Rome, and then entered the French Navel Academy. In the next four years, Savorgnan saw the coast of Africa, and learned the ways of the sea. At this time, King Leopold II of Belgium commissioned the British explorer Henry Morton Stanley to colonize the Congo for him. Savorgnan learned that Stanley used guns, deceit and cheap European goods to win over hundreds of local chiefs. Outraged, Savorgnan presented the French government with a revolutionary approach to Colonialism—he proposed a peaceful mission. The officials were skeptical of Savorgnan's plan to use guns "only if absolutely necessary," but jealous of King Leopold's land grab, they approved Savorgnan's mission. Starting out in 1875, with the aid of native tribes who were seduced by the Italian explorer's charm and sincerity, Savorgnan traveled some 900 miles inland.

When Savorgnan returned from his trip of exploration three years later, the French government was impressed with both his findings and his methods, and immediately commissioned a second mission. On this second trip, Savorgnan reached the Congo River and signed the first treaty of friendship between an African King and a European power, placing almost 200,000 square miles on the Congo's north bank under French protectorate. At this time, Savorgnan also founded the city that is today named Brazzaville, one of the few cities in Africa to keep its Colonial name (out of respect for the only peaceful explorer in Africa's history).

For eleven years, from 1886 to 1897, Savorgnan served as the first Governor of the French Congo. He established schools, hospitals and programs to help the natives, whom he insisted receive a minimum wage from European traders. Meanwhile, across the river in the Belgian Congo, the slaves were treated like animals. The European press gleefully reported the enormous differences, comparing the 'good' Savorgnan with the 'brutal' Stanley, and making him (Savorgnan) famous. In fact, Savorgnan became known as the 'Father of the slaves' for his unprecedented kind and considerate treatment of the natives. Bowing to pressure from an embarrassed King Leopold, the French government fired Savorgnan, who returned to France. Not surprisingly, conditions in the French Congo soon rivaled those across the river in the Belgian Congo. In 1905 the French government convinced Savorgnan to head an inquiry into the scandals caused by the indignities now being imposed on the natives. But, tragically, it was too late. Savorgnan died on his way to the assignment.

In a classic case of French co-opting, Pietro Savorgnani is called Pierre Savorgnan, "the greatest French explorer of his time" in French schoolbooks.

Nick J. Mileti

ELEANORA DUSE

(Born October 5, 1858 in Vigevano, Italy;
Died 1924 in Pittsburgh, Pa.)

Eleanora Duse was the most famous stage actress of her time and the innovator of a new style of acting that has come down to the present.

Before Duse, actors used set expressions to convey various emotions. Not Eleanora. She found the inner truth of the character she was portraying, and expressed it in her own pure, natural way. She showed the world's creative community by example that they too could find their own style by 'elimination of self.' Frances Winwar, her biographer, explains: "She (Duse) did not use make-up. She made herself up morally. In other words, she allowed the inner compulsions, grief and joys of her characters to use her body as their medium for expression, often to the detriment of her health."

Duse famously said: "To save the theatre, the theatre must be destroyed, the actors and actresses must all die of the plague. They poison the air, they make art impossible. It is not drama that they play, but pieces for the theatre. We should return to the Greeks, play in the open air; the drama dies of stalls and boxes and evening dress, and people who come to digest dinner."

Eleanora Duse's father and grandfather were actors, and she joined the troupe at four years of age. Poverty was always lurking, so Duse grew up acting non-stop. She became a mega-star in Italy and then began touring. She started in each town as an unknown, but ended up conquering entire countries—in South America first, then Russia and Europe. In 1896, Duse made a triumphant tour of America. President Cleveland and his wife attended every performance. Shocking Washington society, Mrs. Cleveland gave a tea in Duse's honor, the first ever for an actress. Not even the great Sarah Bernhardt—who was fourteen years Duse's senior—received such an honor. Sarah Bernhardt and Eleanora Duse had a rivalry that began early on. The two actresses were totally different people. Bernhardt was outgoing and imperious, Duse introverted and private. Bernhardt never met an opportunity for publicity she didn't like, while Duse refused to co-operate with the press, preferring to let her acting speak to the public for her. It is for these reasons that Bernhardt is more known today. At the height of their careers, however, George Bernard Shaw saw both Bernhardt and Duse in London in the same play—at different theaters, a few days apart. Again quoting Winwar, "(Shaw) voted unqualifiedly for Duse and defended his choice with trenchant oratory that left Sarah not only less divine but with a sorely wounded vanity."

Over the years, a stunning array of superstars recognized—and paid homage to—Duse's unprecedented acting style and talent. Diverse artistic geniuses including Amy Lowell (the Imagist Poetry Pioneer), Martha Graham, (the Modern Dance Pioneer), and Eva LaGallienne (Actress/Producer/Director) all acknowledge being inspired by Duse.

Eleanora Duse had many men in her life, including Arrigo Boito (Verdi's poet) and Gabriele d'Annunzio, (the famous novelist), who wrote four important plays for her.

Nick J. Mileti

BUTTERCUP DICKERSON

(Born Oct. 11, 1858 in Tyaskin, Maryland;
Died July 23, 1920)
REAL ITALIAN NAME: LEWIS PESSANO

The first Italian-American to play in the major league of baseball changed his name to Buttercup Dickerson because no one with an Italian name like Lewis Pessano was welcome in baseball at that time.

Buttercup's first game in the majors was at the age of twenty, in 1878, when he started in the outfield for the Cincinnati Red Stockings. He measured only 5 foot 6 inches, and weighed only 140 pounds, but his hustle kept him in the majors for seven years. Buttercup's last year in the majors was 1885.

PING BODIE

(Born October 8, 1887 in San Francisco;
Died December 17, 1961)
REAL ITALIAN NAME:
FRANCESCO STEPHANO PEZZULO

Ping Bodie was an excellent major-league baseball player, an inspiration for future stars, and the roommate of the legendary Babe Ruth.

After starring with the San Francisco Seals of the Pacific Coast League, Bodie broke into the majors with the Chicago White Sox in 1911 (where he hit .289 his rookie year), moved on to the Athletics, who were in Philadelphia at the time, and finished with the New York Yankees (batting .295 his final year). Bodie played in the majors a total of nine years.

Closet Italians

An outstanding outfielder, Ping played along side the great Babe Ruth in the New York Yankees outfield. Ruth loved attention, women, and booze—in no special order. In fact, a sportswriter once wrote, "Trying to capture Babe Ruth with cold statistics is like trying to keep up with him on a night out." Ruth's extracurricular antics explain the famous quote by Ping Bodie. When asked what it was like to room with the legendary Babe Ruth, he always replied: "I don't know. I don't room with Babe Ruth, I room with his suitcase." When you think about it, it was poetic justice that Ping Bodie, the Italian-American, who, like Buttercup Dickerson, had to change his name to get into Major League Baseball, gave his famous roommate the nickname 'Bambino'—an Italian name that has stuck with Babe Ruth to this day.

Ping Bodie was also a memorable character—immortalized in his time by the great Ring Lardner in his (Lardner's) popular newspaper column. Bodie is given credit for inspiring other great west coast Italian ball players, including Joe DiMaggio (and his two brothers), Tony Lazzeri, and Frank Crosetti.

Nick J. Mileti

FEDERIGO ENRIQUES

(Born January 5, 1871 in Livorno, Italy;
Died June 14, 1946 in Rome)

Federigo Enriques was a world famous mathematician who founded (with two others) the Italian school of algebraic geometry. He also made numerous other important contributions to geometry and to the foundation and philosophy of mathematics.

After studying in Pisa and Rome, in the early 1890's Enriques began his research on algebraic surfaces with Guido Castelnuovo. In 1896, Enriques was appointed professor of projective geometry and descriptive geometry at the University of Bologna, remaining in that post for twenty-six years, until 1922. While in that position, he introduced History of Science topics into the curriculum.

Although most of his writings were on mathematic subjects, Enriques was also interested in philosophy. In 1906, he published his famous book 'Problemi della scienza' (Problems of Science) in which he explained the connection between physical space and geometry (The important treatise was translated into English in 1914, and reprinted in 1984). The following year, 1907, Enriques co-founded the influential journal 'Scientia,' and 'The Society Filosofica Italiana' (The Italian Philosophical Society), serving as its president for six years. Also in 1907, Federigo Enriques achieved his first taste of fame—it was in the area of differential geometry. Together with F. Severi, he was awarded the prize Bordin of the Academie des Sciences for his work on hyper elliptic surfaces. In the same year, Enriques won the prize of the Academia Nazionale dei Lincei (he was also a member), the oldest, most prestigious scientific society in the world. Enriques' greatest fame, however, came in 1914, when—after working on and off with Castelnuovo on the problem for twenty years—Enriques finally published a classification of algebraic surfaces. This achievement gained Enriques worldwide recognition and prestige.

In 1922, Federigo Enriques left the University of Bologna and relocated to the University of Rome, where he occupied the chair of higher geometry. While in residence at Rome, Enriques attracted many of the brightest scientific minds in the world. During this period, Enriques was president of the Italian Society for Education in Mathematics ('Mathesis') for twelve years, edited the section of mathematics for the Italian Encyclopedia, and wrote textbooks for schools. Numerous buildings and schools throughout Italy are named in honor of Federigo Enriques, including the Department of Mathematics at the University of Milan.

In 1938, Italy passed its disastrous anti-Semitic racial laws, which placed numerous restrictions on Jews, including the expulsion of Jewish students and teachers from all school systems. Consequently, Federigo Enriques, who was Jewish, was forced to leave his University of Rome teaching position during the entire remaining reign of Mussolini's Fascist regime. To compound the tragedy, the great man died (in 1946) only a few months after he was reinstated to his teaching post.

Nick J. Mileti

ALFRED E. SMITH

(Born Dec. 30, 1873 in New York, New York;
Died Oct. 4, 1944)

In 1928, Alfred E. Smith ran for President of the United States, the first Roman Catholic to achieve that honor.

Smith's parents were both immigrants—his mother was Irish and his father was German and Italian. Alfred E. Smith rose from poverty to become the popular Governor of New York State for four terms—he was elected in 1919, and again in 1923, 1925 and 1927. A great liberal in every sense of the word, while Governor, Smith caused legislation to be enacted that helped whom he called 'the little man.' Decent housing and improved factory safety were only two of his passionately pursued reform measures.

In the presidential race of 1928, his friend, and fellow New Yorker, Franklin Delano Roosevelt, nominated Alfred E. Smith for President of the United States on the Democratic ticket. FDR called Smith 'The Happy Warrior,' and the name stuck. Herbert Hoover swamped Alfred E. Smith at the polls—several southern states even voted Republican for the first time since Reconstruction. What caused this stunning defeat? It seems that two emotional issues decided the hotly contested presidential election. First, in 1928, anti-Catholic sentiment in America was rampant. In fact, the vicious anti-Catholicism attacks amazed and disgusted Smith, who naively believed that religious bigotry was dead in America. The second killer was the 'wets versus dries' situation. Hoover supported prohibition, while Smith was against it. In a curious twist of logic, Smith felt that prohibition discriminated against minority groups. This position cost Smith one of his most logical constituencies, the Catholic Church. Smith looked on in disbelief as the Church even campaigned against him. Bishop James Cannon bellowed: "Shall dry America elect a 'cocktail' President?"

After his massive defeat at the hands of conservative Herbert Hoover, Smith reassessed his political views. After careful and exhaustive self-examination, Smith decided that the Protestant majority might use its growing power to discriminate against minorities, especially Catholics. Consequently, Smith decided to reject his old friend FDR and his 'New Deal.' Spelling doom to any possible future political successes, in 1936 and 1940 Smith supported the Republican presidential candidate. Even though he suffered personal embarrassment on the national scene, Alfred E. Smith remained a statesman all his life. Listen to a line from a speech he made in 1933 (five years after his debacle), in which Smith summed-up his political philosophy, and gave an insight into his persona.

"All the ills of democracy,' Smith said, "can be cured with more democracy."

One can only pray that all politicians—of any generation, at any level, in any political party, in any country—would respect the eloquent words of Alfred E. Smith.

Nick J. Mileti

GEORGIA O' KEEFFE

(Born Nov. 15, 1887 near Sun Prairie, Wisconsin;
Died Mar. 6, 1986 in Santa Fe, New Mexico)

Georgia O'Keeffe was, in the words of the New York Times, "the shaper of modern art in the United States."

Georgia's mother, Ida Totto, was Italian. Her father, Francis Calixtus O'Keeffe, was Irish. Georgia was named for Giorgio Totto, her maternal Italian grandfather (her mother's father). As a young man, Giorgio Totto moved from Italy to Hungary. He eventually immigrated to America from Hungary, and, years later, returned to that country. These two facts have caused the erroneous assumption that Georgia O'Keefe's mother was Hungarian.

Georgia decided she was going to be a painter at an early age, and later wrote, "I hadn't a desire to make anything like the pictures I had seen." She painted while she studied art, and while she worked at various jobs—biding her time until she could paint full-time. In 1916, when Georgia was twenty-nine, lightning struck: A friend took a number of Georgia's drawings and paintings to Alfred Stieglitz in New York. At that time, Stieglitz was a famous photographer and interested in new art and artists. When he saw Georgia O'Keefe's work, he famously cried, "At last, a woman on paper!" and immediately displayed the provocative pictures on the walls of his gallery. The critics and the public roared their approval, and Georgia's storybook career began (nine years later, in 1925, Georgia and Stieglitz were married).

Georgia created her first enormous flower painting in 1924. More and more, she created original images—combining an unusual use of color with abstract images (which many critics called erotic). Explaining her style, Georgia wrote in her autobiography, "I often painted fragments of things because it seemed to make my statement as well or better than the whole could . . . I had to create an equivalent for what I felt about what I was looking at . . . not to copy it." In her now legendary career (which spanned almost seventy years), the strong-willed, highly opinionated artist produced over 900 paintings, and in the process, proved that a woman could compete—even excel—in a man's world. The renowned journalist, Edith Evans Asbury, wrote, "In 1970, when she was 83 years old . . . (everyone) made an astonishing discovery. The artist who had been joyously painting as she pleased had been a step ahead of everyone, all the time."

Georgia O'Keefe's paintings hang in museums all over the world. She was a member of the National Institute of Arts and Letters and several other prestigious Academies. She has received numerous Honorary Degrees, and has a museum (and research center) in Santa Fe dedicated to her art. In 1977, Georgia received the Medal of Freedom from the United States Government, and in 1985, she was awarded the National Medal of the Arts.

Nick J. Mileti

GENEROSO POPE, SENIOR

(Born April 1, 1891 near Arpaise, Italy;
Died April 28, 1950)
REAL ITALIAN NAME: GENEROSO PAPA

Businessman and publisher Generoso Pope, Sr., is one of the first Italians to achieve millionaire status in America.

At fifteen years of age, in 1906, Generoso left his parent's farm in Italy and immigrated to America. The hungry—literally and figuratively—young man quickly secured a $3-a-week job carrying water to the men constructing the Pennsylvania Railroad's tunnel under the East River in New York. Generoso worked his way up to foreman in the pits of what became the Colonial Sand and Stone Company. Within ten years, he was running the enterprise. Generoso eventually became owner of the company and made it the largest construction supply firm in America. In 1928, Generoso bought 'Il Progresso Italo-Americano' and made the paper the largest circulation Italian language newspaper in the United States. Generoso Pope, Senior used his newspaper forum to attain great political strength.

GENE POPE

(Born in 1927 in New York City; Died October 3, 1988)
REAL ITALIAN NAME: GENEROSO PAPA, JUNIOR

Gene Pope founded 'The National Enquirer,' the most influential tabloid in history.

Generoso Pope, Sr. was Gene Pope's father. His mother emigrated from Italy. In order to transcend family squabbles, Gene purchased the failing weekly 'New York Enquirer' for $75,000 in 1952. He struggled with what his editorial policy should be, but one day he had an inspiration. "I noticed how a grisly auto accident drew crowds."

'Carnage' (real and imagined) became Pope's key word, and circulation quickly rose to a million copies a week. This 'gore and lurid' editorial policy caused the Enquirer to prosper, but there was change in the air. Newsstands were disappearing. Pope quickly adjusted. He moved his paper into supermarkets and changed his editorial policy accordingly, toning things down. Thus, the Enquirer became a 'Family Weekly'—over six million papers sold when the picture of Elvis Presley lying in his coffin graced the cover in 1977. Spotting another trend, Pope made the Enquirer into the celebrity tell-all, which the paper is today.

Gene Pope is rightly considered the father of America's tabloid journalism. He took a struggling local newspaper and turned it into a much maligned (by jealous rivals), but much copied, and wildly successful, national publication. And that's a fact.

Nick J. Mileti

CHARLES ATLAS

(Born in 1893 in Acri [Calabria], Italy; Died in 1972)
REAL ITALIAN NAME: ANGELO SICILIANO

Charles Atlas was the first person in America to get rich from physical culture. His work paved the way for a multi-billion dollar industry, which is committed to helping people lead healthier, happier lives.

In 1905, Angelo and his parents joined the exodus from southern Italy and immigrated to America. To repel the taunts of the other kids, their skinny little son immediately changed his first name from Angelo to Charles. In his prime, this skinny little kid stood 5 feet 10 inches, weighed 180 pounds, had a chest that measured 47 inches in normal position, a waist that measured 32 inches, and biceps that measured 17 inches.

Physical fitness fascinated young Charles. He first used dumbbells and barbells made from stones tied to sticks, eventually graduating to the real thing at a neighborhood gym. After a long and arduous regimen, the commitment paid off. At twenty-eight, Charles won a photo competition held by the magazine 'Physical Culture', and never looked back. In rapid succession, he won a contest at Madison Square Garden, became a stunt man at Coney Island and worked as an artist's model. While at work at Coney Island one day, Charles noticed that when the lions stretched, their muscles bulged and rippled. He also observed a pitiful, but powerful statute of the Greek God, Atlas. These two observations impressed him, and he couldn't get their images out of his mind. Eventually, Charles put it all together: The work-outs gave him a new body, the statute of Atlas gave him a last name to match his new body, and the animals gave him the idea that was to make him rich and famous.

Labeling his idea Dynamic Tension—pitting muscles against each other and inanimate objects—Charles Atlas joined forces with an entrepreneur named Charles Roman to help him sell it. The marketing campaign they designed is considered one of the best of all time: After sand is kicked in his face by a bully, a 97-pound weakling purchases the Charles Atlas Dynamic Tension Program Kit, develops muscles and knocks the unsuspecting bully on his rear-end. Since 1922, millions and millions of these courses (in seven languages) have been sold all over the world. As part of his marketing strategy, Atlas performed feats of strength most of his life. In 1938, he pulled a 145,000-pound railroad car 122 feet along a railroad track using only one rope. Atlas also accepted students, whom he taught his bodybuilding system. He became the trainer to celebrities who flocked to him from all over the world, including Robert (Believe-It-Or-Not) Ripley, who couldn't believe Atlas's perfect body.

Charles Atlas won the title "The World's Most Perfectly Developed Man" in 1922, and eighty years later, no one has taken the title away from this remarkable man who developed the system and methods now popularly known by scientists and health buffs as isometrics.

JOHNNY DUNDEE

(Born Nov. 22, 1893 in Sciacca, Sicily;
Died April 22, 1965)
REAL ITALIAN NAME: GIUSEPPE CARRORA

Johnny Dundee, a sharp hitter with excellent footwork, fought professionally for twenty-two years. In his first two years, he fought fifty-nine times. In his career, Dundee fought an incredible 330 times (only two fighters in history have had more fights). In the process, Johnny Dundee won both the Featherweight and Junior-Lightweight World Championships. Dundee was so quick he was knocked out only two times in his 330 bouts.

The legendary manager Angelo Dundee (and his brother) took the surname of this great fighter.

LOU AMBERS

(Born Nov. 8, 1913 in Herkimer, New York;
Died April 25, 1995)
REAL ITALIAN NAME: LUIGI D' AMBROSIO

Lou Ambers was one of the top lightweights of the thirties: He was Lightweight Champion of the World in 1936 and 1939. In 104 fights, the amiable Ambers won 90, lost eight and had six draws. A clever fighter, Lou Ambers had a highly aggressive style that prompted writers and fans to dub him "The Herkimer Hurricane' after his hometown, which has named a street and park in his honor.

Closet Italians

WILLIE PEP

(Born Sept. 19, 1922 in Hartford, Conn.)
REAL ITALIAN NAME: GUGLIELMO PAPALEO

Willie Pep was one of the greatest boxers of all time.

A two-time World Featherweight Champion, Pep won his first championship in 1942, when he was only twenty years old. Pep turned professional at the ripe old age of seventeen, and proceeded to win his first 63 fights. Incredibly, he lost only one of his first 135 fights. Willie Pep had a lifetime record of 230 wins (65 were KO's), only 11 losses, and one draw.

Pep was nicknamed 'WILL o' the Wisp' and 'The Artful Dodger' because he was so fast and elusive. In fact, legend has it that Willie Pep once won a round without throwing a punch.

Nick J. Mileti

LOU LITTLE

(Born Dec. 6, 1893 in Boston, Mass;
Died May 28, 1979 in Delray Beach, Florida)
REAL ITALIAN NAME: LUIGI PICCOLO

When Lou Little was inducted into the prestigious National College Football Hall of Fame in 1970, it was generally agreed that he was one of the greatest college football coaches of all time, even though his coaching record was an unimpressive 151 wins, 128 losses and 13 ties, a .539 average.

A close examination of the facts is obviously in order.

Lou Little was hired as football coach by Georgetown University in 1924. In the six seasons he coached the Hoyas, Little compiled a remarkable record of 39 wins, 12 losses and 4 ties, and took the team to national prominence.

Amazingly, there were two matters that transcended even these impressive won/loss statistics at Georgetown.

First, Little upgraded the football program from small college opponents such as Mount Saint Mary's, and replaced them with majors, like Navy and West Virginia. Secondly, as Athletic Director, Little took the entire sports program at Georgetown into the 20th Century.

In 1930, Columbia University lured Lou Little away from Georgetown.

Within four years, Little did the impossible—he took Columbia to the Rose Bowl in Pasadena, California.

Topping the appearance, in one of history's biggest upsets, Little's football team went on to win the Rose Bowl—the nations most prestigious bowl game of the time—beating Stanford by the score of 7-0.

In his first seven years at Columbia, Lou's record was a startling 43-15-3. One of the program's highlights in later years was Columbia's victory over Army in 1947, which snapped the Cadet's thirty-two game winning streak.

Lou Little retired from coaching in 1956 after a total of 27 years at the Ivy League school. Little is considered the greatest coach in Columbia's history. If Columbia hadn't made the classy decision—with which Lou Little agreed—to de-emphasize football, his won/loss record would more accurately reflect his special coaching talent; developing teams that never gave up.

Lou Little received many honors over the years, including being named 'Coach of the Era' by Scripps-Howard Newspapers (sharing the honor with the legendary Pop Warner).

Nick J. Mileti

HARRY WARREN

(Born Dec. 24, 1893 in Brooklyn, N.Y.;
Died Sept. 22, 1981)
REAL ITALIAN NAME: SALVATORE GUARAGNA

Harry Warren was the most successful composer of American popular music in history.

Warren's family emigrated from Calabria in Southern Italy. Like many Italian immigrants at the turn of the century, they anglicized their name to escape the disgraceful prejudice they encountered in America.

Harry Warren was a phenomenon. He wrote the musical score for eighty-one motion pictures, including sixty-four Hollywood Musicals. He was nominated for an Oscar for Best Song in a Motion Picture eleven different years, winning the Oscar three times, for the songs 'Lullaby of Broadway' in 1935, 'You'll Never Know' in 1943, and 'On the Atchison, Topeka & Santa Fe' in 1946. Since four major film studios own the rights to most of his songs, you often hear Warren's music in movies to this day.

More than fifty of Harry Warren's songs have achieved national popularity. Harry James' 'I Had the Craziest Dream'; Bing Crosby's 'You're Getting to be a Habit With Me,' Shadow Waltz,' and 'You Must Have Been a Beautiful Baby'; Dick Haymes' 'You'll Never Know'; Dean Martin's 'That's Amore'; and Tony Bennet's 'Boulevard of Broken Dreams' were a few of the mega-hits written by Harry Warren. Altogether twenty-one recordings of Harry Warren tunes reached Number One on the charts. Three of Harry Warren's songs have been chosen for the Smithsonian collection of American popular songs:

'Jeepers Creepers,' 'I Only Have Eyes for You,' and 'There Will Never be Another You.'

In 1980, David Merrick launched a stage version of Harry Warren's 1933 film musical '42nd Street.' With sixteen classic tunes (including the title song '42nd Street', 'Shuffle off to Buffalo,' and 'You're Getting to Be a Habit With Me), all Harry Warren songs, '42nd Street' was a smash hit and ran eight years. The show continues to be revived on Broadway and around the country.

Harry Warren—who worked with a number of great lyricists, including Johnny Mercer, Mack Gordon and Al Dubin—has had more hit songs than any of his contemporary songwriters, including Harold Arlen, Irving Berlin, George Gershwin, Jerome Kern, Cole Porter or Richard Rodgers.

Why isn't Harry Warren as famous as these other songwriting giants? Harry Warren was a rarity in show business—he was a shy, self-deprecating man who shunned publicity. Also, Warren's working on the west coast in Hollywood out of the media spotlight (which was in New York in those days) was a factor that contributed to his anonymity. Anonymity was fine with Harry Warren. He preferred to let his magnificent, unforgettable music speak for him—yesterday, today and forever.

Nick J. Mileti

WALTER PISTON

(Born January 20, 1894 in Rockland, Maine;
Died November 12, 1976 in Belmont Mass.)
REAL ITALIAN NAME: WALTER PISTONE

Walter Piston was one of the most significant music educators in American history, and is equally renowned as an American music composer.

Piston's grandfather (his father's father) immigrated to America from Genoa, Italy and settled in New England. Like so many others around that time, the family eventually dropped the 'e' from the last name to seem more American.

In 1924, Piston graduated from Harvard University's music program with highest honors. After winning the John Knowles Paine Traveling Fellowship, Piston wisely chose Paris where he was lucky and talented enough to study under Nadia Boulanger—the principle teacher of Aaron Copeland and the most influential music teacher of the 20th Century.

Knowing a good thing when they saw it, Harvard hired Piston when he returned from France in 1926. In a speech some twenty-five years later, the beloved musical genius, known for his humanity, wit and empathy, explained his decision this way: "After graduation (and while in Paris) . . . I discovered that I would probably become a composer. Now it is not from choice that one becomes a composer but rather, it seems, one does it in spite of everything and even against one's better judgment. But writing long-haired music is not a way to make a living so I jumped at the chance offered me to return to Harvard as an assistant instructor in the Music Department. It turned out that I liked teaching very much indeed and found it the best possible occupation for a composer. Teaching . . . acts as a preventative against complacency and stodgy self-satisfaction."

Walter Piston remained on the university's faculty for the next thirty-four years, teaching, composing and writing until he retired in 1960. As a teacher, Piston's pupils included innumerable persons of musical prominence, including Eliot Carter, Leroy Anderson and Leonard Bernstein. As a composer, Piston wrote extensively, composing over forty orchestral works which have been recorded on over thirty record labels. His most famous piece, the ballet 'The Incredible Flutist,' was commissioned by the Boston Pops Orchestra. His style is usually described as sophisticated and witty, combining classical and jazz features. Piston's 'Symphony Number Three' (first performed by the Boston Symphony) and 'Symphony Number Seven' (first performed by the Philadelphia Symphony) earned him Pulitzer Prizes' in 1948 and 1961, respectively.

As an author, Piston's books are considered classics in their fields. The influential texts, used to this day, cover the technical aspects of music including harmony, counterpoint and orchestration, and have been translated into several languages.

Of course, Walter Piston has received innumerable prestigious honors over the years.

Chapter VII

Illustrious Italians With Non-Italian Names
Born Between 1900-1909

Nick J. Mileti

FRANCES WINWAR

(Born in 1900 in Taormina, Sicily; Died in 1985)
REAL ITALIAN NAME: FRANCESCA VINCIGUERRA

Frances Winwar is one of the most important biographers of all time. She was also a novelist and translator, but her greatest fame comes from her biographies of some of the most important people in history. In 1945, George Sand, a critic, wrote: "To my mind it ('The Life Of The Heart') establishes Frances Winwar as the greatest of living biographers."

Arriving in America from Italy at the age of seven, Winwar studied at Hunter College, tutored private pupils in French and Italian, moved on to City College of New York (where she met, and later married, V. J. Jerome) and completed her studies at Columbia. Winwar began writing poems, literary articles, reviews and sketches for New York papers and national magazines. In 1927 her first novel "The Ardent Flame," based on the true story of Francesca da Rimini, was published. Her second novel, "The Golden Round," was also set in the middle ages. Both books foreshadowed her interest in writing biographies.

In 1933, Winwar began her remarkable string of biographies with 'Poor Splendid Wings' (about the Rosettis and their Circle), which won The Atlantic Monthly Non-Fiction Prize and made Winwar famous. She wrote 'The Romantic Rebels' (Byron, Shelly and Keats) in 1935; 'Farewell The Banner' (Coleridge and the Wordsworths) in 1938, and 'Oscar Wilde and the Yellow Nineties' in 1940—for which Lord Alfred Douglas wrote an incredible prologue, defending his life and attacking his biographers, including Winwar. Undaunted, Winwar went on to write 'American Giant' (Walt Whitman and his Times) in 1941; "The Life Of The Heart" (George Sand and her Times) in 1945; 'The Saint And The Devil' (Joan of Arc and Gilles De Rais) in 1948; 'The Immortal Lovers' (Elizabeth Barrett and Robert Browning) in 1950; 'The Haunted Palace' (Edgar Allan Poe) in 1959; and 'Jean-Jacques Rousseau: Conscience Of An Era' in 1961.

In 1951, Winwar met Giuseppe Tusiani, a young college teacher of Italian Literature at New York's Hunter College. Winwar took him under her wing and encouraged her prodigy to write in English if he wanted broad acceptance. "Don't be so emotional about it," she told him. "I had to do it (write in English) and Anglicize my name as well." Tusiani, of course, understood that her Real Italian Name Vinciguerra means Winwar in English. When Winwar and Tusiani journeyed to Italy together in 1954, Tusiani wrote 'The Return' which Winwar surreptitiously submitted to the Poetry Society of England. The long poem garnered the coveted 'Greenwood Prize' for Tusiani and was the impetus to his literary career. In 1956, Winwar wrote 'Wingless Victory' (Gabriele D'Annunzio and Eleanora Duse) which she dedicated to Giuseppe Tusiani. In 1955, Frances Winwar translated 'The Decameron,' by Giovanni Boccaccio—which, to this day, remains the quintessential translation of the classic.

Nick J. Mileti

WALTER LANTZ

(Born Apr. 27, 1900 in New Rochelle, N. Y.;
Died Mar. 22, 1994 in Burbank, Calif.)
REAL ITALIAN NAME: WALTER LANZA

Walter Lantz created one of the world's most famous cartoon characters—Woody Woodpecker. The irascible bird with the trademark laugh made millions of people all over the world happy, and made Lantz rich and famous.

Born into an immigrant Italian family, whose name was botched-up on Ellis Island, Lantz grew up drawing funny pictures. Surprising for the times, young Walter was encouraged in this unusual idea by his parents and went to work at W. Randolph Hearst's New York American. Lantz sought out the cartoonists working for Hearst's King Features Syndicate and hung around them, absorbing all aspects of the cartoon business from the hard-edged newspapermen. At night, he attended classes at an art school. When Lantz was sixteen, Hearst opened an animation studio and hired Lantz. By eighteen, Lantz was doing it all—writing, directing and animating cartoons, as well as acting in the combination live-action/animation shorts. When Hearst closed shop, Lantz moved on to the Bray studios. When Bray closed in 1927, Lantz moved to Hollywood, working odd jobs in and around show biz. In 1928, Lantz "the boy who could do everything in animation" was hired by Universal Studios to run their animation department. Seven years later, he had the savvy to negotiate a deal where he'd leave Universal and supply them with cartoons as an independent contractor. In 1940, he made an even smarter move—he negotiated ownership of the characters he'd been working with, including Andy Panda and Oswald the Rabbit.

While on his honeymoon with Grace (Gracie) Stafford in 1941, a woodpecker kept drilling holes in the asbestos shingles of the lakeside cottage they were staying in. Gracie suggested adapting the woodpecker as a cartoon character. Lantz was skeptical of its potential but decided to try it out. The rest—as they say—is history. All was not smooth, however. Mel Blanc, who developed the legendary laugh, signed an exclusive contract with Warner Brothers after making only three cartoons for Lantz. Lantz tried various other replacements, but was not satisfied with their work and continued to use Blanc's laugh in cartoons and in the 1948 hit record "The Woody Woodpecker Song." Blanc sued Lantz for using his laugh without his permission. Lantz settled the case but now desperately needed a new voice for Woody. His wife, Gracie, volunteered, but Lantz turned her down, pointing out that Woody was a boy Woodpecker. Finally, in 1950, Lantz put out a call for auditions for the voice. Gracie secretly taped her own audition and slipped it into the pile. Lantz held a blind listening session and picked the tape Gracie had snuck into the group. Worried about what people would think if they knew his wife was the voice of Woody Woodpecker, Lantz and Gracie decided to use her maiden name, Grace Stafford, in the credits. Walter Lantz has received innumerable awards and tributes over the years, including a special Oscar in 1979 "for bringing joy and laughter to every part of the world through his unique animated motion pictures."

Nick J. Mileti

GENE SARAZEN

(Born Feb. 27, 1902 in Mamoroneck, N. Y.;
Died May 12, 1999)
REAL ITALIAN NAME: EUGENIO SARACENI

Gene Sarazen was one of the greatest golfers of all time.

To help his father, who emigrated from Italy, Gene naturally did anything he could to help put food on the table. At fifteen, for his health, Sarazen took an outdoor job at a nearby golf club, and began a life-long, passionate love affair with the game. While still in his teens, Sarazen figured out what he needed to do in order to succeed in the WASP world of country clubs (as they existed 100 years ago in America). Exhibiting the intelligence that would help him in all phases of his long life, he gave what must rank as the cleverest reason in history for a name-change. What happened was, after winning his first tournament in 1920, he saw his name in the newspaper for the first time. "My name (Eugenio Saraceni)," he said to the media, "looks too much like a violin player."

By the age of twenty-one, after turning professional, Sarazen had already won three major titles. During the 1930's, winning tournaments and playing exhibitions, Sarazen become the highest paid athlete in the world. He even invented a golf club, today's Sand Wedge. Sarazen's seventy-five year association with Wilson Sporting Goods is a record unlikely to be broken. In his storied career Sarazen won thirty-eight tournaments, and was the first golfer to win all four majors—the U.S. Open and PGA in 1922, the British Open in 1932 and the Masters in 1935—called the Grand Slam today.

While these statistics are impressive, the public will always remember Gene Sarazen for hitting the most celebrated shot in golf history. 'The Shot' (as it has been called ever since) occurred in the 1935 Masters tournament. Sarazen was trailing Craig Wood by three strokes in the final round. Facing almost certain defeat on the par five fifteenth hole, Sarazen, against the advice of his caddy, decided to go for it. Gene Sarazen picked out his 4-wood, and, with his renowned graceful swing, calmly knocked the ball into the hole, scoring a double-eagle (three under par), one of golf's rarest feats.

Here are the ramifications of 'The Shot' (and why it is so famous). First of all, in spectacular fashion, 'The Shot' tied the match when things looked hopeless for Sarazen. It also forced the 18-hole playoff with Craig Wood the next day, which Sarazen won.

Furthermore, his victory in that 1935 Masters rounded out Sarazen's precedent-setting Grand Slam. Lastly, Fred Raphael—who credited Sarazen with inspiring and helping him form the popular Senior Golf Tour—avers that 'The Shot' made the Masters and Augusta National.

Besides his amazing golfing talent, Sarazen was admired for his intellectual approach to the game, his gentlemanly demeanor, his stylish clothing, and his impeccable manners.

Throughout his life, Gene Sarazen was reverently known as 'The Squire.'

Nick J. Mileti

EDDIE LANG

(Born October 25, 1902 in South Philadelphia, Pa;
Died March 26, 1933)
REAL ITALIAN NAME: SALVATORE MASSARO

Eddie Lang was the first internationally known jazz guitarist. A true jazz pioneer, he paved the way for countless great jazz guitar players, including Django Reinhardt, Charlie Christian, Tal Farlo, Barney Kessel and Jim Hall.

Domenico Massaro, Lang's father, was a maker of string instruments. His mother was named Carmella Scioli. Eddie Lang was selected as a stage name because Eddie Lang was a famous baseball player of the time.

From a musical family, Eddie was playing various string instruments his father made for him from the time he was old enough to hold them. He studied violin for a dozen years with the best teachers, but started his career as a banjo player with the Charlie Kerr Band in Philadelphia. Ironically, Lang's brilliant guitar technique and monster reputation eventually made the banjo obsolete in rhythm sections. Musically, Lang teamed up with his South Philly buddy, Joe Venuti (who became the greatest jazz violinist of all time). The pair started playing mazurkas and polkas, but quickly began to improvise. The result was, according to one of the top jazz music critic's in history, Leonard Feather, "a unique style, a tonal finesse and jazz chamber-music quality hitherto unknown in jazz." Lang is most famous for his recordings with Joe Venuti, which are now considered classics.

Because of his flawless technique and his ability to play in any musical style—blues and jazz to classical—Lang became the country's busiest sideman in the 1920s. He played with virtually every jazz and blues legend, including Bix Beiderbeck, Louis Armstrong and Bessie Smith. During this period, he also cut dozens of recordings that were major sellers. In fact, Eddie Lang single-handedly took the guitar out of hillbilly and novelty status and gave the instrument an air of respectability it has never surrendered. Prior to Lang, the guitar was strictly a back-up rhythm instrument, but his revolutionary single string solos and superb technique changed all that. Because of Eddie Lang, the guitar began its climb to become one of the world's most important solo instruments.

In 1929, Eddie joined the Paul Whiteman Orchestra along with Venuti and Beiderbeck. Lang became boy singer Bing Crosby's favorite accompanist. When Crosby answered the siren call of Hollywood, he talked Lang into joining him. Crosby once explained how he picked up his jazz phrasing. "I used to hang around with The Dorseys and Bix and Bunny Berigan and Glenn Miller and Joe Venuti and Eddie Lang—all the musicians I admired—and I was having a helluva good time. I had no idea I was learning anything. But I certainly was."

In early 1933, Lang was suffering from laryngitis. He was talked (reportedly by Crosby) into having an operation to have his tonsils removed. The operation was botched and thirty year-old Eddie Lang died a tragic, and totally unnecessary, death.

Nick J. Mileti

JOHN SCARNE

(Born March 4, 1903 in Steubenville, Ohio; Died in 1985)
REAL ITALIAN NAME:
ORLANDO CARMELO SCARNECCHIA

John Scarne was a world famous gambling expert, and one of the best sleight-of-hand card performers in history.

Scarne was a youngster when he moved to New Jersey with his unemployed Italian-born parents, who went there looking for work. Bored with high school, Scarne dropped out and got his education on the street. In his tough neighborhood, he studied the three-card Monte dealers and other wise guys and gamblers, all of whom were hustling a buck. When he was fifteen years old, Scarne learned the most important lesson of his life. What happened was, he tried his luck in a neighborhood card game. It was fixed. By the time Scarne realized the cards were shaved, it was too late—he had already lost his entire weekly salary. Inevitably, Scarne's mother found out what happened. She sat the teenager down. 'If you like to play with cards so much," she said, "practice to do tricks with them." Scarne, naturally, obeyed his Italian mother.

Scarne devoted countless hours to practicing with cards, and while still in his teens, he perfected what would become his signature feat—cutting four aces from an unmarked deck. In 'The Amazing World of John Scarne,' the master manipulator explains (try to follow this), "I always give the deck one or more riffle shuffles and I hold the cards in such manner that I can glimpse the indices on the cards as they fly past during the shuffle. When I sight an ace I count by feel the number of cards which fall on top of it. Then I calculate the number of cards a player cuts, and I cut down to this total and there is an ace."

By the time of World War II, John Scarne had perfected his ability to manipulate cards. Too old for military service, he did his part on the home front. He mounted a campaign to help young, naive soldiers. Scarne's main thrust was to convince them not to gamble, but if they felt they must, he at least taught them how to spot crooked games and what the true odds were in craps. As Scarne's celebrity status grew, he began writing books on gambling, producing one every few years. His books on dice, poker and other games are considered the authoritative books in their respective fields. Scarne even invented several board games, including one named 'Teeko' that he was particularly keen on. Scarne has appeared on stage, television and in movies. He has fooled everyone with his unequaled handling of playing cards, from the FBI—to whom he demonstrated cheating methods—to the best magicians in the world, such as Harry Houdini and Nate Leipzig. Not easy gentlemen to fool. He has entertained at the White House innumerable times.

True to his mother's early admonition, John Scarne always held actual gambling in disdain. Nevertheless, due to his genius for mathematics and calculations, he still managed to become the world's leading expert on gambling and the best sleight-of-hand performer (particularly with cards) in the world.

Nick J. Mileti

GIORGIO CAVALLON

(Born March 2, 1904 in Sorio, Italy;
Died in New York in 1989)

Giorgio Cavallon was one of America's first 'Abstract Impressionists,' and his paintings are greatly admired for the beauty and spontaneous feeling he achieved with the rich colors he used.

Giorgio always wanted to be an artist, so when he arrived in America at sixteen years of age—from the province of Vicenza in Northern Italy—he immediately began studying art in his spare time from his factory job. Young Cavallon studied art where ever and when ever he could, including private lessons, a stint at the National Academy of Design in New York, a summer with Charles Hawthorne in Provincetown, Mass, and a summer at Oyster Bay, New York after receiving a Louis Comfort Tiffany fellowship. Whenever Cavallon had a few spare moments, he visited museums in Boston, New York, and wherever he happened to be—a practice he continued for the rest of his life. Actually, Giorgio Cavallon never stopped studying all aspects of art, and consequently was known as one of the most erudite artists of his time.

Giorgio returned to Italy in 1930 to paint, and to exhibit his paintings at the Biennale in Venice and his home province of Vicenza. In fact, Cavallon returned to his native Italy numerous times—whenever he could work it into his schedule. In the early thirties, Cavallon was still painting landscapes. In 1933, Giorgio returned to America and subsequently studied with Hans Hofmann for two years. The experience with the painter and teacher—who was a life-long influence—changed the direction of Cavallon's work. He moved toward abstraction.

As Cavallon's work began to evolve and show the influence of the Dutch modernist Piet Mondrian, he began to be associated with William De Kooning and other abstract expressionists. In the late sixties and seventies, Cavallon became concerned with light and all of its ramifications. He began framing his surfaces with small, dark shapes in order to give contrast to the large rectangles of lighter color.

Even though Cavallon spent his life fighting to avoid the labels that art critics love to use to describe artists, Giorgio's style—after his move from early landscapes, which he painted in Italy in the thirties—cannot be described any other way than with the label 'Abstract Impressionism.' Indeed, the geometric forms in his later works have been compared to the early work of Matisse. Through his Hans Hofmann connection, Cavallon exhibited at the 'American Abstract Artists,' group's annual shows for twenty years, starting in 1937. In 1964, Cavallon served as a visiting critic in painting at Yale University.

In 1988, a year before his death, Cavallon was elected a member of the prestigious American Academy of Arts & Letters. Giorgio Cavallon's paintings are exhibited in numerous museums, including the Museum of Modern Art, the Solomon R. Guggenheim Museum, and the Whitney Museum of American Art.

Nick J. Mileti

IRON EYES CODY

(Born April 3, 1904 in Kaplan, Louisiana;
Died January 5, 1999 in Los Angeles, Ca.)
REAL ITALIAN NAME: ESPERA (OSCAR) DE CORTI

Here is a blockbuster of monumental proportions for you. The man who became world famous as the 'American Indian,' whose single tear rolled down his anguished face in the poignant and wildly successful anti-littering television campaign of the seventies, was an Italian actor. The tear was glycerin.

Iron Eye's mother was named Francesca Salpietra. She was a short Sicilian woman, with long black hair and dark skin. In 1902, Francesca was sent from Italy to America, to marry fellow Sicilian Antonio DeCorti. Espera was born two years later. As a child, Iron Eyes dreamed about being an actor. He moved to Hollywood, and, in order to get work, pretended to be an Indian. The tactic worked, and Cecil B. DeMille cast Iron Eyes in an early film. Knowing a good thing when he saw it, Iron Eyes parlayed his Indian character into fame and fortune, appearing as an Indian in over 100 movies and numerous TV westerns. He became the most well known 'Indian' actor of all time, but wisely kept a low profile. When he did go out, Iron Eyes almost always wore his braided wig, beaded moccasins and a buckskin jacket. Eventually, Iron Eyes lived his adult life as an Indian—he married an Indian woman, adopted two Indian children, and worked tirelessly for Indian causes.

In 1971, Iron Eyes Cody gave his greatest performance as an Indian. In a 60-second public service TV spot, Iron Eyes, in beaded buckskin, paddles his birch bark canoe up a polluted river, past belching smokestacks. He lands on a riverbank filled with garbage, walks to the highway, and watches incredulously as a passing motorist tosses a bag of trash out of his car window, which bursts at his feet. The camera moves in and follows a single tear rolling down the 'Indian's' face. An announcer says, "Some people have a deep abiding respect for the natural beauty that was once this country... and some people don't. People start pollution. People can stop it." The image, now an icon, made 'the quintessential American Indian,' Iron Eyes Cody, a worldwide celebrity. The spot won two Clio Awards, and was named one of the top 100 advertising campaigns of the 20th Century by Ad Age Magazine.

In 1982, Iron Eyes, knowing that his Italian heritage was an open secret in Hollywood and his hometown in Louisiana, wrote an autobiography, attempting to legitimatize the lie that he was an Indian. In the book, he claimed, among many things, that his father was a Cherokee and his mother a Cree. After reading the book, a suspicious film historian, Angela Aleiss—with the help of official documents, close associates, and Cody's stepsister—exposed the myth in a newspaper article published in 1996. A friend put things in perspective. "He (Iron Eyes Cody) lived and breathed an Indian lifestyle. In that sense, at least, no one can call him an imposter." Like countless Italians in the early 20th Century, De Corti changed his Italian name to help himself succeed in America. Iron Eyes, cleverly, took it several steps further.

Nick J. Mileti

EMILIO GINO SEGRE

(Born Feb. 1, 1905 in Tivoli, Italy; Died in 1989)

A classical physicist, Nobel laureate Emilio Segre was known as a master of pure theory.

Segre attended the University of Rome planning to become an engineer, but in a classic example of fate taking a person by the hand, he met Enrico Fermi who had only recently established a group for research in atomic and molecular physics. Segre became Fermi's first doctoral student, receiving his degree in 1928. After a two-year stint in the Italian army, Segre returned to Italy where he again joined forces with Fermi at the University of Rome. The group of young Italian scientists worked to discover nuclear energy—they were trying to find a cure for cancer. They conducted experiments where elements such as uranium were bombarded with neutrons, and in 1935, the group discovered slow neutrons, which are important to nuclear reactors.

In 1936 Segre became Director of the Physics Laboratory at the University of Palermo.

In 1938, however, a blow was struck to the heart of Italy's scientific future. The Racial Laws of Italy were passed in that year, and since Segre was Jewish, he fled Mussolini's Fascist rule (Enrico Fermi also fled to America—he was not Jewish, but his wife was).

Segre immigrated to America and became a research associate in the Radiation Laboratory at the University of California at Berkeley. In 1940, Segre was a member of the Seaborg team that discovered plutonium-239 and its fission properties. Following its discovery, Segre determined that plutonium split when struck by fast neutrons, resulting in the release of large amounts of energy. This opened the door to plutonium's use in atomic bombs.

There was still a major problem—the possibility of spontaneous fission in plutonium. In 1943, to investigate this possibility, Los Alamos Director, J. Robert Oppenheimer, invited Emilio Segre and his group to Los Alamos to continue their experiments there. In what became known as 'The Manhattan Project,' the team of scientists—some of the most famous names in the world, including Segre and Fermi—eventually developed the atomic bombs that were dropped on Hiroshima and Nagasaki, Japan, in August of 1945. These were the bombs that convinced the Japanese to surrender, ending World War II.

Segre returned to Berkeley in 1946, and remained at the University for the rest of his life.

In 1959, along with Owen Chamberlain, his colleague at Berkeley, Emlio Segre was awarded the Nobel Prize in Physics for his work in nuclear and high-energy physics—technically they received the prize for the discovery of the antiproton.

In 1983, seventy-eight year old Nobel laureate Emilio Segre joined seventy other scientists in Los Alamos. The prestigious group of scientists, who had all worked on the atomic bomb, pleaded for worldwide nuclear arms reduction. Ironically, with that effort, Emilio Segre's professional life—begun in Italy over fifty years earlier in entirely peaceful pursuits—traveled full circle.

Nick J. Mileti

TONY PASTOR

(Born Oct. 26, 1907 in Middletown, Ct.;
Died Oct. 31, 1969 in New London, Ct.)
REAL ITALIAN NAME: ANTONIO PESTRITTO

Tony Pastor's Big Band—a cross between a novelty group and a swing band, but always with a strong jazz flavor—was popular from 1940 to 1959. Pastor is most famous, however, for discovering Rosemary Clooney (and her sister Betty). The Clooney Sisters (nineteen and sixteen respectively) auditioned for Pastor when the band was passing through Cincinnati Ohio in 1945, and were hired on the spot.

Pastor played the tenor sax and sang. He possessed one of the unique voices of the times and loved to sing tunes with zany lyrics ('Dance With A Dolly With A Hole In Her Stocking'). Before starting his own orchestra, Pastor played with some of the era's best band, including Artie Shaw from 1936 to 1940.

Pastor's band managed to survive the massacre of big bands after World War II—and hang-on until 1959—because of great arrangements and a well-rated radio show. In the Sixties, like most other big band leaders, Pastor formed a small group with his three sons and played Las Vegas and other venues.

Closet Italians

JOHNNY DESMOND

(Born November 14, 1919 in Detroit, Michigan;
Died September 6, 1985 in Los Angeles, California)
REAL ITALIAN NAME:
GIOVANNI ALFREDO DE SIMONE

Johnny Desmond had a successful career as a singer on radio and television.

Johnny worked on Detroit radio as a youth, and formed a vocal group, which performed as the Bob-O-Links with the Bob Crosby Band. Striking out on his own as a solo act, he joined the Gene Krupa Band as a soloist in 1941. Duty called, however, and Johnny joined the Air Force, singing with the Glenn Miller Orchestra in England, where he also hosted his own radio show 'A Soldier and a Song.'

After the war, Desmond starred on radio in various capacities. He was so popular, in the late forties, Johnny turned a guest stint on the immensely popular show 'The Breakfast Club' (which ran for 35 years) into a six-year run.

Some of Johnny Desmond's most popular recordings were 'C'est Ci Bon,' 'The High and the Mighty' and 'Yellow Rose of Texas.' On Broadway, Johnny appeared in 'Say Darling' in 1958, and later in 'Funny Girl' in the role of Nicky Arnstein. "This was a rarity," he later joked, "An Italian playing a Jew".

GIULIO RACAH

(Born 1909 in Florence, Italy;
Died August 28, 1965)

Giulio Racah was a physicist and mathematician, considered by the experts second only to the legendary Enrico Fermi.

In 1930, Racah received his PhD from the University of Florence when he was only twenty-one years old. He then moved to Rome, and studied under Enrico Fermi at the Institute of Via Panisperna (as had Emilio Segre) as a post-doctoral assistant in the nuclear physics group. Racah also studied in Zurich.

In 1932, Racah became a lecturer in Theoretical Physics in Florence, and in 1937, an Associate Professor in Theoretical Physics at the University of Pisa.

Driven out of Italy by the Fascist Racial (anti-Jewish) law, in 1939 Racah immigrated to Israel. He founded the Department of Theoretical Physics at the Hebrew University in Jerusalem and became its first Full Professor. In the forties, Giulio Racah was made Dean of the Faculty of Sciences, and in the early sixties served as Rector and Acting President of the school for five years.

In addition to his teaching chores, Racah was a serious researcher and writer. Reflecting his time with Fermi, Racah's research and publishing was mainly in the fields of quantum physics and atomic spectroscopy. In 1959, Racah wrote the book 'Irreducible Tensorial Sets' with his younger cousin Ugo Fano, who was also a distinguished physicist.

From 1942 to 1951, Giulio Racah made history. He presented his 'Theory of complex Spectra,' a series of five papers on energy levels. These papers presented the possibility of making practical calculations of spectroscopic properties lanthanides and actinides.

During, and even after, his distinguished career, Giulio Racah has received numerous prestigious awards and honors.

In 1958, he was awarded the Israel prize for lifetime contribution to physics (the most highly regarded award in Israel); in 1963 he was made an Honorary Member of the American Academy of Arts and Science; and in 1965 he was made a Commendatore of the Order of Merit from the Republic of Italy.

In 1970, The Racah Institute of Physics was established at the Hebrew University in Giulio Racah's honor.

Nick J. Mileti

DOLORES READE HOPE

(Born May 27, 1909 in the Bronx, New York)
REAL ITALIAN NAME: DOLORES DE FINA

Dolores Hope has been overshadowed all of her life by her famous husband, comedian Bob Hope, but she never let that prevent her from accomplishing her own set of goals in life.

Dolores De Fina began her career as a singer before ever meeting Hope. In 1930, when she turned twenty-one, her agent suggested she change her name to Dolores Reade, because Florence Reed was a popular Broadway actress at the time. When Hope met her in 1933 and got hit by a fulmine (thunderbolt), Dolores was well into her professional singing career on the New York nightclub circuit. The couple was married a few months later and Dolores supported Hope's career for seventy years.

Dolores soon left show biz to raise the couple's four adopted children. When World War II began, however, she joined Hope on his USO tours and helped entertain America's troops around the world. When the Vietnam War broke out, Dolores again joined Hope and again was one of the favorites of the troops. In 1991, in the Desert Storm War, Dolores again joined her husband on tour, and was the only female permitted to perform in Saudi Arabia—a tribute to her as much as to Hope.

Dedicating her entire life to helping her fellow man, Dolores Hope's contributions are legendary. She is the founding President of the Eisenhower Medical Center in Palm Desert, California; she has supported the Hughen School for Severely Handicapped Crippled Children in

Port Arthur, Texas; Saint Anne's Home in Los Angeles; the Helping Hand Organization of Cedars-Sinai Hospital; the Holy Family Adoption Service and Childhelp, USA, to name a only a few of her charitable causes.

Dolores Hope has been honored innumerable times. To give only a few examples, she has been awarded seven Honorary Doctorates; a street has been named for her—Dolores DeFina Hope—in the Bronx, New York; she received the Lifetime Achievement Award for Humanitarian Services from the National Italian American Foundation; and was granted the Ellis Island Medal of Honor.

Dolores Hope received papal honors from Pope John Paul II, Dame of Saint Gregory with Star, only one of four women in the world to be so honored.

In 1993, at the age of eighty-four, after playful nagging from Hope "I wish she'd get steady work," Dolores returned to her first love (after her husband) and re-launched her singing career, having kept in practice by frequent appearances on Hope's television specials. Dolores personally selects the songs for her albums, which are graced with her low and husky voice, which is still beautiful and strong.

Chapter VIII

Illustrious Italians With Non-Italian Names
Born Between 1910-1919

Nick J. Mileti

FRANKIE LAINE

(Born March 30, 1913 in Chicago, Illinois)
REAL ITALIAN NAME: FRANK PAUL LO VECCHIO

In his legendary career, Frankie Laine has sold over 100 million records (including over 20 Gold Records), singing pop, western, blues, country and jazz.

Frankie's parents emigrated from Monreale, Sicily to Chicago, Illinois. Since Frankie was the oldest of eight children, he naturally did what he could to help his parents—working at whatever job he get. But Frankie was ambitious and had music in his heart. Consequently, the youngster entered radio station singing contests on the side. Chasing work, Laine moved to Cleveland, Ohio where he worked in a factory and performed at night. He eventually moved to California, convinced that to make it as a singer he had to be there. But he was careful not to give up his day job in a factory.

One fateful night, at the Billy Berg Club in Hollywood, the great Hoagy Carmichael was present to hear a jazz trio, featuring Nat King Cole. And, as fate would have it, there was also a singer on the bill—it was Frankie Laine—whom the group backed as he sang Carmichael's own song, 'Old Rocking Chair.' Impressed by what he heard, Carmichael took Laine under his wing. He arranged for Laine to get a gig at the Vine Street Club in Hollywood. It was 1947, and Laine introduced 'That's My Desire.' Within weeks, the record was on the charts and selling.

Laine's worked hard at his singing career, and the persistence paid off—but it took a while. In fact, Frankie was forty years old when 'I Believe' became a worldwide hit in 1953. The song made Frankie Laine an international star. 'I Believe' hit a particular nerve in England, where it remained Number One for a record eighteen weeks. Hit after hit followed. Over the years, Laine had an incredible twenty-one Gold Records, including 'Mule Train', 'That Lucky Old Sun', and 'Jezebel.' As is normal in these cases, during his heyday, Laine appeared on radio, television and in movies. When the rock and roll invasion basically shut down Laine's type of singing, he wisely, and successfully, began touring the world in concert and cabaret venues.

Frankie Laine, however, probably remains in the hearts and minds of the public because of an unusual fact. He has recorded title songs for seven motion pictures, including 'Gunfight at O.K. Coral', and Mel Brook's classic western spoof 'Blazing Saddles.' In fact, his rendition of 'Rawhide' has become one of the most popular theme songs of all time.

In 1993, Laine published his autobiography, 'That Lucky Old Son.' Frankie Laine has received numerous awards in his remarkable career, including a Lifetime Achievement Award, presented in 1996 by the Songwriter's Hall of Fame.

Nick J. Mileti

ALFRED DRAKE

(Born October 7, 1914 in the Bronx, New York;
Died July 25, 1992 in NYC)
REAL ITALIAN NAME: ALFREDO CAPURRO

While he has made numerous television and movie appearances over the years, Alfred Drake will always be revered for his roles in musical comedies on Broadway, which he dominated for over a decade.

Rare for stage performers at the time, in 1935 Drake graduated from Brooklyn College (he wanted to be a teacher). Always interested in music—as all young Italians seem to be—before his teaching career began, he auditioned for 'The Mikado,' and landed the part of chorus boy. For the next eight years, Drake worked almost non-stop in various plays and revues. Then in 1943, when Drake was twenty-nine years old, it happened.

Listen to renowned (almost fifty years in the business) Boston theater critic Elliot Norton: "The opening of Oklahoma! was downright daring in its day. The curtain went up on a Midwestern farmyard with old Aunt Eller (Betty Garde) churning butter. No girls, no legs, no dancing! In a moment a voice was heard offstage. Then on walked Alfred Drake, dressed as the cowboy Curly, singing the first and one of the best of all Rogers and Hammerstein hits, 'Oh, What a Beautiful Morning' . . . In that scene and song, American musical comedy took a new turn away from stilted nonsense towards something like truth and beauty. And Alfred, because he got all that into his manner, his bearing, and his exuberant natural singing voice, became in effect the herald of a new era."

'Oklahoma,' and his award winning, robust renderings of the other show-stopping numbers in the groundbreaking, hit musical (including 'Surrey with the Fringe on Top' and 'People Will Say We're in Love'), made Alfred Drake a major Broadway star.

In 1948, Drake scored another award winning Broadway triumph. He played the lead in Cole Porter's 'Kiss Me Kate,' receiving great acclaim for his acting, as well as for his singing. The New York Times said, "Mr. Drake's pleasant style of acting and his unaffected singing are the heart of the show. By hard work and through personal sincerity, Mr. Drake has become about the most valuable man in his field."

It was in 1953, however, that Alfred Drake gave an award winning performance, which will be most associated with him forever. The show was 'Kismet,' and Drake received a sack full of Awards, including a Tony. Richard Watts in the New York Post stated, "He (Alfred Drake) is easily the ablest man in the business at this sort of picturesque swagger, and he is at his best in Kismet, which is saying a lot."

Sadly, as is often the case in Hollywood, when movies were made of his musical triumphs on the Broadway stage, Alfred Drake was not cast in any of the roles.

Alfred Drake was inducted into the Theater Hall of Fame in 1981, and in 1990, he was awarded an Honorary Tony for his lifetime achievement as perhaps "the greatest singing actor the American musical theatre has ever produced."

Nick J. Mileti

ERNEST BORGNINE

(Born January 24, 1915 in Hamden, Connecticut)
REAL ITALIAN NAME: ERMES EFFRON BORGNINO

Ernest Borgnine is a television and motion picture star, best known for his role in the television series McHale's Navy.

Ernest Borgnine's parents emigrated from Italy to the United States. After high school, Ernest served ten years in America's Navy. Discharged after World War II in 1945, he was at loose ends when his mother (like Vittorio Gassman's mother) suggested he try acting. Naturally, Borgnine (also like Gassman) listened to his Italian mother.

In 1951, after Acting School and struggling in and around New York (on Broadway in 1949, he played a male nurse in the play 'Harvey'), he moved to Hollywood to try his hand at acting for movies.

Cast as a heavy in his early screen years, Borgnine's break-through role was as the obnoxious Sergeant 'Fatso' Judson in the 1953 hit movie 'From Here to Eternity.' 'Bad Day at Black Rock' followed the bad guy pattern, but a career-making movie was just ahead.

In 1955, Borgnine was cast and played against type, in the lead role of the award-winning film 'Marty.' Borgnine gave an extraordinary performance as a sensitive butcher named Marty Pilletti ("I don't know, Ang, what do you want to do?"), which earned him an Oscar for Best Actor, and honors from the British Film Academy, the New York Film Critics and the Cannes Film Festival, among others.

Working regularly in feature films—a favorite of directors Robert Aldrich and Sam Peckinpah—Borgnine starred in such films as 'The Dirty Dozen' in 1967, 'The Wild Bunch' in 1969, and 'The Poiseidon Adventure' in 1974. In his extensive career, Borgnine has appeared in over one hundred movies.

The popular star landed the plum lead role of Quinton McHale in the television series 'McHale's Navy,' which also starred the comic genius, Tim Conway. 'McHale's Navy,' which ran on ABC for four years, from 1962 to 1966, has aired regularly in syndication. The mischievous McHale has become Borgnine's defining roll. Borgnine scored a rare theatrical feat when he added an Emmy and Golden Globe Award to his Oscar for 'All Quiet on the Western Front.'

Over the years, Borgnine has received an arm-full of lifetime achievement awards and honorary degrees, but has always retained his down-home, humble approach to stardom. One of the best-loved people in show biz and a favorite with the fans, the warm, gregarious Ernest Borgnine sincerely enjoys touring the country in his forty-foot bus, shaking hands and signing autographs.

Nick J. Mileti

R. S. LOUIGUY

(Born in Italy in 1916;
Died April 4, 1991 in Vence, France)
REAL ITALIAN NAME: LUIGI GUGLIEMI

The Italian, Luigi Gugliemi, wrote what is considered the quintessential 'French' song, 'La Vie En Rose,' in 1947. Luigi Gugliemi became R. S. Louiguy in France (notice the similarity between the real Italian first name and the French adoptation).

Louiguy also wrote 'Cherry Pink and Apple Blossom White' in 1955, which became a huge hit for Prez Prado who recorded the song as a mambo in the same year.

Mack David wrote English lyrics for both 'Cherry Pink and Apple Blossom White' and 'La Vie En Rose.' In 1950, Louis Armstrong made 'La Vie En Rose' popular in America with his famous hit recording of the song. R. S, Louiguy scored a number of French movies, including Jean Gabin's last gangster film.

EDITH PIAF

(Born Dec. 19, 1915 in Paris; Died Oct. 11, 1963)
REAL NAME: EDITH GIOVANNA GASSION

If it isn't shocking enough to learn that the 'French' song, 'La Vie En Rose,' was written by an Italian, listen to this. The quintessential 'French' cabaret singer, Edith Piaf, was half-Italian.

Piaf's mother's name was Anetta Giovanna Maillard who sang under the name Line Marsa. There is disagreement as to whether her mother was a cabaret singer or a 'street singer,' but there is no debate about her nationality. Edith Piaf's mother was an Italian who was born in Italy.

Piaf means sparrow in French. It was a nickname given to her in her youth by nightclub owner, Louis Leplee, who took the singer under his wing and started her on her internationally successful singing career. Edith Piaf became the greatest 'French' chanteuse of all time, which is astonishing, considering that early death cut short her stormy, fabled career.

Edith Piaf herself wrote the French lyrics for 'La Vie En Rose.'

The French reached new highs, or lows—depending on your point of view—with this triple-whammy. They co-opted a song, they co-opted the man who wrote the song, and they co-opted the singer (Edith Piaf) who embraced the song and made it her own.

Nick J. Mileti

DEAN MARTIN

(Born June 7, 1917 in Steubenville, Ohio;
Died Dec. 25, 1995)
REAL ITALIAN NAME: DINO PAUL CROCETTI

Dean Martin achieved mega-stardom in four distinct careers—as a singer, on the stage, in movies, and on television.

Dean's parents emigrated from Italy to America. Just prior to World War II, Sammy Watkins heard young Dean Martin singing in Columbus, Ohio. He immediately brought him to Cleveland as featured vocalist for his popular orchestra. Dean was using the name Martini at the time, but Watkins dropped the 'I.' Dean Martin took Cleveland by storm and became an instant celebrity.

An association with Jerry Lewis began in Atlantic City in 1946 and lasted ten years. 'Martin and Lewis' became one of the biggest acts in show biz, appearing at the top clubs, casinos and in movies. Martin tired of the shtick. According to Nick Tosches, who wrote the definitive biography of the star, Dean felt like the organ grinder to the trained monkey. So, even though the money was flowing, Martin quit and both men went on to important careers. Dean Martin—who sang in the style of Bing Crosby, if Crosby had been Italian—had forty records on the charts from 1950 to 1969. His recordings of 'That's Amore' (written by Harry Warren), 'Memories Are Made of This,' 'Everybody Loves Somebody Sometime,' and 'You're Nobody Until Somebody Loves You,' were all major hits among the 500 records and over 60 albums Martin cut in his career.

Dean's third career was a movie star—he appeared in over fifty films from 1949 to 1984, including those with Lewis. A surprisingly good actor, Dean Martin was always Dean Martin up on the screen—and that was the secret of his success: He was a fun-loving, real man who never took himself, or his impressive talent, too seriously. As for television, 'The Dean Martin Show' was one of televisions most popular shows, lasting almost a dozen years, from 1964 to 1975. Re-runs of Martin's celebrity 'Roasts' are still staples on the tube.

When Dean Martin joined Sinatra and his pals in what was dubbed 'The Rat Pack,' all of the threads of Dean's magical life came together and should have formed one long, sweet, swinging party. Actually, to his millions of fans, it appeared that the ruggedly handsome superstar was living exactly that.

The reality was—again according to Tosches—that as Dean Martin's notoriety and fame grew, he withdrew more and more into himself. Then, in 1987, Dean's son (Dino) died in a military airplane crash, and Dean Martin withdrew totally. For Dean Martin, the eight years from his son's tragic death to his own death were filled with unimaginable pain and despair.

Nick J. Mileti

JOSE GRECO

(Born Dec. 23, 1918 in Montorio nei Frentani [Abruzzi], Italy; Died Jan. 3, 2001 in Lancaster Pennsylvania)
REAL ITALIAN NAME: COSTANZO GRECO

Jose Greco, the greatest Spanish dancer the world has ever known, was one hundred percent Italian. Both parents were Italian and Greco was born in Italy. Here is how history got manipulated.

In 1943, the most important Spanish dancer at the time, the famous La Argentinita, wanted to hire the twenty-five year old Costanzo Greco to perform as her partner. She could see unlimited potential in the young man, but she had a problem.

"It would be better if you had a Spanish name," she said to Greco. "The last name's okay. After all, El Greco, the [Greek] painter is associated with Spain. But Costanzo will never do. How about Jose?" Greco quickly agreed. "After all," he thought, "when people go to see a Spanish dancer, they like to think he's Spanish."

Greco's family immigrated to America when he was ten years old. He was raised in Brooklyn, and originally wanted to be a painter. While studying art in the thirties, at the DaVinci Art School in New York, however, he became interested in dance (to the everlasting joy of the world).

Following his tour with La Argentinita as her lead dancer, after her death Greco and her talented sister Pilar Lopez, formed their own troupe and toured for three years. In 1951, Greco formed his own dance company 'Ballets y Bailes de Espana.' Integrating flamenco with mainstream ballet, the Jose Greco Dance Company toured extensively over the years, performing all over the world. Greco also appeared on television and in movies, choreographing his own dances. The international acclaim and successes earned Jose Greco the universally accepted titles, 'The World's Greatest Flamenco Dancer,' and 'The Greatest Spanish Dancer in the World.'

In 1962, the Spanish government knighted Jose Greco, "in recognition of his worldwide contribution to the culture and performing arts of Spain."

Back to the name. In order to cover-up his pure Italian lineage, myths were promulgated by the Spanish, who co-opted him. The primary myth presented to the public was that Greco was born of mixed parentage—Spanish and Italian. Looking back at the myths, Greco wrote in his autobiography, "I never hid (the fact that I was one hundred percent Italian) but I didn't do enough to deny the myths."

Incredibly, Greco also said that even when he did make the facts clear, he was not always believed—which, of course, is just one reason for writing this book.

Nick J. Mileti

ROBERT STACK

(Born January 13, 1919 in Los Angeles, California;
Died May 14, 2003)
REAL ITALIAN NAME: ROBERT LANGFORD
MODINI

Robert Stack's acting career has spanned six decades of film and television, but he is best known as master crime fighter, Eliot Ness.

Stack first became known as the handsome young actor who gave Deanna Durbin her first screen kiss in the film 'First Love'. Believe it or not, in 1939, this was a significant Hollywood publicity event.

Appearing in Ernst Lubitsch's comic masterpiece 'To Be or Not to Be' in 1942, with Jack Benny and Carol Lombard, Stack was on a fast track in Hollywood. However, World War II slowed the careers of many actors, including Stack. In 1954, Stack rebounded, with the film 'The High and Mighty,' appearing with John Wayne. Then in 1956, with the film 'Written on the Wind,' Stack earned an Oscar nomination for Best Supporting Actor. Over the years, Stack has appeared in over forty feature films.

In 1959, Robert Stack's life made a significant U-turn. In that year he debuted in the ABC television series 'The Untouchables,' playing F.B.I. man Eliot Ness. The series ran four years and made Stack a major star. In 1960, he won an Emmy for his portrayal of Ness.

Stack hit a nerve with the public—he played the part so well, people actually came to believe that Robert Stack was the steely-eyed, resolute Eliot Ness. Stack, however, has a logical explanation. He tells the story of a well-known gangster (Sam Giancana) who, when he saw Stack, hid from him, mistaking him for the real-life Ness. "If you play a character long enough, you become that character in the eyes of viewers. But here's Public Enemy Number One, head of Murder, Incorporated, and he thinks I'm the real Eliot Ness. It can't get any goofier."

Deploring the typecasting, Stack moved to Europe where he lived and worked. In 1980, in an attempt to break the stereotype, and to have some fun, Stack engaged in a hilarious self-parody of his stern, tough-guy image in the hit spoof 'Airplane.' The same year, with Mark Evans, Stack wrote his autobiography 'Straight Shooting.'

In 1988, while Stack was traveling and working between Europe and America, television again delivered an important role to him. Robert Stack was hired as Host and Narrator of the long-running, popular series 'Unsolved Mysteries.' He hosted over 1,200 segments. Stack learned to use his melodious voice dramatically when he appeared on Radio in the early days of his career.

Robert Stack received the Hollywood Legend Award in 2001, and in 2002 he received the Society for Cinephile's Career Achievement Award.

Nick J. Mileti

HARRY CARAY

(Born March 1, 1919 in St Louis;
Died Feb.18, 1998 in Rancho Mirage, Calif.)
REAL ITALIAN NAME:
HARRY CHRISTOPHER CARABINA

In the rarefied world of legendary sports radio play-by-play men such as icons Chick Hearn (Los Angeles Lakers), Ernie Harwell (Detroit Tigers) and Joe Tait (Cleveland Cavaliers and Indians), Harry Caray not only held his own professionally, he became a larger-than-life symbol of baseball—when baseball really was 'the national pastime.'

Overall, Caray spent over fifty years broadcasting baseball games, beginning his career when television was just a dream and radio was king. In the early days before announcers traveled with the teams, broadcasting Saint Louis Cardinals games Caray would 're-create' the play by play. He did this by reading the coded 'ticker tape' and (for example) announcing, "Here comes a foul ball, watch it . . ." and banging his fist on the table. "Holy Cow, that was close" (Caray coined the phrase "Holy Cow").

During his eleven years with the White Sox and sixteen years with the Cubs, Caray became a major celebrity in Chicago, where he was as famous for leading a full and colorful life as he was for being the top broadcaster in town. Frequenting the watering holes of fabled Rush Street whenever the teams were playing at home, Harry was a Damon Runyon character idolized by the fans and politicos alike. In fact, Caray was so well known and admired, he was called 'Mayor of Rush Street.' He once laughed, "Oh, I get a little tired now and then, but knowing my life style, that's only natural."

Harry Caray's tell-it-like-it-is style of play-by-play delivery was always on target. Sometimes he was critical, but he was never malicious. Sometimes he made mistakes, as all announcers do, but Caray always laughed at himself when he did.

The highlight of the fan's day was listening to the singing of 'Take Me Out to the Ballgame' by Harry Caray. For an Italian, Caray sang surprisingly off-key—but it probably was just an act to have fun and be 'one of the guys.' "I would always sing it (Take Me Out to the Ballgame)," he once explained facetiously, "because I think it's the only song I know the words to," cleverly illustrating his dedication to the sport.

One of the most famous announcers in all of sports—certainly the most colorful—Harry Caray was named The Sporting New's 'Baseball Announcer of the Year' seven straight years. In addition to his place in the prestigious Baseball Hall of Fame, Caray has been inducted into the American Sportscasters Hall of Fame.

Every year, on February 19 (the day after he died), in a perfectly appropriate gesture, Harry Caray is saluted in bars, pubs, restaurants and lounges everywhere: A unique worldwide toast is offered to the memory of the unique Harry Caray.

CHAPTER IX

Illustrious Italians With Non-Italian Names
Born Between 1920-1929

Nick J. Mileti

YVES MONTAND

(Born in 1921 in Monsummano Alto, Italy;
Died Nov. 9, 1991 in Senlis, France)
REAL ITALIAN NAME: IVO LIVI

Here's yet another shocker. Yves Montand is Italian. You read that right—Yves Montand is another classic case of co-opting by the French.

The great 'French' actor/cabaret singer/political figure is one hundred percent Italian. His lovely mother was named Giuseppina Simoni and his father was Giovanni Livi. Montand was born in a small town in Tuscany, which his family left in 1924 to escape the Fascists. They settled in Marseilles, France, where Montand began his career performing in the nightclubs of the port city. When Yves was seventeen years old, he was beginning to make a name for himself when a promoter, Francois Trottobas, persuaded him to "Invent a stage name that sounds good," because his name (Ivo Livi) wouldn't look good on a Music Hall program in France.

In 1945, Montand became the prodigy (and lover) of Edith Piaf, opening for the legendary cabaret singer while slowly and carefully developing his own stage act. When Montand began to make movies, he met the famous actress Simone Signoret, and married her in 1951. Montand's cinema break-through was his role in the 1953 thriller 'The Wages of Fear,' which propelled him into international stardom. As usual, the siren call of Hollywood pulled Montand to America. In 1960, in his first American film, he co-stared with Marilyn Monroe in 'Let's Make Love,' which they did, to the delight of the pulp press and consternation of the long-suffering

Signoret. In 1986, Yves Montand capped his career of over fifty years with two show-stopping performances in the films 'Jean De Florette,' and its continuation, 'Manon of the Spring.'

A communist from his youth (because of his father and brother), Montand famously rejected the ideology in 1968 and became an out-spoken critic of the Soviet regime for the rest of his life.

Most people not only mistakenly believe Yves Montand is French, when they learn his Real Italian Name is Ivo Livi, they also mistakenly believe he is Jewish. Not surprisingly, his name was a recurring problem in France during World War II. A delightful story—which may or may not be true—is told about a Gestapo agent who cornered Montand backstage at a theatre in which he was performing.

"You are Jewish," the German agent said. "Your name is Levy, not Livi. You have changed two letters in your name."

"That's absurd," Yves Montand replied. "If I had changed anything at all I would have changed the whole thing and called myself Dupont." The Gestapo agent roared with laughter and allowed Montand to remain free.

Nick J. Mileti

ANGELO DUNDEE

(Born August 30, 1921 in Philadelphia, Pennsylvania)
REAL ITALIAN NAME: ANGELO MERENA

Angelo Dundee is the greatest fight trainer of all time. In his unprecedented career he trained fifteen world champions.

Angelo's older brother Joe adopted the surname Dundee in honor of the great fighter Johnny Dundee, and Angelo, interested in boxing from when he was a kid, followed suit. After World Was II, Angelo moved from South Philly, where he grew up, to New York. Dundee quickly found famed Stillman's Gym. He hung around, and watched, and learned in what was, in essence, his school and training ground. Dundee and his brother Chris, a Hall of Fame promoter, moved to Miami Beach and bought the 5th Street Gym, which they owned for over forty years. Dundee was chief trainer and achieved worldwide fame there, making the gym as famous as Stillman's in the world of Boxing.

Some of Dundee's champions include Carmen Basilio, Jimmy Ellis and George Forman (during his second career). Incredibly, in 1963, two of his fighters—Sugar Ramos and Luis Rodriguez—won titles on the same card. Later that year, in 1963, two more of his fighters—Ralph Dupas and Willie Pastrano—won titles. In 1969, Jose Napoles, another of the fighters Dundee trained, won the welterweight title.

But it was in 1960 that Angelo Dundee became a household name, because in 1960 he was hired to train Muhammad Ali. A great fighter, but a difficult man to handle in those days, Dundee was more than a trainer to

Ali. During his twenty-year tumultuous on-again off-again association, Dundee had a major role in Ali becoming a boxing legend. In spite of the volatility of the relationship, Ali always respected Dundee, recently calling him, "The greatest trainer of all time." For his part, Dundee has always been known for his intelligence and common sense in a field not known for those traits. For example, when asked about his fighter's conversion and membership in the Nation of Islam, and changing his name from Cassius Clay to Muhammad Ali, Dundee said. "What's in a name? To me, he's still the same guy."

In 1976, Dundee again entered the high-profile arena—he was hired to shape the career of Sugar Ray Leonard. A quick thinker and master motivator in the corner, his "You're blowing it, son" pep talk to Sugar Ray, just before he knocked out Thomas Hearns, has become more famous than the fight itself. When asked by ABC Sports if there were any similarities between Ali and Sugar Ray, Dundee said, "None. None whatsoever . . . You can't make a fighter be like a clone of the other fighter, because it won't happen. The reflex is different, the balance is different, the approach is different, and the height is different. So much goes into play there. And it's a complete study." Dundee was named the Manager of the Year in 1968 and 1979 by the Boxing Writers Association of America, and was granted their Long and Meritorious Service Award in 1996. In 1994, Dundee was elected to the International Boxing Hall of Fame.

Nick J. Mileti

RAY ANTHONY

(Born January 20, 1922 in Bentleyville, Pennsylvania)
REAL ITALIAN NAME: RAYMOND ANTONINI

The Ray Anthony Orchestra was one of the best dance bands of the last century, and Anthony has worked tirelessly in his later years to keep alive the phenomenon known as the Big Band Era.

The Antonini family, which had emigrated from Italy, settled in Cleveland, Ohio when Ray was a little boy. Ray's father started to teach him to play the trumpet at the age of five, and he was soon performing in the family band.

Ray attended John Adams High School, where he played in the highly respected school band, which was quite famous in the area at that time (legend has it that Ray was kicked out of the group for improvising). He also played with several local professional bands, including those led by Vince Patti and Jack Crawford. "I learned a lot from Vince," Ray said later, "and the first time I went on the road I was with Jack's band. (But) I always kept coming back to Cleveland which was my home town."

After a stint with the Al Donahue Band, in 1940, Anthony was playing first trumpet with the Glenn Miller Orchestra. During his year-and-a-half stay with Miller, the group recorded most of the tunes that will forever be associated with the Miller Orchestra, including 'Chattanooga Choo-Choo', written by Harry Warren. With sales of over one million, RCA presented Glenn Miller a golden disc of the record—the disc was actual gold, a first.

Ray joined the Navy in 1942 and led a service band in the Pacific. When he came out of the Navy in 1946, Anthony formed his own band, featuring Tony 'Ace' Parisi on first trumpet, and his brother Leo on sax. "We were searching for our own identity as a band," he said later, "and until we got one, we took the best of the best. We took the sax sound of the Glenn Miller Band, we took the trombone sound from Tommy Dorsey. I, being a trumpet player, was naturally compared to Harry James at the time and so we felt the combination of sounds might be one of our own."

In 1949, Anthony signed with Capital Records (which he describes as "a lucky break") and recorded with them for nineteen years. The Ray Anthony Band was ranked as the Number One Band in the country in all the trade magazine polls from 1950-1955. Million sellers included 'The Bunny Hop' and covers of the 'Dragnet' and 'Peter Gunn' themes. Over the years, Anthony toured extensively and released hundreds of hit albums.

In 1960, Ray Anthony—like the other big bands—was forced to form a small group to perform in nightclubs; his group (The Bookends) toured the world for over twenty years. The warm and likeable Ray Anthony also enjoyed success in motion pictures and television, which both featured his music.

Nick J. Mileti

JOEY MAXIM

(Born March 22, 1922 in Cleveland, Ohio;
Died June 2, 2001)
REAL ITALIAN NAME:
GIUSEPPE ANTONIO BERARDINELLI

Joey Maxim was the World Light Heavyweight Champion from 1950 to 1952, but is most famous for having beaten Sugar Ray Robinson in one of the most memorable boxing matches in history.

After a successful amateur career, Joey turned pro in Cleveland in 1941, at the age of eighteen. In his seventeen-year professional career (he retired in 1958), Maxim won 82 bouts, lost 29 and drew 4. When Joey Maxim was inducted into the Boxing Hall of Fame in 1994, here is how he was described: "What Joey Maxim lacked in power, he made up for it with outstanding boxing ability. Although he only scored 21 knockouts in his 115 career bouts, he managed to beat some of the best fighters of his era."

In 1950, Joey went to England to challenge Freddie Mills, who was the World's Light Heavyweight Champion at the time. Maxim was a huge underdog, and the hometown crowd was stunned when he knocked out Mills in the tenth round. Suddenly, nine years after turning pro, Joey Maxim was the Light Heavyweight Champion of the World (he relinquished the title to Archie Moore in December 1952).

On June 25, 1952, Maxim traveled to New York City to defend his crown against Middleweight Champion Sugar Ray Robinson. Robinson, one of the greatest boxers in history, was trying to win a World Title in a third weight class. A crowd of 48,000 boisterous, partisan New York fans filled Yankee Stadium to cheer for heavily-favored Robinson. They figured Maxim didn't have a chance, and they came to see blood. One writer at the time wrote, "Robinson saw no reason he couldn't best Maxim. Joey Maxim wasn't a particularly colorful fighter and wasn't much of a puncher. He was, however, a smart fighter and a first-rate boxer . . . So he lacked Robinson's charisma and aura, but he wasn't a stiff, either."

At ringside, when the fight started at eight o'clock, the temperature was 104 degrees. Robinson, in his usual fashion, danced around Maxim, who was slower than Robinson, taking round after round. It was so hot, the referee quit after the tenth round. Even though he was too far down on points to win, however, Joey Maxim never quit. "I knew I could stand the heat better than Robinson could, so I just let it do its work . . . I was way behind and I knew it. But I also knew I had him if I didn't run out of rounds."

When the bell rang for the fourteenth round, Maxim came out, but Robinson didn't. Joey Maxim retained his crown by what is called a TKO, a technical knockout. For the only time in 202 fights, Sugar Ray Robinson had been knocked out.

The biased New York press claimed the heat, not Maxim, beat Robinson. "I don't know," Joey Maxim later laughed. "It was hot on my half of the ring, too."

Nick J. Mileti

VITTORIO GASSMAN

(Born Sept. 1, 1922 in Genoa, Italy;
Died June 29, 2000 in Rome)

In private, a timid and reserved man, you would never know by talking with handsome Vittorio Gassman that he has appeared in over one hundred films in his remarkable international movie career. His stage career in Italy is equally impressive.

The Austrian father explains the Gassman surname and the Italian mother explains Vittorio's first name and his career.

Vittorio was studying law when his mother encouraged him to become an actor. Naturally, listening to mamma as all good Italian boys do, he entered the National Academy of Dramatic Art in Rome in 1941.

Almost immediately, Gassman became a star on the Italian stage—appearing in over forty productions of mostly classical works before he was twenty-four years old. At that time, Gassman decided to try his talents in motion pictures.

After a few false starts in forgettable movies, in 1949, Vittorio hit pay dirt in the international hit 'Bitter Rice,' also starring Silvana Mangano. The movie made Gassman an international star.

As is usually the case, Gassman heeded the siren call of Hollywood and made his way to Southern California. While there, in 1952, he married Shelly Winters. She made some decent movies, while the MGM people had no clue about how to utilize Vittorio's considerable talent, focusing on his blinding good looks, instead of his acting abilities.

After appearing in several mediocre films—and divorcing Winters—Vittorio returned to Italy. Gassman formed his own stage company, 'Teatro Popolare Italiano,' which was very successful in Italy.

By now, however, movies were in his blood, so, in a mirror image of his earlier career, Gassman began making Italian movies again. Just as 'Bitter Rice,' established Gassman as an international star, in 1956 he had another international hit in the film 'Big Deal on Madonna Street.' It re-established Gassman's position as an international movie star. In the seventies, Gassman again appeared in several American films, including 'A Wedding,' in 1978 and 'Quintet,' in 1979.

In 1975, Gassman received the Best Actor Award at the Cannes Film Festival for his work in 'Profumo di Donna', which was copied in America in 1992 as 'Scent of a Woman,' again starring a great Italian actor, Al Pacino.

Vittorio Gassman's ability to play serious and comic roles on the stage as well as the screen, caused him to be dubbed 'The Lawrence Olivier of Italy."

Nick J. Mileti

EARL HAMNER

(Born July 10, 1923 in Schuyler, Virginia)

Earl Hamner is a film, television, and novel writer, who is most famous for having created the television series 'The Waltons.'

Doris Giannini, Earl's Italian mother, encouraged her oldest son to write—which he started to do when he was six years old (the poem was published). After attending a number of schools and serving in the Army in World War II, Earl graduated from the University of Cincinnati.

Working in New York as a radio writer, nights and weekends Earl wrote novels. He has had six published to date, including his first, 'Fifty Roads To Town,' and the best seller 'Spencer's Mountain,' which Warner Brothers made into a movie with an all-star cast.

Earl's books have been translated into ten languages.

Needless to say, as the radio market dried up and television began to take over, Earl made the switch with his writing. Then, in 1961, the change became complete as Earl moved to Hollywood, following the television industry to the west coast.

Hamner has written for the numerous television shows, including 'The Today Show,' 'The CBS Playhouse,' and 'The Twilight Zone,' for whom he wrote eight episodes.

While in Hollywood, Earl (naturally) wrote a number of feature films, including 'Where the Lillies Bloom' and 'Palm Springs Weekend.'

However, it was Hammer's short novel, 'The Homecoming,' that brought him fame and fortune. First a Christmas special was made based on the material, and then, in 1970, Lorimar Productions hired Earl to write a television special based on it. The rest, as they say, is history.

The special was well-received by the public, and turned into the wildly successful series, 'The Waltons.' The show ran on CBS for eight years and, it appears, will run forever in syndication. The sweet, family show collected thirteen Emmys and numerous other awards over the years.

Later, Hamner wrote and produced the pilot for 'Falcon Crest,' which also had an eight—year run on CBS.

Earl Hamner has won numerous awards for his writing, including, in 1972, the George Foster Peabody Award for Distinguished Journalism, and an Emmy for Best Program (The Waltons) in 1974.

Nick J. Mileti

GUY WILLIAMS

(Born Jan. 14, 1924 in New York City;
Died May 8, 1989 in Buenos Aires, Argentina)
REAL ITALIAN NAME: ARMANDO CATALANO

In the late 1950's, Guy Williams, playing Zorro on television, was the most popular personality in America.

Guy Williams' parents emigrated from Italy to America shortly before he was born. As a youth, they tried to steer their son into a business career, but the tall (6 foot, 3 inch) handsome youngster had other ideas.

Guy slipped into a career as a photographic model and found immediate success—he was featured in commercials placed in the leading magazines of the day, including Vogue and Harper's Bazaar. In the early fifties, answering the siren-call of Hollywood, Williams moved to Los Angeles. He made a number of appearances in television shows and performed in several feature films, but nothing much came from either.

Finally, however, Guy William's got the big break. In 1957, answering a cattle call, the thirty-three year old Williams was thrilled—and surprised—to be selected as a finalist for the lead in a new television show Disney Studios was producing for NBC, to be called 'Zorro.'

A two-month battle over the casting of Zorro commenced between Walt Disney and Norman Foster, the director/producer of the show. Walt Disney, as the boss, naturally did not lose many arguments, but when Foster, the creator of the project, finally stated that he wouldn't make the show unless Guy Williams played Zorro, Disney capitulated and Williams was cast as Zorro.

Norman Foster was right. The series was a smash hit. It also made Guy Williams a cult-favorite and a star. Zorro sprouted up everywhere. Zorro merchandise flooded America. Kids slashed Z's everywhere. Amiable Guy Williams made frequent personal appearances in his Zorro costume. His wife, Jan, says, "He'd put his costume on and go into the wards where the children were (at the children's hospital) and talk to them and pick them up and carry them around and spend time with them. It gave him a lot of pleasure and the children were in seventh heaven when Zorro showed up."

After the third season, unfortunately, the popular show was caught in the crossfire of a legal dispute between Disney and the network, and 'Zorro' was canceled.

In his other major role, Williams played Professor Robinson in the television series 'Lost in Space' for three years, from 1965 to 1968. Following this assignment, Williams basically retired to Argentina.

In recognition of his achievements in television and movies, Guy Williams was awarded a star on the Hollywood Walk of Fame.

Nick J. Mileti

MARCELLA HAZEN

(Born in 1924 in Cesenatico [Emilia-Romagna], Italy)
REAL ITALIAN NAME: MARCELLA POLINI

Marcella Hazen, through her groundbreaking cookbooks and cooking classes, has almost single handedly made authentic Italian food fashionable, in America, and around the world.

When Marcella married Victor Hazen in her hometown of Cesenatico, Italy in 1955, she cooked for the first time in her life and something magical happened—Marcella loved cooking for Victor and Victor loved Marcella's cooking. After marriage, the couple moved to New York where Marcella was shocked and dismayed by the lack of understanding of her native Italian cuisine. She decided to have some fun and teach her friends Italian cooking in her apartment. The cooking classes grew steadily by word of mouth, and when Craig Claiborne, the New York Times food editor, gave her cooking and recipes a rave review, business really boomed, and Marcella was on her way.

Eventually, Marcella felt a need to serve a larger audience. She decided to write down her favorite recipes, and soon the project had a life of its own. With her husband Victor's help, Marcella devoted her prodigious energy to the project (she tests each recipe at least five times), and in 1973, Marcella Hazen produced a groundbreaking cookbook. At this point, however, few people knew it existed. Named 'The Classic Italian Cookbook,' the volume's initial impact was minimal, because for the Hazans, every author's greatest fear came true. No promotion, no sales. Julia Child (thankfully, for the Hazans, and lovers of fine Italian food all over the world) suggested a new editor (Judith Jones) at a new publishing house (Knopf). Jones not only signed up Marcella for her next book, she also surprisingly arranged for her publisher to buy the rights to Marcella's first book. In 1976, Knopf reissued 'The Classic Italian Cookbook,' and the rest, as they say, is history. Fine, authentic Italian cuisine was on its way to becoming ubiquitous all over the world.

The Hazens moved back to Italy and established cooking schools in Bologna, and then Venice. Marcella and Victor became world-renowned culinary teachers, attracting celebrities, professionals and amateurs to their classes (even James Beard was a student). Marcella published four more award-winning Italian cookbooks, one more successful than the other. Julia Child once praised Marcella as "my mentor in all things Italian", and Craig Claiborne called her "a national treasure."

The warm and enduring nature of the relationship of Marcella and Victor Hazan is unique, particularly between two such highly creative people. Victor has served as his wife's translator, writing partner, taste tester and confidant for almost fifty years. In fact, the dedication of her fifth book (Marcella Cucina) published in 1997, reads, "For, and because of, Victor."

Victor Hazan is also an authority on Italian wines and has written extensively on the subject for prestigious magazines and in his own books.

Nick J. Mileti

FELICE BRYANT

(Born August 7, 1925 in Milwaukee, Wis;
Died April 22, 2003 in Gatlinburg, Tenn.)
REAL ITALIAN NAME:
MATILDA GENEVIEVE SCADUTO

Felice Bryant and her husband Boudleaux Bryant were one of the most successful and prolific songwriting teams in history.

Both Felice and her husband wrote music and lyrics. Together they penned some 800 songs and helped define the careers of Little Jimmy Dickens, The Osborne Brothers and The Everly Brothers; yet, they are most famous for a song named 'Rocky Top,' a University of Tennessee fight song, which is played at every game and was eventually adopted as Tennessee's Official State Song.

Felice was a musical prodigy who began composing lyrics set to traditional Italian tunes at ten years of age. In her teens, she branched out and began singing around town. She met her classically trained husband in 1945 in Milwaukee; both were simultaneously hit by the "fulmine" (thunderbolt), and the couple eloped shortly after meeting. The duo began writing songs between Boudleaux's gigs with various jazz and country bands. After Little Jimmy Dickens made their tune 'Country Boy' a Country Top Ten hit in 1949, the couple moved to Nashville, Tennessee and began writing songs full time. In fact, Felice and Boudleaux Bryant are considered the first individuals to move to Nashville to make their living solely as songwriters, starting a trend that seemingly will never abate. In their first half-dozen years, the couple's first hits were country songs, including 'The Richest Man in the World,' which the legendary Eddie Arnold recorded.

The country hits were mere warm-up, however. In 1957, one of those historical fortuitous meetings occurred. The Bryants supplied an up-and-coming act named The Everly Brothers with their first two hits, 'Bye Bye Love' and 'Wake Up Little Susie.' Over the next few years, they fed the group most of their hits, including 'Problems' and 'Take a Message to Mary.' Over the years, their songs have been recorded by numerous stars, including Elvis Presley, the Beatles and Bob Dylan. Also innovative in business, in 1966 the Bryants regained publishing rights to their earlier material (unheard of at the time) and formed their own publishing venture, House of Bryant.

Felice and her husband have received innumerable awards and honors in the course of their extraordinary four-decade-long career, including induction into The Nashville Songwriters Hall of Fame in 1972, The National Academy of Popular Music Hall of Fame in 1986, and the Country Music Hall of Fame in 1991. Together, Felice and Boudleaux Bryant have earned fifty-nine BMI Pop, Country, and R&B Awards, and recordings of their songs have sold over 500 million copies worldwide.

Incidentally, her new husband bestowed the nickname Felice on the beautiful Matilda. In Italian, the word means (depending on how and where used) happy, contented, pleased, fortunate or lucky. That Boudleaux certainly had a way with words.

Nick J. Mileti

TONY BENNETT

(Born August 3, 1926 in Queens, New York)
REAL ITALIAN NAME:
ANTHONY DOMINICK BENEDETTO

Tony Bennett's singing has had enormous appeal to young and old alike—he has received a total of nine Grammys in a career spanning more than five decades.

Because his father died when he was a young child, Bennett worked a variety of jobs to help support his working mother. Creative from the start, in his teens Bennett studied to be a commercial artist before being drafted into the Army. This turned out to be a break—in the Army Bennett sang with several military bands and realized his calling was singing, not painting.

Home from military service, Bennett studied music and received his second big break when he won a spot on Arthur Godfry's television show, 'Talent Scouts.' When Mitch Miller, then the head of Columbia Records, heard Bennett sing, he signed him to an recording contract. Starting in 1951 with 'Because of You,' which went to Number one on the charts, Bennett had a string of Number One Hits, including 'Boulevard of Broken Dreams' (written by Harry Warren), 'Because of You' and 'Rags to Riches.' Tony Bennett, with his instinct for a phrase, and his warm husky voice, was a star.

One of Bennett's greatest accomplishments was overcoming the rock trend in the sixties. What he did was develop a nightclub act that relied heavily on previous hits and standards, and secondly, he kept recording good, well-written songs. His rendition, in 1962, of 'I Left My

Heart in San Francisco' became a smash hit that will always be identified with Tony Bennett, and came at a propitious time in his career. He received his first two Grammys for the single (Record of the Year and Best Solo Vocal). In the sixties, Bennett's albums consistently made the charts, and his singles of 'Who Can I Turn To?' and 'If I Ruled the World' have become classic standards.

In the eighties, nineties, and beyond, Bennett has risen to even new heights by adding every generation of young people to his immense worldwide following. Most people agree that the reason Bennett can transcend generations is because of his jazz orientation. This jazz dimension has had the subtle effect of giving his pop music a sharper edge and a sense of spontaneity. Bennett has consistently performed and recorded with numerous jazz legends, including Count Basie and Stan Getz.

Like most singers of his style, Bennett spent most of his life in the shadow of Frank Sinatra, the greatest saloon singer of all time. The landscape changed in the nineties, however. Frank kept singing instead of retiring as his health deteriorated in the nineties, but somehow, Bennett seemed to get stronger as he aged.

Tony Bennett never lost his love of art, and has become a highly respected painter. He signs his works Anthony Benedetto—which, of course, is his Real Italian Name.

Nick J. Mileti

ED MC BAIN

(Born October 15, 1926 in New York, New York)
REAL ITALIAN NAME: SALVATORE A. LOMBINO

Ed McBain has written more than one hundred books of fiction in five decades, and has sold over one hundred million books world-wide—that's 100,000,000 +.

In fact, in addition to his writing talent, McBain might be the champion of pseudonyms, having used, besides Ed McBain, John Abbot, Curt Cannon, Hunt Collins, Ezra Hannon, Evan Hunter and Richard Marston. McBain explains: "I began using pseudonyms early in my career, when I was being paid a quarter cent a word for my work, and I had to write a lot to earn a living. Sometimes I had three or four stories in a single magazine without the editor knowing they were all by me." Curiously, although he has written using seven different names, he has never written under his Real Italian Name, Salvatore Lombino.

Like Tony Bennett, McBain initially studied to be an artist, but World War II and the Navy interrupted his art studies. While in the service, McBain began to write, liked it, and when he was discharged after the war, started to write seriously, at night after work, and on weekends. In 1954, McBain's commitment to his craft paid off handsomely when 'The Blackboard Jungle,' was published. Writing as Evan Hunter, the novel was the first of McBain's many bestsellers—and it allowed him to concentrate on writing. The hit movie was released the following year.

Piling success upon success, two years later McBain

virtually invented the 'group of detectives' genre with his '87th Precinct' police procedure novels. Beginning with 'Cop Hater' in 1956 (through 'Fat Ollie's Book' in 2003) he has written an incredible fifty-two books in what must be the longest and most popular crime series ever. Sadly, Ed McBain's groundbreaking form has been shamelessly ripped-off in television by numerous series—such as Hill Street Blues and N.Y.P.D. Blues—with no payment of a fee, with no acknowledgment, with not even a thank you. A prolific writer, McBain has written in most every genre, including short stories, plays, children's books, novels about Private Investigators (twelve feature Matthew Hope) and screenplays (Alfred Hitchcock's 'The Birds' has become a cult classic). Over a dozen films have been made of McBain's books. His novels have been bestsellers in over two-dozen countries, from Brazil to Sweden, from Russia to England, from Japan to Italy.

Ed McBain has received numerous awards, including the Diamond Dagger award from the British Crime Writer's Association (its highest award), which was presented at a formal ceremony at the House of Lords in London, England in 1998. He is the only American to ever win the award. McBain also received the Mystery Writer's of America Edgar Allan Poe award in 1957 and its prestigious Grand Master Award in 1986 for Lifetime Achievement

Nick J. Mileti

KAYE BALLARD

(Born November 20, 1926 in Cleveland, Ohio)
REAL ITALIAN NAME: CATHERINE GLORIA BALOTTA

As a singer, actor and comedienne, Kaye Ballard has had a long and distinguished career, on the stage, in movies, on television and especially in cabaret.

In 1943, during World War II, while at John Adams High School, the effervescent Ballard broke into show biz at fifteen years of age, singing in a USO show in her native Cleveland. She was offered a scholarship to nearby Kent State University, but opted to join a burlesque company instead. She sharpened her skills in vaudeville—where she caught the attention of Spike Jones and soon graduated into a solo act.

Appearing in various stage productions in the forties and fifties, Kaye made her break-through national impact in the 1954 Broadway production of 'The Golden Apple,' which landed her on the cover of Life Magazine, the day's ultimate honor.

As is often the case, however, it is a television series (the 1960's 'The Mothers-In-Law') that made Kaye Ballard a household name. Even though the show only lasted two seasons, her sparkling wit earned her a legion of loyal fans, which the trooper has never disappointed in a career that has spanned over sixty years.

Over the years, Kaye has been a regular guest on the top television variety and talk shows, and has appeared in some twenty movies. She has also cut numerous record albums, both singing and comedic.

In the seventies, Kaye Ballard returned to her first love, performing live. She played in the most prestigious cabaret venues around the world, such as Mr. Kelly's in Chicago and the Plaza and St. Regis Hotels in New York. She has worked alongside the biggest names in the business. At the Blue Angel, when it was one of the top nightclubs in the country, Kaye worked with Harry Belafonte and Pearl Baily, among many other stars.

Both of Kaye's one-woman shows in New York (Kaye Ballard—Working Forty Second Street At Last, and Hey Ma . . . Kaye Ballard) received nominations for the Drama Desk and the Outer Critic's Circle Awards.

In 2003, a street in Rancho Mirage, California was named for the affable and talented star. Considering that the list of other celebrities who have had that singular honor includes icons Bob Hope and Frank Sinatra, Kay Ballard, while not as well known as those show-biz giants, is deservedly in their rarified company.

Nick J. Mileti

HUGO PRATT

(Born June 15, 1927 near Rimini;
Died August 20, 1995 in Pully, Switzerland)

Hugo Pratt, one of the 20th Century's best illustrators and writers, is famous for creating the comic book character Corto Maltese, a lonesome, wandering seaman and adventurer, whom Pratt placed in real historical contexts.

Pratt's mother was from Venice and his father was from the Rimini area.

After the World War II, Pratt (with two friends), created his first comic book character 'Asso di Picche,' a hooded man of justice. In 1959 Pratt began traveling the world, creating comics and developing his detailed, dramatic and cinematic drawing style. His full-color images are a beauty to behold—he is a genius at creating atmosphere. His chief inspiration was the American cartoonist Milton Caniff, who is known as "the Rembrandt of the comic strip' because of his mastery of drawing. Also impressed by Caniff's method of characterization and dialogue in comics like 'Terry and the Pirates,' Pratt developed his story sense during this period and began writing his own scripts. Back in Italy in 1967, Pratt created 'A Ballad of the Salt Sea,' in which Corto Maltese made his first appearance (as a side character). Lightning struck. An instant hit, the character was so well received by the public, Pratt soon made Corto Maltese a main character— he featured the adventurous rogue, with his own set of ethics, in approximately a dozen graphic novels, or 'albums' as Pratt called them.

Pratt was a voracious reader—his library contained over thirty thousand volumes—and Corto's stories reflect both Platt's adventurous personal life and his deep scholarly research. His work is mysterious, esoteric and complicated, like a Joseph Conrad novel. The worldwide locations of Corto Maltese's stories are exotic, but the stories all have an intellectual underpinning. Platt combines fact with fiction, and sets the action against true historical crises in the early 20th Century. Corto interacts with everyone from Rasputin to Stalin, from Lawrence of Arabia to the leaders of the Irish Revolution—almost always on the side of the underdog. Not surprisingly, Pratt's work appeals more to adults than children. In fact, Corto Maltese and his creator, Hugo Pratt, have achieved cult status in both Italy and France— over five million copies of his comic books have been sold in these two countries alone. Around the world, Corto has already prompted over seventy Doctorate theses. Several plays, novels, and full-length movies have been made featuring Corto. In Thailand, there is a resort "modeled after the concepts and ideas from the famous Corto Maltese Cartoons of Hugo Pratt." Continuing the on-going love affair with the character, in 2003, a dramatic tango entitled 'Les Tangos de Corto' debuted.

In addition to providing thoughtful entertainment for millions of people over the years, Hugo Pratt's approximately forty 'albums' (including Sgt. Kirk, Ernie Pike, Anna of the Jungle and Jesuit Joe) have been a major inspiration to comic artists all over the world. The Swiss have co-opted Hugo Pratt.

Nick J. Mileti

CARDINAL JOSEPH LOUIS BERNARDIN

(Born Apr. 2, 1928 in Columbia, S. Carolina;
Died Nov. 14, 1996)

Cardinal Joseph Louis Bernardin spent his life promoting peace and human rights. Using common sense and seeking common ground instead of confrontation, he helped bring the Catholic Church in America into the twentieth century.

Cardinal Bernardin's parents emigrated from Primiero [Trentino], Italy to America.

Joseph entered the seminary at the age of twenty-four, and in 1966—at thirty-eight years of age—he became the youngest Bishop in his adopted country when he was named Auxiliary Bishop of the Archdiocese of Atlanta, Georgia.

Six years later, in 1972, Bernardin was appointed Archbishop of Cincinnati. In a series of unprecedented moves, he applied the gospel to real life in America and the world, and helped bring the Catholic Church into the mainstream. For example, Bernardin shocked his constituents by openly criticizing then President Nixon for the Vietnam War. Compared to his conservative fellow Bishops, Bernardin was a flaming liberal.

In 1974, Bernardin was elected to a three-year term as President of the United States Bishop's Conference, which means he was the head of the Catholic Church in America.

Eight years later, in 1982, Bernardin became the Archbishop of Chicago, the largest Archdiocese in America, numbering over 2.3 million Catholics.

In 1983, Joseph Louis Bernardin was named Cardinal by Pope John Paul II, the first Italian-American to be so honored. Bernardin's appointment as Cardinal was hailed by many as a turning point for the Catholic Church in the United States. The feeling at the time was that his appointment signaled the end of the Irish-American domination of top clerical positions.

Cardinal Bernardin always worked for justice in the larger picture (opposition to nuclear armaments, for example), while at the same time he personally tended his flock (administering to condemned men on death row, for example).

Cardinal Bernardin advocated universal medical care, and at the same time worked to ensure that the Catholic schools of his diocese served every child enrolled, regardless of background.

In 1996, just prior to his untimely death, Cardinal Bernardin was presented with the Medal of Liberty by then President Clinton. In 1998, the Cardinal was the subject of a compelling hour-long PBS documentary entitled 'Bernardin.'

In 1982, while still Archbishop of Chicago, Joseph Louis Bernardin was named Time magazine's 'Man of the Year.'

Nick J. Mileti

BRUCE KIRBY

(Born April 24, 1928 in New York, New York)
REAL ITALIAN NAME:
BRUCE GIOVANNI QUIDACIOLU, SR.

The character actor Bruce Kirby is perhaps the most recognizable face with the least recognizable name performing in movies and on television today.

Bruce made his television debut late in life—he was thirty-three in 1961 when he played the role of Sergeant Kissel in the television series 'Car 54, Where Are You.'

Several roles on Broadway followed, but Bruce's career has been primarily in television.

Interestingly, Bruce actually seems to specialize in cop roles—capturing the nuances of that character perfectly. For example, in the long running series 'Columbo', starring Peter Falk, Bruce played Sergeant Kramer, the long suffering cop who does the grunt-work while Columbo solves the cases. Also, Bruce is perhaps best known for playing yet another cop—District Attorney Bruce Rogoff—in 1986 in the TV series L.A. Law.

In addition to his numerous TV guest appearances (yes, often as a cop), Bruce Kirby has appeared in some twenty theatrical motion pictures, including playing a cop in the Danny DeVito/Billy Crystal hilarious comedy 'Throw Mamma From the Train.'

BRUNO KIRBY

(Born April 28, 1949 in New York, New York)
REAL ITALIAN NAME:
BRUNO GIOVANNI QUIDACIOLU, JR.

Bruno Kirby is the son of Bruce Kirby, and, like his father, is an outstanding supporting and character actor.

Bruno has made numerous television appearances and appeared on stage, but, unlike his father, Bruno Kirby's real success has come in feature films.

Bruno's first break came in 1974, when he played young Clemenza, along side Robert DeNiro, in Francis Ford Coppola's award winning classic 'Godfather, Part II.' His second break didn't come until 1987, when he was cast as the humorless Lieutenant Hauk, the officer who is bedeviled by Robin Williams in 'Good Morning Vietnam.'

Although Bruno Kirby has successfully played many diverse roles in his career—including those in 'Birdy' in 1984, and 'Donnie Brasco' in 1997—his performances as Billy Crystal's buddy in 'When Harry Met Sally,' released in 1989, and 'City Slickers,' in 1991, firmly established him as an outstanding comedic actor.

Nick J. Mileti

BILLY MARTIN

(Born May 16, 1928 in Berkeley, Ca.;
Died Dec. 25, 1989 in Johnson City, N.Y.)
REAL ITALIAN NAME: ALFRED MANUEL PESANO

In his sixteen-year career as a manager in major league baseball, Billy Martin had a fine .553 winning percentage, which includes five divisional titles, two American League Pennants and one World Series.

When one considers the pathetic teams Martin inherited, his won/loss record is even more impressive.

As a kid, Billy was small and awkward. For the aggressive youth, however, this was an inspiration, not a handicap. He concentrated on sports to prove to his schoolmates that he was as tough as they were. Billy put all of his energy into baseball—the game seemed to fit his physical and mental framework. His hard work paid off because as soon as he graduated from high school, Billy was signed by the minor-league Oakland Oaks. By the happiest of coincidences, Casey Stengel was the manager of the team.

The legendary Casey Stengel performed two miracles with Martin—one was relatively easy and one would have been impossible for a lesser man than Casey Stengel. Stengel taught Billy Martin how to win—that was the easy accomplishment. Harnessing Billy Martin's explosive energy—that was the coup.

When Stengel moved up to manage the New York Yankees, he called on Billy to be his second baseman. Billy Martin helped his mentor win championships in 1950, 1951, 1952, 1953 and 1956.

After being traded from the Yankees in 1957, Billy eventually became a manager, and he was as feisty a manager as he'd been as a player.

He took the Minnesota Twins from a seventh place finish in 1968 to a American League West title the next year—and got fired.

Same story in Detroit with the Tigers.

Ditto with the Texas Rangers and Oakland Athletics.

Billy Martin was hired to manage the New York Yankees in 1975, and within two years Billy became the only Italian-American to lead a team to the World Championship. The Yankees beat the Los Angeles Dodgers in the World Series and Billy was fired. Incredibly, Billy's four additional stints with the Yankees ended in the same way. Through it all, in 1986, the Yankee's retired Billy Martin's Number (which was #1).

Nick J. Mileti

VIC DAMONE

(Born June 12, 1928 in Brooklyn, New York)
REAL ITALIAN NAME: VITO FARINOLA

Vic Damone's singing career lasted a full fifty years. He graduated from the famous Lafayette High School in Brooklyn, which produced numerous famous people, including baseball stars Ken and Bob Aspromonte.

Damone was only nineteen years old when he hosted his very own radio show. In the same year, 1947, Damone signed with Mercury Records. While his initial songs were successful to a point ('I Have But One Heart' was a hit), Damone was only warming up. In 1948, he broke-through with his recording of 'Again,' and 'You're Breaking My Heart,' which were both million record sellers. In the fifties, like many pop singers, Damone appeared in numerous forgettable films. Bucking the rock and roll trend in the sixties, however, Damone kept working and recording. His version of 'On the Street Where You Live' from the smash musical 'My Fair Lady" was a hit, as was 'An Affair to Remember' (written by Harry Warren). Through the years, Vic Damone performed all over the world, and was considered a consummate professional right up until he retired to Florida at the turn of the century. Near the end of his career, Damone was often placed in Frank Sinatra's league—not bad for a singer who began his career as a Sinatra copyist.

BOBBY DARIN

(Born May 14, 1936 in The Bronx, New York;
Died Dec 20, 1973 in Los Angeles)
REAL ITALIAN NAME: WALDEN ROBERT CASSOTTO

You think you have problems? Listen to the Bobby Darin story. While fighting rheumatic fever as a child, he was told he wouldn't live past the age of sixteen. What would you do? Here's what Darin did. He proclaimed that he wanted to be a legend before he was twenty-five ("like Frank Sinatra"), and pack as much as possible into his life. Darin did just that. He sang in every genre, but pop was his real love—his smash-hit 'Mack the Knife' was Record of the Year in 1959. He wrote some twenty songs for himself and others—'Splish, Splash' was only one of many hits. He appeared on stages across the country. He made more than a dozen movies—his role in 'Captain Newman, M.D.' earned him an Oscar nomination in 1963. He got married twice, the first time to teen movie idol Sandra Dee in 1960. Then, incredibly, in 1968, when Bobby was thirty-two years old, he learned that the woman he knew as 'mother' was his grandmother, and the girl he knew as his 'sister' was his mother. His Italian family engineered this farce "To Prevent Scandal," but obviously no one considered Bobby's feelings when the scheme was hatched. Five years later Bobby Darin was dead at thirty-seven years of age.

Officially, Bobby Darin died of complications after his second open-heart surgery.

Nick J. Mileti

VINCE EDWARDS

(Born July 7, 1928 in Brooklyn, New York;
Died March 11, 1996)
REAL ITALIAN NAME: VINCENT EDWARD ZOINO

Since 1961, in America, Vince Edwards has been Ben Casey, and Ben Casey has been Vince Edwards.

Vince found a fascinating world outside of Brooklyn when his parents—who had both emigrated from Italy—allowed him to leave home and accept a swimming scholarship to The Ohio State University in Columbus, Ohio.

Bored by the Mid West, Vince returned to New York to attend the American Academy of Dramatic Arts. For a dozen years he was cast in minor rolls on Broadway and in movies. Although he worked regularly, Vince realized that he was being cast based solely on his great looks and imposing physique and he resented it. Determined to make it based on his acting ability, Vince immersed himself in acting classes once more, and discovered 'method' acting.

Vince's commitment paid off when he was cast as the lead of the ABC television series 'Ben Casey' in 1961, a roll that brought Vince instant stardom. As he stated in an interview in 1988, "My picture was on the cover of Look and Life magazines. I went from obscurity to fame. What a cultural shock that was. It just exploded. (When it happened) I was living in a room at a friend's house."

Playing a dedicated, but difficult, physician who battled disease and the medical establishment in equal doses, Vince combined his brooding good looks with his brooding good acting. Vince Edwards made 'Ben Casey' an overnight sensation. With his portrayal of a television antihero, Vince had hit a hot button with the public at a time it was looking for antiheros. 'Ben Casey' ran five years, from 1961 to 1966 (an eternity in television), passing its rival show, Doctor Kildare—which starred Richard Chamberlain—in the ratings. Besides acting, Vince Edwards enjoyed directing; he worked behind the camera in some 20 of the 154 'Ben Casey' episodes.

After 'Ben Casey', Vince did more directing and other acting—he appeared in over twenty forgettable movies in his career. He even tried his hand at singing (recording six albums and playing Vegas), but his fate seemed to be tied to his signature role.

The intensity of a big-city hospital as pioneered by the show 'Ben Casey' has been copied ad nauseam, but Ben Casey, 'the surly surgeon who fought to get things done,' will always be remembered as the original, and it will always be Vince Edwards' private property.

Vince Edwards was a warm, fun-loving man who never let fame go to his head. He remained loyal to his many friends and enjoyed good food, the racetrack, and life—in no special order.

Nick J. Mileti

JOE PASS

(Born January 13, 1929 in New Brunswick, N.J.;
Died May 23, 1994 in Los Angeles)
REAL ITALIAN NAME: GIUSEPPE PASSALAQUA

Joe Pass was one of the greatest jazz guitar players of all time. By mastering the technique known as fingerpicking, or single-line playing, the virtuoso could actually give the impression he was accompanying himself on his solos.

When Joe was a child, his Sicilian father, Mariano Passalaqua, moved the family to Johnstown, Pennsylvania to get work in a steel mill. He was determined Joe shouldn't join him in the filthy, degrading work that is inherent in making steel, but initially wasn't certain how to direct the boy. When he heard Joe on his first guitar at the age of nine, however, a light went off in his head— Mariano realized Joe had musical talent. From that historic moment on, Joe's father became a world-class nudge, literally forcing his son to practice every moment of his spare time. Joe came to hate the guitar, but thanked his father in later years for forcing him to practice seven or eight hours a day, "until the instrument in my hand felt like an extension of myself." In fact, in an interview in the nineties, Joe said, "He (my father) deserves all the credit for how I play today."

The reason for that statement is Joe eventually came to appreciate *how* he was forced to practice. For example, his father would sing or whistle an Italian tune and then say "OK, learn this song." After Joe would find the notes, his father would say, "Fill it up; don't leave any spaces." If a song came on the radio or was played on the record player, Joe was told to copy it—and after he became adept at copying, he was pushed to add to it. His father would bring home music books and make Joe learn every song in the book. Sometimes, Mariano would say, "Play me a song—make it up." Later Joe said. "That was the way I learned to play, by actually playing a lot and filling in all the spaces and not leaving gaps in the music."

By the time Joe was fourteen, he was playing weddings and dances, but he never stopped practicing. He studied the great jazz improvisers of the time and moved to New York to be part of the bop scene. Unfortunately, life in the fast lane spun out of control and Pass threw away what could have been very productive years. By the mid-sixties, Joe was clean, living in Los Angeles and playing with some of the best musicians in town. His monster break-through came when Norman Granz signed Joe to his Pablo Records label in 1973. Joe cut several solo albums, accompanied Ella Fitzgerald on some of her best recordings, and worked with every one of Granz's staggering stable of great jazz artists.

For the next twenty years, Joe Pass became sought after for recordings, concerts and festivals all over the world, working in duos and various small groups. It was as a soloist, with his warm tones and exceptional technique, that he garnered the most attention. Not surprisingly, Joe's unique style inspired guitar players all over the world to emulate him, and because of his willingness to help others, the modest musical genius jazz guitar player also became a highly successful guitar teacher.

Nick J. Mileti

PAT COOPER

(Born July 31, 1929 in Brooklyn, New York)
REAL ITALIAN NAME: PASQUALE CAPUTO

A comedian's comedian, the public has loved burly-chested Pat Cooper since his big break in 1963 when he appeared on The Jackie Gleason Show.

Cooper is best remembered for his 'comedic anger'—that is, saying what he thinks in an extremely funny way. A favorite of talk-show hosts, Cooper has said what he thinks on The Tonight Show with Johnny Carson and The Late Show with David Letterman, among many others. Pat has made innumerable television appearances on shows such as Seinfeld and L.A. Law, and has made half-a-dozen comedy albums, including the record with the fascinating title 'You Don't Have to Be Italian to Like Pat Cooper.'

Cooper's real strength is in his live appearances. With his commanding stage presence and inherent sense of comedic timing, Pat has the unique ability to bring live concert audiences back for more. His style is the classic 'stream of consciousness', with candor and anger—but always hilarious. Cooper has appeared solo in concert innumerable times and has also enjoyed opening for the biggest names—including Frank Sinatra and Tony Bennett—at the top venues in Las Vegas, Atlantic City and New York.

Pat Cooper changed his name when he began to perform. "My father hated that I changed my name," he said later. "(He felt) I betrayed him. I betrayed my heritage." No one but a person with Pat Cooper's inherent intellectual honesty would have the courage to admit that fact publicly.

Closet Italians

DON CORNELL

(Born April 21, 1919 in the Bronx, New York;
Died Feb. 23, 2004 in Florida)
REAL ITALIAN NAME: LUIGI FRANCISCO VARLARO

Don Cornell was one of America's biggest singing stars in the fifties. During his salad days, a critic, describing his lush voice, wrote, "Don Cornell could make a gal swoon if he sang the phone book."

When Cornell landed a job with the Sammy Kaye Orchestra as the 'boy singer' (as they were called in those days), his career was on its way. In 1950, when he recorded 'It Isn't Fair,' it was a huge hit and the song made Cornell a star. Not surprisingly, the handsome high baritone then decided to strike out on his own, and what a decision that turned out to be. Between 1950 and 1962, Don Cornell had twelve gold records, averaging one per year, including 'I'm Yours,' and 'I'll Walk Alone.' His singing career led to work in television, movies, supper clubs, dinner theaters and musical comedy.

In 1963, in recognition of having sold over fifty million records, Cornell was awarded a star on the Hollywood Walk of Fame.

CHAPTER X

Illustrious Italians With Non-Italian Names
Born Between 1930-1939

JERRY VALE

(Born July 8, 1930 in The Bronx, New York)
REAL ITALIAN NAME: GENARO LOUIS VITALIANO

In his teens, Jerry Vale won a talent contest and has never stopped singing.

Vale's father's family is from Calabria, and his mother's family is from Naples—both of which are in Southern Italy.

Jerry's big break came when he was recommended to Mitch Miller—the A & R head of Columbia Records at the time—who signed him. In the fifties and sixties, Vale had a parade of hits—mostly Italian favorites, which seemed just right for his melodic baritone voice. His choice of material seemed to strike a cord with the post-war public, and especially with Italian-Americans. Italian love songs, such as 'Innamorata' (Sweetheart), written by Harry Warren, 'O Solo Mio' (My Sunshine), 'Chitarra Romana' (Roman Guitar), and, of course, 'Volare' (I'm Flying) are just some of his best-selling hits over the years. Vale has maintained his association with Columbia, and is one of their most consistent selling artists worldwide.

Over the years, Jerry has performed in New York venues as diverse as Carnegie Hall and the Copacabana, for whom he had the honor of opening their season from 1964 to 1974. For the entire decade of the seventies, Vale headlined at the Sands Hotel in Las Vegas. Jerry Vale was one of the few crooners to withstand the rock and roll revolution of the sixties and even prosper in the process. Into the 21st Century, Vale continues to sing and has been one of Atlantic City and Las Vegas's most consistent and adored performers.

He has appeared on innumerable television shows, and has been seen playing himself in several movies, including 'Casino' and 'Goodfellows.'

Jerry Vale has a unique distinction. Over the years, his recording of America's National Anthem has been played at more baseball games than any other rendition—live or recorded—in history. At one point, a dozen teams preceded their games with Vale's rendition. As a tribute to this success, Jerry Vale's Gold Record of the song is on display in Cooperstown, New York, at the Baseball Hall of Fame.

In addition to his hectic concert schedule, Jerry Vale, with Rita, his wife of over forty years, is active in a number of charitable institutions, including the Cancer Society, the Heart Fund and the Arthritis Foundation. Vale has received numerous awards, including the prestigious Medal of Honor from the National Ethnic Coalition of New York, which was presented on Ellis Island in an impressive formal ceremony. When home in Beverly Hills between club and concert performances, every lunch hour the amiable and popular showman Jerry Vale can be found bonding with his show-biz friends at his favorite restaurant, the celebrity hangout 'Cafe Roma' in Beverly Hills, California, owned and operated by the debonair, handsome brothers, Gigi and Gianni Orlando.

Nick J. Mileti

ERIK AMFITHEATROF

(Born in 1931 in Milan, Italy)

Erik Amfitheatrof is a writer who has achieved his greatest fame as a journalist for his in-depth, insightful magazine reporting and coverage of world leaders and world issues.

Erik's father, the Russian Daniele Amfitheatrof, was a respected music conductor and composer who worked primarily in Italy and America (he became a naturalized Italian citizen in 1922). Erik's mother, May C. Semenza, was Italian, born in Milan. The couple married in 1930 and emigrated from Italy to America when Erik was seven years old

Erik graduated from Harvard, worked in Rome, and from 1967 to 1970 was a Time-Life correspondent for the Far-East. He spent the next several years as a writer for the excellent Time-Life Books series.

In 1973, Erik wrote the non-fiction book 'The Children of Columbus: An informal History of Italians on the New World.' The book tells the story of Italian-Americans from the age of Columbus through the 1930's. In 1980, he wrote a second book, 'The Enchanted Ground.' This book tells of Americans in Italy from 1760-1980.'

Beginning in 1981, and for the next four years, Erik held the prestigious position of Moscow Bureau Chief for Time Magazine. While serving in that position, during one of the most sensitive periods in modern history, Erik gave the world his unique insight into Soviet politics and life. He reported on—and wrote numerous in-depth articles on—Russian military strength, the ultra-secret KGB, the shifting tastes of the Russian people and even the funerals of the leaders of the world's second superpower. Erik was the key reporter on Time Magazine's 1983 Man of the Year story. Published January 1, 1984, the cover story named Ronald Regan and Yuri Andropov 'Men of the Year.'

Following his stint in Moscow, Erik moved to Time's Rome Bureau. In 1996, he was a member of the jury for the Barzini Prize in Italy.

In 1997, upon the death of Princess Diane of England, the editors of Time ran a reprint of Amfitheatrof's story on the nineteen-year-old Lady Diana, which he had written for the magazine in 1981, sixteen years earlier. This was a highly unusual move and was a bow to Erik's brilliant reporting. While living in Rome, in May of 2002, Erik was the key reporter on a major Newsweek Magazine article "Sex and the Church."

In addition to his writing, Erik Amfitheatrof teaches journalism (magazine writing) in the Notre Dame Institute/Saint Mary's College program in Rome, Italy.

Nick J. Mileti

ANNE BANCROFT

(Born September 17, 1931 in the Bronx, New York)
REAL ITALIAN NAME: ANNA MARIA ITALIANO

Anne Bancroft is one of the best stage and screen actors of the last century.

After studying at the American Academy of Dramatic Arts, Anne Bancroft left New York and went to Hollywood. She made her film debut in 1950 in the movie 'Don't Bother to Knock.' The movie was aptly named because nothing much came of that effort, nor of the films she made in the following years.

Disappointed with Hollywood's lack of understanding of her aspirations and talent—she was being touted as a bimbo—Bancroft made an inspired career move and returned to New York.

Although Bancroft was beautiful, she was no bimbo. She was very bright and very talented, which she showed the world in 1958 when she was cast opposite another Italian, Henry Fonda, in the Broadway drama, 'Two For The Seesaw'. Living proof of the show biz saying, "I worked twenty-seven years to become an overnight hit on Broadway," Bancroft received a Tony Award for Best Actress for her performance.

Two years later, again on Broadway, Bancroft won even greater acclaim for her portrayal of the half-blind Annie Sullivan in 'The Miracle Worker,' garnering both a Tony and a New York Drama Critic's Award. Then, in 1962, in an achievement that borders on the impossible—at least in Hollywood, where, remember, Audrey Hepburn replaced Julie Andrews in 'My Fair Lady'—Bancroft was not only cast in the film version of 'The Miracle Worker,' she won an Academy Award for her performance.

While the great Meryl Streep understandably receives most of the accolades for her extraordinary mastery of dialects and accents, listen to what author Edwin O'Conner said about Anne Bancroft after seeing her in his play 'The Miracle Worker.' He said: "This is the most astonishingly accurate Irish accent I've ever heard. It sounds as if she'd been born in Galway."

After another Oscar nomination in 1964 for 'The Pumpkin Eater', Anne Bancroft helped forge the psyche of an entire generation when she delivered her signature performance as Mrs. Robinson in 'The Graduate', for which she was again honored with a Best Actress nomination. Bancroft was nominated for Best Actress two more times after 'The Graduate': In 1977 for 'The Turning Point' and in 1985 for 'Agnes of God'. In addition to her Broadway appearances, Bancroft has appeared in numerous television movies and series, and some forty-feature films in her highly successful career.

Anne Bancroft has been married to actor/writer/producer/director/music hummer and all-around genius Mel Brooks since 1964.

GAY TALESE

(Born February 7, 1932 in Ocean City, New Jersey)
REAL ITALIAN NAME: GAETANO TELEZA

Gay Talese, one of the most respected non-fiction writers in the world, is credited with creating what is called 'new journalism'—combining dialogue with non-fiction writing.

In 1922, Talese's father, who was a tailor, emigrated from Maida (which is in Southern Italy) to America, where he met and married Catherine DePaolo, an Italian-American. In 1982, Talese published the best selling book 'Unto the Sons,' an account of the massive turn-of-the century Italian immigration to America.

His nine-year stint as a reporter for the New York Times, from 1956 to 1965, helped sharpen his writing skills. Frustrated by the space limitations of a daily newspaper, in 1965 Talese joined Esquire Magazine and wrote some of the most respected, and interesting, profiles in history—many of which were republished in anthology form forty years later. Moving on to novel writing, in 1969, Talese's earliest bestseller, 'The Kingdom and the Power,' chronicled the history and influence of his old employer, the New York Times. Stories with real names, Talese says, represent his own highly personal response to the world as an Italian-American outsider. "(I) come from an island (Protestant, WASP, Ocean City) and a family (Italian, Catholic) that reinforced my identity as a marginal American, an outsider, an alien in my native nation."

The suave and always immaculately dressed Talese (his father's influence) credits his mother for helping him develop, in his tender years, the listening and interviewing skills that have served him so well. While Talese disavows his pioneering role in the 'new journalism,' there is no escaping the fact that he is indeed a unique writer with unique talents. He has been able to interview and write about real people ordinary writers are not even lucky enough to meet. Talese been able to create a successful career out of reporting difficult, even forbidden, subjects, by perfecting what he calls "the fine art of hanging out." That is, he listens with patience and care and never interrupts. Secondly, he gains the confidence of his subjects, and that can take time. For example, it took Talese some five years to gain the trust of Bill Bonanno, but his patience paid off handsomely when the relationship evolved into Talese's revealing story about the mob, the best-selling 1971 book, 'Honor Thy Father.' 'Thy Neighbor's Wife,' which he wrote in 1980, was a runaway best seller. Yes, sex sells.

Eventually, Talese gets to know his subjects in such depth he confidently describes their thoughts and feelings as well as their actions. When Talese infuses his writing with quotes and dialogue, however, lesser talented, jealous writers (and critics) collapse into spasmodic fits—which, not surprisingly, they breathlessly share with the general public. Gay Talese's modern classics have sold millions of copies worldwide. His success is a tribute to exhaustive research, an elegant writing style, and a dogged adherence to the truth—no matter what the consequences, or what those others might say or think.

… *Nick J. Mileti*

CAROL LAWRENCE

(Born in 1933 in Melrose Park, Illinois)
REAL ITALIAN NAME: CAROLINA MARIA LARAIA

Carol Lawrence is a singer, dancer and actress, most famous for portraying 'Maria' in Leonard Bernstein's 1957 Broadway smash hit, 'West Side Story,' a show that has become a classic of American theater.

As soon as she could stand and walk, Carol began to dance. Obviously, this is not so unusual. What's unusual is that she danced whether or not there was music playing. A devoted pupil, she studied voice and dance throughout her youth. A beautiful, artistically precocious child, Carol signed with her first agent at the age of thirteen. It was at this time that her father insisted she change her name: "People can't read Laraia," he said. "So they won't remember it, too many vowels in a row" (reminiscent of Emperor Joseph II telling Mozart one of his pieces had "too many notes").

Carol's first part on Broadway was in the chorus of the revue 'Borscht Capades,' starring Mickey Katz. After honing her craft in other productions, her major breakthrough came when she was cast as 'Maria' in 'West Side Story,' a part that would define her career. After she left the show, Carol starred in the national tours of a number of important productions, including 'Funny Girl,' The Unsinkable Molly Brown,' 'Sweet Charity,' 'The Sound of Music' and 'Sugar Babies.'

In 1963, Carol married singer/actor Robert Goulet, and for several years the couple toured the United States in their personal stage show. The marriage unraveled and ended in acrimony and an extended, bitter divorce.

Carol has appeared in several movies; has made innumerable television appearances; and has had a popular solo nightclub act that has toured the world. In addition, she has been a guest performer with some of the countries top symphony orchestras.

Sandwiched between her grueling professional schedule, Carol has been one of the country's leading advocates for children. She has hosted numerous telethons for needy children, particularly the charity World Vision. Carol was named City of Hope's Woman of the Year in 1984 and has been honored many times for her charitable work.

In 1990, Carol wrote her autobiography, entitled 'Carol Lawrence: The Backstage Story," and in 1996 she wrote a cookbook entitled 'I Remember Pasta." The versatile artist even produced an aerobic video, which she named 'Broadway Body Workout.'

Carol Lawrence has been honored with a star on the Hollywood Walk of Fame, in the Live Theater Category.

Nick J. Mileti

REGIS PHILBIN

(Born August 25, 1933 in New York, New York)

Regis Philbin is a television performer who made the near impossible leap from star, as a daytime talk show co-host, to superstar, as host of the wildly popular primetime show 'Who Wants to be a Millionaire.'

Philbin's father was Irish and his mother, Florence, was Italian, her parents having emigrated from Italy. While still a youth, Regis and his family moved to the Bronx and lived with his Italian grandmother and uncle in his great aunt's house. "With that combination [Irish and Italian] is it any wonder I'm feisty?" he says mischievously.

And is it any wonder he's a good talker, one might add. Philbin basically invented his own style of 'talk-show host,' combining warmth, wit (that is never malicious), charm, and enthusiasm (that is never false). Philbin's television career has spanned four decades. Working his way through the ranks, he had his first national recognition as Steve Allen's replacement on Westinghouse's syndicated late-night talk show, and as Joey Bishop's second banana on 'The Joey Bishop Show.'

Philbin took the morning talk show, 'A.M. Los Angeles,' from last place to Number One; it remained on top for seven years. Not surprisingly, Regis was convinced to move to New York and do a morning talk show there. Three years later, the successful show segued into the nationally syndicated "Live! with Regis and Kathie Lee." Although there has been much speculation about riffs between Philbin and Gifford (fueled, to a great extent, by the press), in 1995, she wrote for Philbin's memoir 'I'm Only One Man' "I just know that he is the absolute best at what he does. Nobody tells a story better then Regis. Nobody works an audience better than Regis. And nobody puts more of himself into what he does . . . Please don't tell him any of this, because it would spoil everything, but the fact is I love him to pieces." Kathie Lee left the show in the year 2000 after twelve years with Regis on national television. The show continued, first called "Live! With Regis" and now "Live! With Regis and Kelly."

In 1999, the impossible happened. Regis took his highly successful career to new heights when he was selected by ABC to host a rip-off of a British television show. Regis had to lobby for the position of host on "Who Wants to be a Millionaire?" He says not only was he not on the short list, he wasn't on any list. The Disney ownership thanks its lucky stars for having listened to Regis, because the explosive audience response to 'Who Wants to be a Millionaire?' (fueled primarily by Philbin's warmth and charm) rocketed ABC to Number One in the ratings in its time slot, and then the show basically took over the network. Philbin has written four books—all bestsellers—two of which are memoirs. Regis Philbin has received numerous awards and honors over the years, including the TV Guide Award for Personality of the Year in 2001, and an Honorary Doctor of Laws Degree from his alma mater, Notre Dame University, for his on-going contributions to the school.

Nick J. Mileti

SOPHIA LOREN

(Born September 29, 1934 in Rome, Italy)
REAL ITALIAN NAME: SOFIA VILLANI SCICOLONE

Sophia Loren is a true international star in every sense of the word, and has even been honored as the most beautiful woman in the world.

An illegitimate child who grew up in the slums of Naples, Sophia was so starved and skinny as a child she was called 'Stechetto' (stick). But Sophia wasn't a stick for long. By age fourteen she was winning beauty contests and was discovered by the producer Carlo Ponti, who realized Sophia had talent as well as looks.

In 1961, the great Italian director Vittorio De Sica cast Loren in the now classic 'Two Women,' for which she won Best Actress Awards from the New York Film Critics Circle, the Cannes Film Festival, the British Film Academy, and the Academy of Motion Picture Arts and Science. In 1964, De Sica also directed Loren in 'Marriage Italian Style,' for which she received a second Oscar nomination.

Throughout her entire career, the ageless Loren moved between Hollywood and Italy, making movies and becoming a legend in the process.

In 1990, Sophia Loren was awarded an Honorary Oscar as "one of the genuine treasures of world cinema." In all, Sophia has received more than a dozen Lifetime Achievement Awards in her dazzling career, including one from the Berlin Film Festival (its Silver Bear) in 1994, from the theatre owners (NATO/ShoWest) in 1996, and from the Venice Film Festival (its Golden Lion) in 1998.

Sophia Loren oozes class even when she plays her favorite part of housewife, cooking pasta for her beloved husband of some forty years, movie producer Carlo Ponti. The Ponti/Loren saga goes back to the early fifties. The world watched breathlessly as the Italian government and Catholic Church made fools of themselves.

What happened was, Carlo obtained a Mexican divorce from his first wife and married Sophia in Mexico (by proxy) in 1957. The Italian government, however, refused to recognize Ponti's divorce. The Catholic Church said Ponti and Loren were living in 'concubinage.' The international press loved the scandal and milked it for all it was worth. Ultimately, in Italy, the couple was charged with bigamy and their Mexican marriage was invalidated.

In 1965, the first Mrs. Ponti finally cooperated and obtained a divorce in a French court, on the grounds of her husband's adultery. Carlo and Sophia quickly renounced their Italian citizenship, turned in their Italian passports, and became citizens of France, where they were legally married in 1966. This one the French got right.

Nick J. Mileti

GARRY MARSHALL

(Born November 13, 1934 in The Bronx, New York)
REAL ITALIAN NAME: GARRY KENT
MARSCHARELLI

Garry Marshall is a movie producer, director, writer and actor, but he is best known as creator, writer and producer of the television series 'Happy Days,' 'Mork and Mindy,' 'The Odd Couple' and 'Laverne and Shirley'—some of the longest running and most successful series in television history.

In Garry's tight-knit Italian family, he was known as "the sick one" (Garry presently has 128 known allergies, and is still counting). Persevering, Garry graduated from Northwestern University with a degree in journalism. Journalism, however, was not creative enough for him, so Garry drifted into gag writing for some of the top comedians of the day. Eventually, Garry, and his partner, Jerry Belson, wrote more than 100 episodes for situation comedies, including the classic 'Lucy Show,' 'Danny Thomas Show,' and 'Dick Van Dyke Show.'

A prime-time legend, Marshall has spent his life making people laugh—he has created and developed fourteen series, and executive produced more than a thousand half-hour episodes, a record that will probably never be broken.

For the multi-talented Garry Marshall, television was only a start. He then made the next to impossible transition from television sitcoms to directing theatrical motion pictures—at the advanced (for Hollywood) age of forty-seven.

Transferring his well-known passion for clean humor from television to the movies, Garry has directed dozens of films, including such up-lifting, warm movies as 'Pretty Woman,' 'The Flamingo Kid,' and 'Overboard.'

Garry could have become one of Hollywood's most successful comedic actors if he'd gone that route—as his 'right-on' hilarious scene with Albert Brooks in 'Lost in America' attests (Garry plays the Casino Boss).

In typical Italian fashion, Garry has strong family loyalties—he is notorious for employing his family as producers, actors and in any other way possible. For example, his daughter Lori was co-writer on his autobiography 'Wake Me When It's Funny.' "I try to make nepotism an acceptable art form," Garry jokes. With his well-known eye for talent, the Hollywood establishment is happy to oblige the comedic icon.

Garry Marshall has been feted innumerable times over the years, including receiving the Producer's Guild of America David Susskind Television Lifetime Achievement Award. He has been inducted into the Television Hall of Fame, and has received a Star on the Hollywood Walk of Fame.

Nick J. Mileti

FREDERIC TUTEN

(Born c. 1935 in the Bronx, New York, New York)

Frederic Tuten is an award-winning writer of rare talent whose writing achieves cult status among the cognoscenti.

Tuten was raised by his Sicilian mother and her parents. In fact, only Italian was spoken in the household—except on those rare occasions when his WASP father came home. His mother, who left school at fifteen and supported the entire family, was an avid reader. Tuten's inspiration to become a writer, however, was his mother's mother, Francesca Scelfo, his Sicilian grandmother, with whom he shared a cot in the family's modest living room and who helped him develop his story sense.

Tuten received his Doctorate in 19th century American Literature from New York University, concentrating on Melville and Whitman, although his greatest inspiration (after his grandmother) was Hemingway. "No young writer today can imagine the power Hemingway's prose had for us then," he once said. "You could take one of his sentences and twist it and shake it and slice it, and it would always return to its original shape. It was you who was misshaped at the end, turning even laundry instructions into a Hemingway line."

Tuten's book of experimental fiction "The Adventures of Mao on the Long March" was published in 1971, but was written while Tuten was enveloped in the change and turmoil of the Sixties. The book received rave reviews and is now considered a classic; John Updike wrote a forward for the book when it was reissued in 1997. Later, Updike said this about Tuten's first published book: "(When I read it in 1971, The Adventures of Mao on the Long March) seemed to me original, droll, and mysteriously precious . . . a deadpan amalgam of quotation, parody, history, and fanciful fiction."

Frederic Tuten directed the Graduate Program in Literature and Creative Writing at City College in New York for fifteen years. He also taught literature and American cinema at the University of Paris, France. Tuten writes short stories and articles on art, literature and film for various prestigious publications. Back to writing fiction some twenty years after his first novel, Tuten's books include "Tallien: A Brief Romance" (1994), "TinTin in the New World: A Romance" (1996), Van Gogh's Bad Café: A Love Story" (1997) and "The Green Hour" (2002) for which he received an Award in Literature from the Academy of Arts and Letters. The citation reads in part: "(Tuten) has consistently produced an oeuvre which is courageous, adventurous, intelligent and highly original, and has moments of haunting lyrical power."

Frederic Tuten was named a Guggenheim Fellow in Creative Writing in 1973 and received the prestigious DAAD Prize from Berlin in 1997. Tuten was a Pulitzer Prize nominating juror for fiction in 2002.

Nick J. Mileti

JOSEPH CERRELL

(Born June 19, 1935 in New York, New York)
REAL ITALIAN NAME: JOSEPH CERRELLA

In the rough and tumble world of big-time politics, Joseph Cerrell shines like a beacon.

That is to say, Cerrell is one of America's leading political consultants who operates in an honest, low-key, straight forward manner.

Cerrell graduated from the University of Southern California in 1961, and within a few years, established Cerrell Associates, Inc. (CAI) in Los Angeles. The firm has prospered and today is one of the most prestigious and successful in its field, sporting a blue-chip client list.

Over the years, Cerrell has played an increasingly important role in California politics, specializing in Democratic candidates and liberal judges. The affable Cerrell has been an important player in most of the presidential campaigns of the last forty years—from John F. Kennedy to Albert Gore.

The fact that California has voted Democratic most of this time is due in great part to the enthusiasm and expertise of Joseph Cerrell.

Always anxious to serve and assist his fellow man, the busy Cerrell has always found time to teach. He served as adjunct professor in Southern Cal's Jesse Unruh Institute of Politics for fifteen years, and is a Distinguished Visiting Professor in Political Science at Pepperdine University. Cerrell is also in great demand nationwide as a speaker.

Proud of his Italian heritage, Joseph Cerrell has served several terms as President of the thirty-year-old National Italian-American Foundation (NIAF), an organization committed to assisting the millions of people with Italian blood living in America, concentrating on the young.

Cerrell is also active in numerous other Italian-American, professional, and civic organizations, most of which have elected the natural-born leader to executive positions.

Not surprisingly, Joseph Cerrell has received innumerable awards in his lengthy career, including The Ellis Island Medal of Honor from the National Ethnic Coalition of Organizations (NECO) in 2002, and the Lifetime Achievement Award for Outstanding Contribution to Campaign Consulting from the American University Campaign Management Institute in 2004.

Lee Cerrell, Joseph's wife, is Executive Vice-President of CAI and has been a critical part of Joseph Cerrell's success.

Nick J. Mileti

RENATA TREITEL

(Born c. 1935 in Switzerland, of Italian parents)
REAL ITALIAN NAME: RENATA MINERBI

Renata Treitel is a teacher and poet. It is as a translator, however, that she has garnered her greatest fame.

Renata was educated in Italy, Argentina and America. While in Buenos Aires, she met German born Sven Treitel, who received his Doctorate from MIT in 1958 and has become a leading geophysicist. Renata moved with her husband to Tulsa, Oklahoma in 1960, where she has lived all her life. Treitel taught Italian and Spanish at the University of Tulsa, and in 1983, she published a chapbook of poetry entitled 'German Notebook.' Treitel has been the recipient of several Witter Bynner Foundation Translation Grants. In 1994 she translated, from the Spanish, Susana Thenon's 'distancias' (Distances) for which she also wrote the Introduction and Afterward. Treitel also translated Thenon's last book, 'Ova Completa.'

In 1996, Treitel translated from the Italian 'Splendida lumine solis' (The Blazing Lights of the Sun) written by Rosita Capioli, for which, the following year, she won the Oklahoma Book Poetry Award for her translation. In 1997, she translated 'Furore delle rose' (Wrath of the Roses) also by Rosita Capioli. In addition, Treitel wrote the Introduction to the book.

Just as a restorer of art must be a great artist in his or her own right, in addition to having the language skills, a translator of poetry must first be an accomplished poet.

Paying tribute to the skills necessary in a translator, the poet Cynthia Tedesco, wrote to Treital:

"I just wanted to write you to tell you how magnificent your translations of Rosita Capioli's poems are. I believe every poem is a translation and that every translation is another poem to be treasured when done so beautifully as yours."

In 1998, Treitel translated the photography books 'Artificial Illuminations Artificial Illuminations' by Enrico Ghezzi, and 'Sarajevo,' by Tom Stoddart, and in 2000, Treitel published the short poem 'The Burden of Silence.' Later, Treital translated from Spanish 'Las Cacerias' (The Hunts) by Amelia Biagioni. Treital also wrote the Introduction and explanatory notes.

In 2001, Renata Treital was First Runner-Up for the Bordighera Poetry Prize for 'Oklahoma Baroque,' her first full poetry manuscript. The Distinguished Poet Judge Dorothy Barassi wrote: "These are brave inventive poems . . . I admire the intelligence of these poems, and the rueful imagination that is edgy, but never smug or disaffected."

Nick J. Mileti

NEIL LEON RUDENSTINE

(Born 1935 in Ossining, New York)

Neil Rudenstine was the twenty-sixth President of Harvard University, serving from 1991 until he retired in 2001.

Half Italian, Rudenstine's mother's family emigrated from Campobasso in Southern Italy. His mother's name was Mae Esperito.

Rudenstein's family moved to Danbury, Connecticut when he was five years old. He attended Danbury public schools, but his parent's dream was to send him to the private Wooster School in their hometown for his high school years. His father worked as a federal prison guard and his mother labored as a part-time waitress in pursuit of the dream. Young Neil did his part by applying himself to his studies, and, inspired by the love of his family, Rudenstine made his parents proud by earning a scholarship to Wooster School. Eager to continue pleasing his parents, Rudenstine applied himself, and upon graduation from Wooster School in 1952, received a scholarship to Princeton, where he received his B.A. in 1956. He moved to England as a Rhodes scholar, studying at Oxford University. While living in England, Rudenstine met his future wife, a fellow student, Angelica Zander. Rudenstine returned to America, and received his Ph.D. in English Literature from Harvard in 1964. After a four-year stint teaching English at Harvard, Rudenstine moved to Princeton where he taught English and rose to become Dean of Students, Dean of the College, and finally, Provost. In 1988, Rudenstine was lured out of academia to become Executive Vice President of the Andrew W. Mellon Foundation.

Interested in again working directly with young people, Rudenstine accepted the appointment as Harvard's President in 1991. Coming from a background that taught him the value of a dollar—as well as the need for money to accomplish goals—shortly after having been sworn in as President Rudenstine inaugurated an ambitious (to put it mildly) fund-raising program for Harvard—the 2.1 billion dollar goal was the most any college had ever sought to raise. By the time the drive ended, the university had raised $2.6 billion, half-a-billion dollars over its goal. Rudenstine explained that the money was simply an instrument for expanding the school's range of studies—which he did across the board over his ten-year tenure, improving most every department and aspect of the university. His tenure as President of Harvard is considered a tremendous success.

In his active retirement, the scholar of Renaissance literature is Chairman of a major, non-profit enterprise he formed, named "ArtSTOR." Funded by the Mellon Foundation with whom he was previously affiliated, the new venture develops, stores and distributes digital images to scholars, teachers and students who study art, architecture and related fields, and use images as an important aspect of their work. Neil Rudenstine has written several scholarly books, and, not surprisingly, sits on numerous boards and has received numerous honors and awards in his lifetime.

Nick J. Mileti

JAMES DARREN

(Born June 8, 1936 in Philadelphia, Pennsylvania)
REAL ITALIAN NAME: JAMES ERCOLANI

James Darren is an actor, singer and television director best known for his roles in the 'Gidget' movies in the early sixties.

After studying acting in New York, Darren answered the siren call of Hollywood in 1955. A number of forgettable films followed, but a short four years later, his big-break came. In 1959, Darren starred opposite Sandra Dee in the teen movie 'Gidget,' in which he sang the title song. The song was a hit and the movie was so successful, two sequels were made—'Gidget Goes Hawaiian' (1961) and 'Gidget Goes To Rome (1963).' Darren starred in both sequels. Of the dozen films Darren appeared in, the best known is 'Guns of Navarone,' released incongruously in 1961, in the middle of the Gidget trilogy.

Darren had several other pop-hit records, including 'Goodbye Cruel World.' In the sixties, Television began to occupy Darin—he had important roles in 'The TimeTunnel' and 'T.J. Hooker'—and TV directing kept the multi-talented star occupied for two decades. James Darren's first love has always been music, however, and in the nineties he has begun concert appearances and record production.

Closet Italians

MARIA MULDAUR

(Born September 12, 1943 in New York, New York)
REAL ITALIAN NAME: MARIA D'AMATO

Maria Muldaur is a singer of jazz, gospel and blues who is best known for her smash pop hit 'Midnight at the Oasis.'

Maria began singing at the age of five and has never stopped developing musically—singing and experimenting with different forms of music for her entire life. Starting with a jug band, she moved on to classical blues, Christian, and later even incorporated blues, R & B, and what is known as Louisiana music, into a genre known as 'bluesiana.'

In 1974, Maria recorded her first solo album, which included 'Midnight at the Oasis,' which went platinum. Her follow-up recording of 'I'm a Woman,' was well received by the emerging feminist movement of the mid-seventies, and has served as Maria's theme song for thirty years—in fact, she opens every concert with it. In 2003, Maria released 'A Woman Alone with the Blues (Remembering Peggy Lee),' a collection of twelve of Lee's greatest songs. The album was a labor of love because Lee was one of Maria Muldaur's earliest musical inspirations. The classy Peggy Lee would be proud of the wonderful, exciting, result.

Nick J. Mileti

RICHARD CELESTE

(Born November 11, 1937 in Cleveland, Ohio)

A Democratic liberal—in the highest sense of the word—Richard Celeste has devoted his life to serving his fellow man in numerous prestigious elected and appointed positions, including Governor of Ohio and United States Ambassador to India.

Celeste's Italian father, Frank P. Celeste, was Mayor of Lakewood, Ohio (a suburb of Cleveland) for many years, and was also a force in Ohio's Democratic politics.

After graduating with honors (Magna Cum Laude) from Yale University in 1959, Celeste moved on to Oxford University in England, where he studied as a Rhodes scholar. After graduation from Oxford, Celeste was anxious to help the needy and unfortunate, so he joined the Peace Corps as a Staff Liaison Officer. Following his stint in the Peace Corps, Celeste served for four years in New Delhi as Special Assistant to Chester Bowles, United States Ambassador to India.

Lured back to his native Ohio, in 1970, Celeste ran successfully for State Representative. He served in that capacity for four years. A four-year term (from 19774 to 1978) as Lieutenant Governor of Ohio followed. Then, in a rare political defeat, Celeste ran for Governor and lost. In 1979, President Jimmy Carter made the perfect move when he appointed Richard Celeste Director of the Peace Corps (for which organization, you will recall, Celeste had previously worked). Celeste ran the worldwide humanitarian organization for two years, and as Director, he streamlined the Peace Corps and inaugurated numerous policies that remain in place today. Returning to Ohio, Richard Celeste ran again for Governor in 1982—this time winning the State's top post. An extremely popular official, Celeste was re-elected Governor of Ohio in 1986. Because the Ohio Constitution limits the term of the Governor to two successive terms, Celeste was barred from running for a third term. After a lifetime of public service, Celeste (understandably) decided to have a little privacy and make some money. He served on numerous boards and established a company that advised some of the top corporations in the country. Although Celeste was extremely successful in the private sector, this was 'strictly business' and did not—could not—last long. Richard Celeste wanted (in his own words) "to make a difference again."

Consequently, in 1997, Richard Celeste accepted the appointment by President Bill Clinton to be the United States Ambassador to India (another perfect appointment because of Celeste's previous service in that country). Celeste served in that important post for four years. During his tenure, relations between the two countries reached an all-time high, culminating with an historic visit from then President Clinton, which Ambassador Celeste, and his gracious wife, Jacqueline, hosted.

In 2002, Richard Celeste was appointed President of Colorado College, a prestigious independent liberal arts and sciences institution, located at the foothills of the Rocky Mountains.

Nick J. Mileti

MARLO THOMAS

(Born November 21, 1937 in Deerfield, Michigan)

An actor and author, Marlo Thomas became famous and, simultaneously, a symbol of strength and confidence to a generation of young women in the turbulent sixties, because of her character in the television series 'That Girl.'

Marlo's father was Lebanese (the famous entertainer Danny Thomas), and her mother, Rosemarie (Rosie), was Italian.

Both parents had a major influence on her.

Marlo credits her father with inspiring her—he implored her to break out from the 'Danny Thomas' daughter chokehold' and "run your own race." Of her Italian mother, Marlo says: "My mother left us the joy of life. (Also) she used to say to my sister, brother and I, 'take care of each other,' and we sure do."

After graduating from the University of Southern California (USC) with a teaching degree, in a major breakthrough for women at the time, Marlo conceived, produced and starred in—as one of television's first independent women—'That Girl,' which ran on ABC from 1966 to 1971. She has appeared in numerous movies and television shows over the years, and occasionally guest stars on the sitcom 'Friends' as Rachel's mother.

For her work on television, Marlo has received four nominations for Golden Globe Awards, winning once.

She has also won four Emmys, received the Peabody Award and been inducted into Broadcasting Hall of Fame.

As an author, she has written three bestsellers, 'Free to Be . . . You and Me,' and 'Free to Be . . . a Family,' and, in 2002, the innovative 'The Right Words at the Right Time,' an inspiring collection of essays written by prominent individuals, describing the moment when words changed their lives—literally. All of the money from the book goes to the Saint Jude Children's Research Hospital, which was founded by her parents.

The facility is known throughout the world for its mission to find cures for children with catastrophic illnesses through research and treatment. Marlo's mother and father are buried in a memorial garden on the grounds.

With this heritage, it is not surprising that Marlo has been active in social causes her entire life. She is most proud of the work she and her family do for Saint Jude, where she serves as the Outreach Director and sits on the Professional Advisory Board.

Marlo Thomas remains a positive role model. Her influence now extends beyond young ladies to women (and men) of all ages.

Nick J. Mileti

CONNIE STEVENS

(Born August 8, 1938 in Brooklyn, New York)
REAL ITALIAN NAME:
CONCETTA ROSALIE ANN INGOLIA

Brilliantly parlaying her fame as a singer and movie star, Connie Stevens has accomplished what many performers dream about for the later stages of their show biz careers—she has achieved great success as a businesswoman.

Connie started out as a singer. She formed a vocal group called 'The Foremost'—the three male back-up singers went on to fame as 'The Lettermen'—and then appeared in an all-girl group named 'The Three Debs.'

Stevens performed in numerous forgettable feature films, and then, when she was twenty-one, struck pay dirt in television. Connie's break out role was as 'Cricket Blake' in the television series 'Hawaiian Eye,' which ran on ABC for four years, from 1959 to 1963. This was followed the next year by a role in the short-lived series 'Wendy and Me,' with George Burns. The teen idol of the sixties moved on to nightclub appearance, summer theatre and concert performances. Connie's appearances for the USO, often with Bob Hope, have made her a serviceman's favorite in three wars.

In 1989, responding to demands by her fans who were awed by her beautiful, youthful appearance, Connie Stevens entered the business world, forming 'Forever Spring,' a cosmetic company that she created and runs as president. The company sells hundred of items—including men and woman's fragrances, hair care, makeup, bath and body products, cosmetics, candles and potpourri, gift sets and gift baskets—and has become a force in the business. Her 'Ginseng Facial Feed,' which is part of her acclaimed six-step beauty system, is a particularly popular product. 'Forever Spring' was one of the top-selling lines of its kind on television's 'Home Shopping Network,' serving a clientele of millions of women.

'The Garden Sanctuary,' Connie's luxurious day spa and boutique in Los Angeles, pampers the rich and famous with soothing facials, body wraps, and a full line of health and beauty services, all served up in a garden-like setting by an attractive, attentive staff. In a cross promoter's dream, the popular boutique at the spa features 'Forever Spring' products.

In addition to her demanding business commitments (and occasional singing and acting jobs), Connie Stevens works tirelessly for the disadvantaged—particularly Native Americans (through project 'Windfeather'), and people with disabilities (through 'Dignity' of Jackson Hole)—and says proudly, "A large portion of my sales are given to charity."

Not surprisingly, Connie has received numerous awards in recognition of her community service efforts, including the Shriner's 'Humanitarian of the Year' Award in 1991 and the Humanitarian Award by The Sons of Italy Foundation in the year 2000.

Nick J. Mileti

CONNIE FRANCIS

(Born December 12, 1938 in Newark, New Jersey)
REAL ITALIAN NAME:
CONCETTA ROSEMARIE FRANCONERO

Pop singer Connie Francis has fought for everything she has—including her life.

After winning her first talent show as a child playing the accordion, Connie quickly turned exclusively to singing. Then, early in 1958, star-maker Dick Clark, on 'American Bandstand', while introducing Connie and the song, 'Who's Sorry Now,' said the magic words:

"No doubt about it, this new girl singer is headed straight for the number one spot."

For the next several years Connie seemed to work twenty-four hours a day and it paid off; she was a star and made the most of it. She had hit records and made movies, stage and television appearances. More importantly, Connie was one of the first to see the potential for sales of her records worldwide. She has recorded in German, Greek, French, Portuguese, Spanish, Hebrew, Japanese and Italian. "It was easy for me," she said. "I did it phonetically. I had a flair for it". Connie is bigger in Europe than in the United States—she has recorded more than seventy albums for America, but more than twice that number for Europe.

Then, tragically, in 1974, while on tour at the Westbury Music Fair, in Westbury, New York, an intruder broke into Connie's motel room. Held at gunpoint, she was the victim of a violent sexual assault and robbery.

After overcoming her depression, Connie sued the hotel for lack of security and became a strong advocate for victims' rights. Not surprisingly, the high-profile case caused the hotel industry to become much more serious about security: They began installing dead bolts and viewing ports, among other things—all because of a slight, but highly determined, and principled, pop singer from Newark, New Jersey.

JONI JAMES

(Born September 22, 1930 in Chicago, Illinois)
REAL ITALIAN NAME: JOAN CARMELLO BABBO

Joni James was a pop singer who recorded for MGM Records from 1952 until 1964. Her second release "Why Don't You Believe Me?" was Number One on the Pop Charts and sold over a million records. The hits came fast and furious for James—she hit the Top Ten four more times in the next three years with songs like "Have You Heard?" and "Your Cheatin' Heart," but then the hits stopped coming.

PATRICIA DE STACY HARRISON

(Born May 1, 1939 in Brooklyn, New York)
REAL ITALIAN NAME: PATRICIA DI STACIO

Patricia is one of the Republican Party's best fundraisers, as well as an effective spokesperson for the political party.

Her grandfather immigrated from the south of Italy and had his name changed from Nunziato Di Stacio to Charles De Stacy at Ellis Island.

A graduate of American University, Patricia has always had a public conscience. In the nineties, Patricia and her husband, E. Bruce Harrison, established a public affairs company that specialized in environmental public policy.

Patricia's wide-ranging business and political talents were acknowledged when she was appointed Co-Chairman of the Republican National Committee, serving from 1997 to 2001. Patricia was the first person—man or woman—of Italian heritage to assume that position. One of her missions, which she attacked with her usual enthusiasm, was to recruit more women and minorities.

Late in 2001, President George W. Bush appointed Patricia Assistant Secretary of State for Educational and Cultural Affairs.

A firm believer in equal rights for all, Patricia has written the book with the intriguing title 'A Seat At the Table: An Insider's View of How Women Can Move to the Leader's Table and Enjoy the Trip." She is also the author of 'America's New Women Entrepreneurs.'

Patricia was a founder of the National Women's Economic Alliance, which is an organization committed to identifying qualified people, who happen to be women, for leadership roles in business and politics, and for appointment to corporate boards. Patricia has served on the President's Export Council of the Department of Commerce, the U.S. Trade Representative's Service Policy Advisory Council and chaired the International Committee of the Small Business Advisor Council.

An outstanding public speaker, known for her honesty, and dynamic telling-it-like-it-is style, Patricia is in great demand by non-profit, business and political organizations.

Patricia de Stacy Harrison has received numerous awards and honors, and in 1997 she was named one of the "50 Most Influential Women in Politics," by the Ladies Home Journal.

Proud of her heritage, Patricia relishes the time she served on the Executive Committee of the National Italian American Foundations, the non-profit, non-partisan foundation that represents America's twenty-six million Italian-Americans.

DION

(Born July 18, 1939 in the Bronx, New York)
REAL ITALIAN NAME: DION FRANCIS DIMUCCI

Dion's singing career has spanned forty years. Although he has changed his style many times, he is best known for his string of doo-wop hits in the late fifties, recorded with his group, Dion & the Belmonts (three neighborhood Italian buddies).

Growing musically over the years, Dion constantly reinvented himself, turning to Rhythm and Blues (R&B) in the sixties, folk and gospel in the seventies and eighties, and rock in the nineties. "I didn't get stuck in an era or stuck in a period," Dion said recently. "To me its always been this way: If you grab someone's ear, you can take them on a trip . . . I just want to take them to a cool place."

In 1989, Dion was inducted into the Rock and Roll Hall of Fame, located in Cleveland, Ohio.

HENRY FIOL

(Born January 16, 1947 in New York, New York)

Henry Foil is one of the best-known salseros—Latin singers—in the world. By blending the country sound—what he calls 'son montuno'—with an urban flavor, Fiol has touched a nerve with his Latin fans.

Henry Foil's mother is Italian and his father is Puerto Rican.

For Foil, the Italian-Puerto Rican combination made his life difficult while growing up in Manhattan's Washington Heights, which was very Irish. "There was a sprinkling of Italians around," Foil said later, "and they were sort of acceptable. But Puerto Ricans or Latinos . . . they were like garbage." Foil spoke Italian before he spoke English, and to fit in as a youth he denied his Puerto Rican heritage. Then, after visiting Puerto Rico as a teenager, he denied his Italian heritage.

Foil has been recording and performing since his early twenties and has become a cult favorite of Latin music buffs all over the world. Songwriting, singing and playing a host of instruments, Foil's provocative lyrics often depict the world of harsh urban realities. This, not surprisingly, makes him particularly popular in countries with problems of that nature. Foil has toured Columbia—where he is extremely popular and his recordings are bestsellers—Mexico, the Caribbean, Central and South America. In 1992, Henry Foil took his Latin music throughout Europe on a successful tour. While in Italy, he visited his grandparent's village in Calabria in Southern Italy. Foil was as impressed with the Italian culture as he was with that in Puerto Rican when he first visited the island as a teenager.

Nick J. Mileti

ELEANOR SMEAL

(Born July 30, 1939 in Ashtabula, Ohio)
REAL ITALIAN NAME: ELEANOR MARIE CUTRI

Eleanor (Ellie) Smeal is one of America's most influential women. For over thirty years, she has been in the forefront of the drive for woman's equality, both as President of the National Organization for Women (NOW) and as a founder and President of the Feminist Majority Foundation.

Born of immigrant Italian parents, Eleanor graduated with honors from Duke University and received her masters in political science from the University of Florida. She married Charles Smeal in 1963.

In 1970, Smeal joined the National Organization for Women, and the organization quickly rewarded her leadership abilities. She was elected to the National Board three years later, National Board Chair in 1975 and National President in 1977, serving three terms in that office. Under Smeal's leadership, NOW became the premier feminist organization in the country. As President, one of Smeal's priorities was the passage of the Equal Rights Amendment. In that campaign she organized what has been called 'the largest nationwide grassroots and lobbying campaign in the history of the modern feminist movement.'

Smeal was the first to identify the so-called 'gender gap,' the difference in the way men and women vote. She wrote "How and Why Women Will Elect the Next President," which was published in 1984. In that book, she predicted that women's votes would be decisive in presidential politics—a revolutionary concept at the time. In 1986, Smeal led 100,000 people in the first national abortion rights march in Washington, D.C. Smeal has played a leading role in several landmark court cases, including NOW v Scheidler.

In 1987, Smeal felt NOW was becoming too conservative, so she joined with four others to found The Feminist Majority Foundation. The group's campaigns included the defense of abortion clinics and lobbying for approval of the French abortion drug, mifepristone.

While Smeal's campaign encouraging law enforcement to recognize violence against abortion clinics as a major crime have earned her a substantial amount of publicity, her shifting of women's organizations strategies from targeting key contests to working to get the largest possible number of women to seek—and then help them win—political office is equally significant (and more successful with each passing election). Always a pioneer, Smeal conceived and organized a national feminist convention, called Expo '96 (and again in 2000), bringing together all sectors of the woman's movement for the first time in history. In 1997, Smeal took her organization global, fighting for women's rights in Afganistan.

Nick J. Mileti

FRANKIE AVALON

(Born September 18, 1939 in Philadelphia, Pennsylvania)
REAL ITALIAN NAME: FRANCIS THOMAS AVALLONE

BOBBY RYDELL

(Born April 26, 1942 in Philadelphia, Pennsylvania)
REAL ITALIAN NAME: ROBERT RIDARELLI

FABIAN

(Born February 6, 1943 in Philadelphia, Pennsylvania)
REAL ITALIAN NAME: FABIANO ANTHONY FORTE

In the early 1940's, there must have been something extremely potent in the Chianti wine of South Philly— three bona-fide teen pop singing idols, Frankie Avalon, Fabian and Bobby Rydell, were born within a four-year span.

Amazingly, each of the three handsome Italian youngsters went to the same high school and lived within a few blocks of each other. They each also had successful, if brief, singing careers in the late fifties and early sixties that led to Hollywood and the movies.

Frankie Avalon is best known for his 'beach' films, which have become cult classics. 'Beach Party' in 1963,

'Bikini Beach' in 1964 and 'Beach Blanket Bingo' in 1965, were all made with Annette Funicello and were hits.

Bobby Rydell had nineteen Top 30 Hits and thirty-four Top 40 Hits.

Fabian was voted most promising vocalist in a poll in 1959.

All three were products of Dick Clark's American Bandstand. When the British Invasion of the early sixties occurred, the hit-making days were over for the popular pop trio, as well as for most others in the pop, crooner and swing categories.

In 1985, Dick Clark worked his creativity and magic once more and reunited Avalon, Fabian and Rydell in a nostalgic revue named 'The Golden Boys of Grandstand.' The three performers were well received—cheered lustily by their graying fans all over America for over a decade.

Chapter XI

Illustrious Italians With Non-Italian Names
Born Between 1940-1949

PATRICK J. LEAHY

(Born March 31, 1940 in Montpelier, Vermont)

As a politician, Patrick Leahy is a phenomenon. In 1974, when he was 43 years old, Leahy was the youngest person ever elected to the United States Senate from the State of Vermont. He is a liberal Democrat in the notoriously Republican state (he is the only Democrat ever elected to the U.S. Senate from Vermont), and a Catholic in predominantly Protestant Vermont. Leahy was re-elected in 1980, 1986, 1992 and 1998, when he received a full 72 % of the vote.

Leahy's mother was Italian. His mother's parents, who were from Friuli, in Italy, immigrated to Vermont to find work in the state's granite quarries. Leahy's father was Irish.

One of the most powerful—and respected—members of the Senate, Leahy is interested in nutritional standards, protection of privacy, and open government. He considers his work to ban the use of landmines his most important achievement.

MARY LANDRIEU

(Born November 23, 1955 in Arlington, Virginia)

Mary Landrieu is the first Italian-American woman elected to the United States Senate. After serving as Louisiana State Representative (1979-1987), and then State Treasurer (1988-1995), Mary, who is a Democrat, was elected to her first term as U. S. Senator from Louisiana in 1996.

In 2002, in Mary's bid for re-election, journalists on both sides of the political fence framed her bitterly contested race in a larger context. The closely watched election attracted national attention and interlopers, and was generally considered to be a sort of bell weather for the presidential elections of 2004 in America.

"When President Bush threw everything except poisoned gumbo into the fight to defeat Sen. Landrieu in Saturday's runoff," E.J. Dionne, Jr. wrote in the New York Times after the election, "she didn't fold . . . Losers allow their opponents to set the terms of the competition. Winners change the terms—and, yes, fight back. That's Mary Landrieu's lesson to her party." That's right, in December 2002, in a startling victory, Mary Landrieu was re-elected to the United States Senate for a second six-year term.

Mary had good teachers. She learned her political lessons from her father, 'Moon' Landrieu, popular ex-mayor of New Orleans. Her Italian ancestry filled in the blanks. Mary Landrieu thinks for herself, and crosses party lines when her conscience dictates—a combination that bodes well for her political future.

Nick J. Mileti

BILL PARCELLS

(Born August 22, 1941 in Englewood, New Jersey)

Bill Parcells is one of the National Football League's most successful coaches, retiring and un-retiring himself into football history.

Duane Charles Parcells, as Bill Parcells was christened, is half-Italian—his mother's maiden name was Ida Naclerio.

In 1983, Parcells began his head-coaching career when he was named Head Coach of the New York Giants. In the next eight years, he led the Giants to Super Bowl wins twice—in 1987 and 1991.

Shortly after the second Super Bowl, Parcells retired from coaching.

After two years in television, however, Bill Parcells un-retired in 1993.

Parcells joined the New England Patriots as Head Coach and led the previously hapless Patriots to the Super Bowl in 1997.

Once again, shortly after his Super Bowl appearance, Parcells retired.

Later that same year, Bill Parcells un-retired.

He joined the New York Jets as Head Coach for the 1997-'98 season. Parcells took the pathetic 1-15 Jets to

AFC East Champions in two years—the Jet's first Division Title in twenty-nine years.

After one more season with the Jets, Parcells retired from coaching for the third and final time in the year 2000.

In 2003, Bill Parcells un-retired.

Parcells became the Head Coach of the Dallas Cowboys.

Bill Parcell's lifetime record as a Head Coach is 149 games won, 106 lost and one tied. Though impressive, as with Lou Little, numbers only tell part of the story. First of all, Parcells took players who were losers and made them believe in themselves. Secondly, like Vince Lombardi before him, Bill Parcells is a tough and uncompromising coach who teaches his players how to win—in football, and in life after football.

Here is Bill Parcells summing-up his coaching philosophy (and his philosophy on life). "In the end, I've found, people like the direct approach. It's much more valuable to them to have a leader who's absolutely clear and open than to have one who soft-soaps or talks in circles."

Nick J. Mileti

FEDERICO FAGGIN

(Born December 1, 1941 in Vicenza, Italy)

Federico Faggin, along with Ted Hoff and Stan Mazor, designed and built the world's first microprocessor, which many people believe will eventually be recorded as the most important development of the 20th century.

Faggin graduated from Instituto Industriale at Vicenza in 1960 and went to work for Olivetti. "I worked with transistors and memories, core memories and I understood the first order approximation of how those things worked," Faggin later explained. "But I wanted to go deeper. I had questions. In fact, that's why I did physics and not engineering. I chose physics because it would allow me to ask questions of how things worked. That was the essence." Consequently, the twenty-year old attended the University of Padua where he received a Doctorate in Physics in 1965 (four years being the shortest time possible to earn the degree).

In 1968, Faggin immigrated to America to join Fairchild Semiconductor in its Research and Development (R & D) Laboratory in Palo Alto. At Fairchild he led the development of the original Metal On Silicon (MOS) silicon gate technology. His group also designed the world's first commercial integrated circuit to use that technology. In 1970, Faggin was lured to the Intel Corporation in Santa Clara. At Intel, Faggin led the design and development of the world's first microprocessor, the Intel 4004. Federico Faggin's initials (F.F.) adorn the surface of this famous microprocessor. The only set of initials present, they graphically underscore Faggin's leadership role.

This microchip made the personal computer revolution possible.

An entrepreneur as well as a physicist and inventor, Faggin co-founded Zilog, Inc. at the end of 1974, and was its President and CEO until 1980. Zilog was at the forefront of microprocessor technology under Faggin's leadership. He conceived and designed the Z80 microprocessor family and supervised the design of the Z80 microprocessor, considered the most successful 8-bit processor ever produced. In 1982 Faggin co-founded Cygnet Technologies, Inc. and was President and CEO until 1986, where he developed the Communicaton CoSystem, an intelligent voice and data peripheral for the personal computer. In 1986, Faggin co-founded Synaptics, Inc. in San Jose, California, where he is currently President and CEO. Synaptics makes touch-screen technologies and Chinese-language handwriting recognition systems.

Faggin has received numerous awards and honors over the years, including the 1988 International Marconi Fellowship Award for his contributions to the birth of the microprocessor, the 1988 Gold Metal for Science and Technology from the Prime Minister of Italy, and the IEEE W. Wallace McDowell Award in 1994. In 1996, Federico Faggin was inducted into the National Inventors Hall of Fame for his role in the invention of the microprocessor.

Nick J. Mileti

DONNA LEON

(Born September 29, 1942 in Montclair, New Jersey)

Donna Leon is one of the most successful crime writers in the world today. Her novels are published in over 25 countries—from China to the United Kingdom, from Spain to Russia—but she is most successful in Germany, Switzerland and Austria.

Donna was born into an Italian-American family. "People tend to think the name Donna Leon is a nom de plum. It's not. It's real," she recently told the New York Times. In college, Donna majored in English Literature (Jane Austen was the subject of her doctoral dissertation). Donna moved to Italy in 1965, when she was 23 years old. From Italy, the bold, adventurous young woman moved around the world, teaching English literature in Iran, China and Saudi Arabia, among other countries.

Returning to Italy in 1978, Donna moved to Venice and taught classes at a nearby U. S. military installation. "And ending up in Italy, I guess I made some kind of connection with something that was there all the while in my blood, my family." She has lived in Italy since 1978, and says she has no plans to leave Italy or return to America to live.

About ten years after settling in Italy, Donna embarked upon an unusual course for an academician—"for fun," she wrote a crime novel. A well-known opera connoisseur, she set the story in La Fenice, the Venice opera house. The German-born conductor is found dead between acts, and she invented a series of characters around her hero,

Closet Italians

Commissario Guido Brunetti. Donna plunked the manuscript into a desk drawer, where it remained for over a year. Eventually, she sent the book off to a competition, and won. 'Death at La Fenice' was published in 1992, and since then, Donna Leon has published a Guido Brunetti book every year, for a total of twelve to date. In 2000, 'Friends in High Places,' won the Crime Writers Association (of England) Silver Dagger Award for fiction.

Donna Leon has been translated into nineteen languages, but not Italian, one of the few countries where she is not published. All of her books are all set in Venice, and the Italians begrudgingly admit she writes about Venice like an insider, meaning she captures perfectly the whole of the Italian way of life (including the corruption). And therein lies the problem. Donna says the Italians don't mind Italians writing about the corruption in their legal system, but resent hearing about it from an outsider.

In 2003, Donna Leon's latest novel, "Uniform Justice" was the first to be published in the United States. Her publishers expect her to become a household name in America as she is in Germany—where most of her novels have been made into television specials.

A private person, the modest writer claims discussion of her considerable success is usually overblown. She says things like "Murder mystery is a craft, not an art," and "I'm not a violin maker, I'm a carpenter." Obviously, the millions of Donna Leon fans don't agree with her, and more importantly, even if what she says is true, they don't care.

Nick J. Mileti

MICHAEL BENNETT

(Born April 8, 1943 in Buffalo, New York;
Died July 2, 1987)
REAL ITALIAN NAME: MICHAEL DI FIGLIA

Michael Bennett spent his entire professional life working on Broadway. Possessing an unprecedented combination of talents, Bennett was successful on Broadway as a director, choreographer, producer, writer and performer, although his greatest successes were as director and choreographer.

Starting out as a dancer on Broadway, Michael's first big hit came in 1968 when the twenty-five year old choreographed 'Promises Promises'. The musical comedy ran on Broadway over three years. The show's success seemed to invigorate Bennett—he worked non-stop over the next few years. Bennett choreographed and directed Katherine Hepburn in 'Coco' in 1969. The next year he provided the musical staging for 'Company' and the following year he choreographed and directed 'Follies', both Stephen Sondheim musicals.

Being an ex-dancer, and understanding the suffering and frustration of rejection the nameless dancers (the 'gypsies') routinely endure, Bennett rented a studio and invited a group of dancers to talk about their experiences, in and out of the theatre. The sessions were recorded and the rest is history—literally. 'A Chorus Line,' a new kind of musical—one that integrated the story line with all of the other elements of the show—opened in the Shubert Theatre in July of 1975. Conceived, choreographed and directed by Michael Bennett, the original musical ran an unprecedented fifteen years on

Broadway, closing in April of 1990 after 6,137 performances.

In addition to breaking box office records, 'A Chorus Line' won an incredible string of awards, including the Pulizer Prize for Drama, nine Tony Awards, five Drama Desk Awards, the New York and Los Angeles Drama Critics Circle Awards, and a Gold Record Award from Columbia Records.

For the three years following the Broadway opening, Bennett personally supervised productions of 'A Chorus Line' all over the world. He auditioned, rehearsed and even directed the smash hit, always striving to maintain the show's integrity. The musical has been produced in over twenty countries.

It is obvious, even to a casual observer of the theater, that Michael Bennett had no role in the disappointing 1985 film version of his theatrical classic.

In 1981, Bennett had his last big hit in 'Dreamgirls' (he produced, choreographed and directed), which the New York Times said, "solidified the reputation of Michael Bennett as one of the greatest directors of American musical theatre." He received his seventh and final Tony for the show, which ran over three and a half years, and capped Michael Bennett's unique and extraordinary Broadway career.

Nick J. Mileti

PENNY MARSHALL

(Born October 15, 1943 in the Bronx, New York.)
REAL ITALIAN NAME:
CAROLE PENELOPE MARSCHARELLI

Penny Marshall is an actor and director who is best known for her portrayal of Laverne DeFazio in the long-running sitcom 'Laverne and Shirley.'

Penny received her first acting break on television from her brother, Garry Marshall, who cast her in his sitcom 'The Odd Couple,' which ran from 1971 to 1975. In 1976, Penny was writing scripts with her friend Cindy Williams, when Garry asked Penny, and her friend Cindy, to guest star on 'Happy Days, another of his hit shows.

The public response to the girls was phenomenal, and inspired the creative genius, Garry Marshall, to create yet another smash hit, the sitcom 'Laverne and Shirley.' Penny embraced and helped shape the role of Laverne and went on to stardom. She also cut her director's teeth on several episodes of the series, which ran until 1983.

Penny acted in numerous television movies and then—in her forties (mirroring her brother's career change) made the monster jump from television to directing feature films. Her first directorial effort was the 1986 movie 'Jumpin' Jack Flash,' starring Whoopi Goldberg. Like her brother Garry's films, Penny Marshall's movies also have positive themes. 'Big,' nominated for an Oscar for Best Picture in 1988, and 'A League of their Own,' in 1992, are only two of Penny's successes as a director.

CINDY WILLIAMS

(Born August 22, 1947 in Van Nuys, California)

Cindy Williams is an actor and producer whose signature role is the eternally optimistic brewery worker Shirley Feeney in the hit blue-collar sitcom 'Laverne and Shirley.'

Cindy's mother, Francesca Bellini, is Italian, and encouraged the petite brunette to follow her dreams. From early childhood, Cindy dream was to be an actor. Her big break came in 1973, when George Lucas cast her as Ron Howard's girlfriend in 'American Graffiti.' Several juicy parts in feature films followed, but they were merely prologue to her second major break—being cast as Shirley in the smash sitcom 'Laverne and Shirley.'

Cindy left the show in 1982 and continues to act, mostly in made-for-TV movies. In a switch of careers, she is achieving success and satisfaction as a movie producer, co-producing the hilarious Steve Martin hit 'Father of the Bride,' and its sequel.

Nick J. Mileti

MICHAEL CRISTOFER

(Born January 22, 1945 in Trenton, New Jersey)
REAL ITALIAN NAME: MICHAEL PROCACCINO

Michael Cristofer is an award-winning playwright, screenwriter, actor, and director of stage, screen and television, but his greatest fame lies in the recognition heaped upon him for writing 'The Shadow Box,' a play about three terminally-ill patients.

Prior to his success as a playwright, Cristofer spent a decade as an actor, appearing in television and feature films. He best efforts as an actor, however, were on the stage—he won an Obie for his performance in 'Chinchilla' at the Phoenix Theater and a Theater World Award for his role in 'The Cherry Orchard' at Lincoln Center.

Cristofer's play, 'The Shadow Box,' was produced on Broadway in 1977, and won a Tony Award for Best Play. More significantly, Cristofer was awarded a coveted Pulitzer Prize for the play in which the characters struggle to find meaning in their last moments before they die—to reassure themselves that their lives were worth living.

When the play was produced for television—starring Joanne Woodward and directed by her husband, Paul Newman—it was awarded a Golden Globe Award and an Emmy nomination.

Since the early eighties, Cristofer has had a successful screenwriting career, and has consequently pretty much abandoned his acting career. Like most screenwriters, he receives little recognition outside of Hollywood for his successes in the challenging occupation of script writing.

Cristofer's first effort to make it to the big screen was an original screenplay—the 1984 film 'Falling in Love,' starring Meryl Streep and Robert DeNiro. Since then, Cristofer has written several well-known movies, including the adaptation of John Updike's best selling novel, 'The Witches of Eastwick,' in 1987, starring Jack Nicholson, Cher, Susan Sarandon and Michelle Pfeiffer. Screenplays for 'Mr. Jones,' starring Richard Gere in 1993, and 'Breaking Up,' in 1997, followed.

When Cristofer tried his hand at directing, his efforts were also highly acclaimed. His screenplay, 'Gia,' presented on HBO in 1998, received six Emmy nominations and Cristofer received a Director's Guild Award. Angelina Jolie received a Golden Globe Award for her starring role. Cristofer has since directed 'Body Shots' in 1999, and 'Original Sin' (which he also wrote), starring Antonio Banderas and Angelina Jolie.

Concentrating once more on the theatre, Cristofer signed on as artistic advisor (and later, co-artistic director) of River Arts Repertory. The company produced American premiers of new plays, and Cristofer wrote and directed several stage adaptations, which he directed.

Nick J. Mileti

MICKEY DOLENZ

(Born March 8, 1945 in Hollywood, California)

A versatile showman, Mickey Dolenz is best known for being a member of the Beatles copycat group known as The Monkees.

Mickey Dolenz was born into a show biz family. His father was the actor George Dolenz, who was born in Trieste, Italy, and achieved a measure of success in Hollywood as the lead in the 1956 movie 'The Count of Monte Cristo.' Mickey's mother was an actress.

The classic 'child actor pushed by his parents,' Mickey was doing screen tests at the age of six, and at age ten made his television debut as Corky in 'Circus Boy.' He toured the country with his elephant show biz partner to promote the television show, which ran several years. In his teens, Mickey performed and honed his professionalism.

Then, like in a movie script—meaning thousands wouldn't believe it—Mickey's life-altering break came in 1965.

What happened was, he answered a 'cattle call' for a television show about a rock band. As is normal in these cases, hundreds and hundreds of hopefuls tried every trick in the book to get noticed and selected, but Mickey auditioned by coolly playing the guitar and singing—old hat for the twenty-year old veteran performer.

And just like in the movies, Mickey Dolenz was selected—along with Michael Nesmith, Peter Tork and Davy Jones—

to be the drummer, even though he didn't know how to play the drums. The group became The Monkees, a made-up pop musical group (actually, none of them was a musician) manufactured by Hollywood. The four youngsters were made the stars of a TV show with the same name, and the series became an instant hit in 1966, when irreverence, no matter how benign, was popular. The show ran for two years and won an Emmy for Best Comedy its first year.

The Monkees pretended to record a hit, 'Last Train to Clarksville,' which soared to Number One on the charts. Two more hits, 'I'm a Believer' and 'Daydream Believer,' followed. In 1969, The Monkees starred in 'Head,' a movie written by Jack Nicholson, but by this time the fad had faded, and the movie flopped at the box office. In the seventies, Mickey Dolenz went on to become one of the most successful 'voices' for numerous Hanna-Barbera movies and cartoons, including Scooby-Doo.

After acting and directing in England for a decade, in 1986 Mickey participated in a re-incarnation of The Monkees that successfully toured the world for almost four years. With almost as many retirements and un-retirements as Bill Parcells, in 1996, the group again recorded and toured. All of his life—literally—Mickey Dolenz has continued performing (he learned to play the drums), singing, acting and directing. He has even written his autobiography.

Nick J. Mileti

DAVID CHASE

(Born August 22, 1945, in Mount Vernon, New York)
REAL ITALIAN NAME: DAVID DE CESARE

David Chase is the writer, director and producer of one of the most critically acclaimed television series in TV history, the phenomenally successful 'The Sopranos.' The show has become a social phenomenon, and, amazingly, unlike virtually every other movie or television series, it is the product of one person's creativity.

Both of David's grandparents were born in Southern Italy. His father's family is from Naples, and his mother's family is from outside of Naples. "My mother was defiantly Italian," David said later, "when it was not easy to be."

When he was five, David's parents moved to New Jersey. The youngster absorbed the Jersey environment into his very being—a fascination with American gangsters, and American gangster movies, took root almost immediately. After completing the graduate film program at Stanford University, Chase became one of the writers and producers of the 'The Rockford Files.' In the eighties, Chase directed one of the episodes he wrote for another show. He immediately knew, instinctively, that his creative talents had to be all-inclusive. In rapid succession, the new 'hyphenate' wrote, produced, and directed segments of the TV series 'Almost Grown,' 'I'll Fly Away,' and 'Northern Exposure,' all of which received critical acclaim.

And then, in 1999, when David Chase was in his fifties, everything came together. His Italian and New Jersey backgrounds bubbled over and 'The Sopranos' was born.

New Jersey is Italian-American," he once said. Chase structures each season, writes and co-writes several episodes, polishes every segment, and overseas every aspect of every show. The man who bought the show for HBO explains it this way, "He's the intellectual, creative, spiritual, conscious and unconscious leader of the show." 'The Sopranos' focuses on the crew and family of a contemporary mob boss. And what a crew and family they are. Both groups are filled with fascinating, complex characters, and Tony Soprano, their leader, is the most fascinating and complex character of them all. In a strange way, the charm of the series is its believability. In addition to the constant dramatic tension, the viewer never knows what is going to happen next. And unexpected things keep happening. Drama and uncertainty—just like in real life.

In the four years the series has been on the air, the HBO television network has never had higher ratings. In addition to its commercial success, David Chase (and the show and actors) has received unprecedented recognition, including Emmys, Golden Globes, DGA, SAG, Peabody, and numerous other nominations and awards. A self-effacing, down-to-earth gentleman, regarding the awards David Chase recently stated, "'The Sopranos' has gone into the American people's lexicon . . . It seems to have had a really deep social impact . . . (The awards are wonderful and appreciated, but) the fact that the audience finds it compelling is enough for me."

Nick J. Mileti

LIDIA BASTIANICH

(Born in 1946, in Pula, Istria, Italy)
REAL ITALIAN NAME: LIDIA MATTICCHIO

Lidia Bastianich is considered one of the foremost chef and restaurant owners in America. She is also an author, teacher, and television personality.

Lidia was born in Italy in Istria, which is about 90 miles northeast of Venice. The peninsula was taken from Italy after World War II and given to Yugoslavia—it is now part of Croatia. Uncomfortable with the chaos in the region, in 1958 Lidia's family left Istria and immigrated to America. Inspired by her mother and grandparents—who owned a trattoria and grew most of the food they served—Lidia opened a restaurant named Buonavia in Queens at the tender age of 24. After opening a second restaurant nearby, her successes inspired her to make her move to the big time of dining—Manhattan. At the age of 35, she opened the restaurant 'Felidia' on East 58th Street. Lidia cooked, and her Croation husband, Felice, worked the front of the house. Lidia's Italian food, with recipes from her northeastern Italian birthplace subtly adjusted for the American palate, drew serious foodies (before the term existed) from all over the world. 'Felidia' is considered one of the premier Italian restaurants in America and has been honored numerous times over the years.

Passionate in equal parts about food and her native Italy, Lidia is also scholarly. She is the author of three cookbooks, hosts a popular PBS television series which is seen worldwide, writes a monthly syndicated column, has two lines of tomato sauce and owns a travel company which specializes in gastronomic and cultural tours of Italy. Lidia, herself, has been the recipient of numerous awards, including, in 1999, American Express Best Chef, New York City, by the James Beard Foundation.

JOSEPH BASTIANICH

(Born in 1968, in Queens, New York)

Joseph Bastianich is Lidia's son. After becoming an expert in the field of Italian wine, Joseph made Felidia's wine list one of America's largest and strongest—featuring Italian selections, of course. Possessing his mother's entrepreneurial spirit, Joseph has opened several restaurants, with his mother as partner, including 'Becco,' not far from 'Felidia.' Joseph then partnered with chef Mario Batali and opened several wildly successful NYC restaurants (Babbo, Lupa and Esca), established a retail Italian wine store (Italian Wine Merchants) and purchased vineyards in Italy (one in the region where his mother was born and one in southern Tuscany). Joseph has also written a book on Italian wine. "I've had the opportunity to learn from the best," Joseph said recently. "Now I want to keep expanding on that and continue to share the real Italy with people here in the U.S."

SUSAN SARANDON

(Born October 4, 1946 in New York, New York)

Susan Sarandon is a highly talented movie star. She is also a highly motivated person who has the courage to be politically incorrect and fight for the rights of her fellow human beings.

Susan is half-Italian. Her given name was Susan Tomaling, from her Welsh father. Her mother, Leonora Criscione, was Italian. Susan married Chris Sarandon in 1967 and has retained his name throughout her highly successful career.

A classic case of Hollywood not knowing how to utilize talent, it took ten years, and more than a dozen movies, before thirty-two year old Susan Sarandon was cast—by famed French director Louis Malle—in a decent role. It happened in 1978. The film was 'Pretty Baby,' and the role was the mother of a young prostitute (played by Brooke Shields).

In 1980, Susan starred opposite Burt Lancaster in the film 'Atlantic City.' Her complex performance, again elicited by director Louis Malle, was acknowledged by the Academy of Motion Arts and Sciences, which awarded Susan her first Oscar nomination.

In 1987, the 'Witches of Eastwick' thrust Susan into the minds of the Hollywood powers. The successful 'Bull Durham' followed, and then in 1991 came the female 'Butch Cassidy and the Sundance Kid'—'Thelma and Louise'—for which Susan was again nominated for an

Oscar. The next year, she was nominated for an Oscar once more for her role in 'Lorenzo's Oil.'

In 1993, as a presenter in front of a worldwide Oscar television audience, Susan famously spoke about the plight of the Haitian refugees and the problem of AIDS in that country. Not an 'I am a Movie Star So Now I Care' activist, Susan has been politically active all of her life, opposing the war in Vietnam, supporting Civil Rights and so on. Nevertheless, she was banned from all future Oscars.

But Susan Sarandon had a secret weapon—talent—and two years later she was awarded the Oscar for Best Actress for her moving role in 'Dead Man Walking.'

In a feature article about Susan in the New York Times—ostensibly about the improbability of three Sarandon movies opening within a three-week period in 2002—writer Karen Durbin focused on the human side of the beautiful, talented actor. The article is entitled 'She Breaks the Rule That Says Actresses Can't Age,' and the sub-head says 'Susan Sarandon stays sexy because, like her male contemporaries, she takes charge.' As Walt Kelly's comic strip character 'Pogo' used to say, "Noble spoke."

Into the new Millennium, Susan Sarandon continues to care—and because of her activism, we all live in a better world.

Nick J. Mileti

SONIA GANDHI

(Born December 9, 1946 in Orbassano [near Turin], Italy)
REAL ITALIAN NAME: SONIA MAINO

Sonia Gandhi, whose parents were both Italian, is one of the most popular, and important, political leaders of India—the world's largest democracy.

Sonia arrived in India in 1968, the twenty-one year old bride of Rajiv Gandhi—the son of Indira Gandhi, India's Prime Minister—who she met in England. A quiet and unassuming person, Sonia jealously guarded her privacy and the privacy of her family: she stayed in the background, running her household, and the household of her mother-in-law, the Prime Minister. Over the years, Indira Gandhi pressured her son (Sonia's husband) to follow his famous family into politics but he was steadfast in his refusal. Enchanted by the country and its warm, wonderful people, in 1983 Sonia became an Indian citizen. In 1984, her mother-in-law, Indira Gandhi, was assassinated by her own bodyguards. After the assassination, Rajiv reluctantly stepped in and and won an easy victory to become Prime Minister. Sonia continued to stay in the background, concentrating on running the household and raising the couple's son, Rahul, and daughter, Priyanka. Seven years later, in 1991, a suicide bomber assassinated Rajiv. Sonia was heartbroken and went into mourning. "He gave me the love that made my life complete," she said.

After the back-to-back tragedies, the Congress Party— the Party of Nehru and Gandhi that had taken the lead in India's struggle to win freedom from the British—fell into disarray. They desperately needed a strong person, one with national recognition. It took them seven years, but in 1998, Congress Party officials finally convinced Sonia to take the Party's leadership. Sonia's innate honesty and common sense made her an instant hit with the voters: she brought a renewed unity and cohesion to the unwieldy and moribund Congress Party. Sonia was imbued with the political philosophy of her dynastic Indian family, which included showing equal respect to all religions. "My mother-in-law received 32 bullets in the chest in the name of this country's unity," she said while campaigning. "My husband sacrificed every cell in his body for the same principle. I will keep their idea (that the soul of our nation is inclusive, secular and united) alive as long as I live and breath."

Sonia Gandhi was elected a Member of Parliament in 1999, and Parliamentary Leader in 2004. Most significantly, Sonia's stunning victory occurred in spite of the virulent political attacks against her for being Catholic and Italian— 'a foreigner.' The people of India obviously ignored the incendiary comments. Sonia was offered the post of Prime Minister of India but, surprisingly, turned the offer down. "I am following my inner voice, my conscience," she said. Her children, who had lost their father, were relieved.

In a goosepimply replay of history, Sonia followed the lead of her mother-in-law and encouraged her son to join her in serving their country. In 2003, the reluctant Rahul won a seat in Parliament and is now considered the rising star of the Congress Party.

Nick J. Mileti

MARISA BERENSON

(Born February 15, 1947 in New York, New York)

While Marisa Berenson is mainly known as a high-fashion model and jet setter, she is a good actress and has appeared in over thirty movies.

Marisa's mother was Italian, and had the improbable nickname of Gogo. Marisa's grandmother (and Gogo's mother) was the famed haute couture fashion designer, Elsa Schiaparelli.

Glamorous and beautiful, Marisa had a successful career as a top fashion model, appearing regularly in Vogue and other important publications. Although no one took her seriously—she had much too much money and social cache—Marisa was serious. She wanted to be an actor, and Luchino Visconti gave her a chance. In 1971, he cast her in 'Death in Venice,' where Marisa proved she could act. Over the years, Marisa has appeared in both made for TV and feature films in America and abroad. Cinema fans cherish the performance Bob Fosse coaxed from her as the Jewish lady in the landmark film, 'Cabaret,' which was released in 1972.

Marisa had a beautiful, loving sister, Berinthia (Berry) Berenson. Berry died tragically at 53 years of age, on September 11, 2001, aboard American Airlines Flight 11, the first plane to strike the World Trade Center in the terrorist attack on America.

Closet Italians

ELSA SCHIAPARELLI

(Born September 10, 1890 in Rome; Died November 13, 1973)

Inspired by the art and architecture of GianLorenzo Bernini while growing up in Rome, Elsa Schiaparelli's clothing and accessory designs were as revolutionary as Bernini's sculpture when first introduced. But, while Bernini famously refused to be seduced by the French, Schiaparelli encouraged them after moving to France.

As Yves Saint Laurent wrote: "She (Schiaparelli) slapped Paris. She smacked it. She tortured it. She bewitched it. And it fell madly in love with her . . . But (you say) she was an Italian. She wasn't an Italian any longer, she was a Parisienne. Paris had adopted her. And Paris was wrong, for she proceeded to devour it."

Schiaparelli was the design trend-setter of the twenties and thirties who popularized brilliant colors, especially shocking pink. Some of the biggest name artists of the time worked with Elsa, including Dali, Cocteau, Dufy, and Duchamp. In her twilight years, Elsa came full circle. She reverted to the Italian language and spent endless hours just sitting and talking with her family.

Even though her name is obviously Italian, Elsa Schiaparelli appears in this book (as an exception) to expose and record the French attempt to co-opt her.

Nick J. Mileti

PETER CRISS

(Born December 20, 1947 in Brooklyn, New York)
REAL ITALIAN NAME: PETER CRISCOULA

Peter Criss is a rock star most people would never recognize because, for most of his career, he wore bizarre make-up on his face as a member of the rock group KISS.

When Criss became a teenager, his musical career was triggered by his father, an antique dealer (possible sign outside the shop, 'We Buy Junk, We Sell Antiques'). What happened was, Joseph Criscoula gave his son an old snare drum that he had taken into his shop in Brooklyn. Criss not only displayed a natural musical talent on that old drum, he fell in love with drums, period.

The youngster saved his pennies until he could afford to buy a set of 'Radial King Singerlands,' drums that were just like Gene Krupa's. Peter wouldn't let the drums out of his sight—he even carried them around in his little red wagon. To this day, critics love to point out that Criss looks like Krupa when he plays the drums.

When Peter was twenty-five, in 1972, his world changed forever as he entered the Rock and Roll Revolution in a major way. In that year Criss joined Gene Simmons and Paul Stanley as the third member of KISS (Ace Frehley became the fourth).

The group was unique and wild and caught the imagination of the kids in a time of change in America. The musicians decked themselves out in outrageous make-up and elaborate costumes. Their performances were equally bizarre, with the music enhanced with smoke bombs, lasers, blood spitting, fire breathing, dry ice and whatever else was handy. The young people couldn't figure out which they loved more, the group or the show. No matter, KISS was named the most popular band in America in a 1977 poll, helped along by Peter Criss's hard-driving ballad, 'Beth,' which he wrote and sang.

For eight hard-driving years, the Rock group KISS was a dominant force in the business, releasing half-a-dozen platinum albums for Casablanca Records. 'The Cat Man,' as Criss has been called ever since, wrote and selected songs for the group, played the drums and sang. His spectacular drumming, influenced by soul and rhythm & blues, was one of the major factors in the band's success.

The exciting times for the group ended when Criss, in 1980, tired of the make-up gimmick and anxious to try a solo career, left KISS. He produced a solo album and formed several bands, but somehow his heart wasn't in it.

In the mid-nineties, when Gene Simmons and Paul Stanley asked Criss if he wanted to re-unite with the original KISS, Peter Criss (with Ace Frehley) jumped back in with both feet and found his groove once more.

Nick J. Mileti

BERNADETTE PETERS

(Born February 28, 1948 in
Ozone Park [Queens], New York)
REAL ITALIAN NAME: BERNADETTE LAZZARA

Bernadette Peters began her singing and acting career at 3 1/2 years of age and has been performing regularly ever since.

Working on the stage throughout her teen-age years, Peters made it to Broadway in 1967 when she was only nineteen years old. Although her initial show has been largely forgotten, Peters was on her way. The next year she won both a Theater World Award for her roll in the musical 'George M,' and a Drama Desk Award for her work in "Dames at Sea,' an off-Broadway musical. Peter's theatrical career has been replete with honors. She won a Tony Award and The Drama Desk Award in 1985 for her performance in Andrew Lloyd Weber's 'Song and Dance.' She was nominated for a Tony for her performances in 'Into the Woods' and 'The Good-by Girl.' Then, in 1999, Peters was awarded a second Tony for her roll as Annie Oakley in the Broadway revival of 'Annie Get Your Gun.' She also received her third Drama Desk Award and an Outer Circle Critic's Award for that performance. Called "A beloved eternal daughter of the American musical" by Ben Brantley of the New York Times, Peters received her greatest accolades for her role as Momma Rosa in the revival of the classic musical 'Gypsy.'

In addition to her extensive body of work on Broadway's musical stage, Peters has also been honored for her work in television and film. She draws rave reviews for her concert appearances and has recorded a number of cast and solo albums for which she has also been honored. A committed and tireless contributor to the community, Bernadette Peters has been presented numerous awards. She is the youngest performer to have been inducted into the Theater Hall of Fame.

PAULA PRENTISS

(Born March 4, 1939 in San Antonio, Texas)
REAL ITALIAN NAME: PAULA RAGUSA

Paula Prentiss is a fine comedic actor who sacrificed her career to raise her family.

Paula attended Northwestern to study drama. While there, she met Richard Benjamin, whom she married in 1961 (Benjamin developed into a comedic motion picture actor and director of some note). Metro Goldwyn Mayer signed Paula to a contract, and to the studio's credit, they didn't try to re-invent the beautiful brunette. Paula's first roles played to her strength—comedy. She made her film debut at the age of twenty-one, in 1960, in the film 'Where The Boys Are," with Jim Hutton. While Paula acted in over twenty movies, it was in Neil Simon's 1972 romp, 'Last of the Red Hot Lovers,' that Paula, playing an adorable hippie, delivered her most memorable performance.

Nick J. Mileti

STEVEN TYLER

(Born March 26, 1948 in the Bronx, New York)
REAL ITALIAN NAME: STEVEN VICTOR
TALLARICO

Steven Tyler is the charismatic lead singer in the rock band Aerosmith.

Tyler's father was Italian, and his mother the fascinating combination of Russian and Cherokee Indian. His protruding lips could have been his downfall due to teasing by schoolmates, but Steven says it benefited his musical life because he would immerse himself in writing songs and playing music to escape the ridicule. An accomplished musician, Tyler plays drums as well as guitar and all keyboards. In 1970, Tyler, along with Joe Perry, Tom Hamilton, and Ray Tabano began what later became the rock group Aerosmith. Later in the year, Brad Whitford replaced Tabano and Joey Kramer signed on as drummer so that Steven Tyler could move from behind the drums to become the group's lead singer. The following year, after they moved to Boston, Clive Davis saw the group and signed them to a recording contract for Columbia/CBS.

In 1973, the band released its first album to limited success. Ditto their number two album. But like Bruce Springsteen, the third album was a charm. Released in 1975, the album 'Toys in the Attic,' rose to the top of the charts and sold over six million copies. With it, Aerosmith became a real force in the world of rock-and-roll. Throughout the remainder of the seventies, the band—which combines pop, heavy metal, and blues—enjoyed multiple platinum albums and was one of the most popular touring rock and roll groups in the world. In 1976,

Steven Tyler appeared on the cover of Rolling Stone magazine. Turmoil followed success, however, and in 1979, Joe Perry left the band. The following year Brad Whitford did the same. Steven Tyler kept the band together with mixed results, and in 1984, both musicians rejoined Aerosmith. The group persevered and eventually overcame personal and changing taste problems. Before the end of the eighties, Aerosmith was again selling records, filling music venues and gathering awards. In April of 1990, the band appeared on the cover of Rolling Stone, signaling the completion of their remarkable comeback. In the nineties, Aerosmith enjoyed greater success than ever. Steven Tyler, 'The Demon of Screamin,' whose unique piercing voice has been best described as soulful, continues to howl after over thirty years in the trenches. The group has received a basket of awards since its reincarnation, and in 2001, Steven Tyler's band, Aerosmith, was elected to the Rock and Roll Hall of Fame in Cleveland, Ohio.

LIV TYLER

(Born July 1, 1977 in New York City)

Liv Tyler, Steven's beautiful daughter, first starred as a model, and then turned to acting. She has appeared in over a dozen movies, including the three "Lord of the Rings." Liv remains best known for her role in Bernardo Bertolucci's 1996 film 'Stealing Beauty.'

Nick J. Mileti

MIKE MARAN

(Born March 11, 1949 in Edinburgh, Scotland)

Mike Maran's first career was as a successful musician and folk-singer. Today, in his roles as a troubadour—that is an actor, storyteller, producer and director—he is presenting award-winning theatre to international acclaim.

Maran's father's parents were born in Picinisco, Italy, and his mother's parents (maiden name Gasperinin) hail from Borgotaro, Italy, making Maran a second generation Scots-Italian, Scotto-Italian, or Italian-Scot, whichever you prefer.

Joining the hot musical scene in London in the early seventies, Maran began touring with some of the biggest names in rock, opening for Uriah Heep and ELO (The Electric Light Orchestra), among others. He also wrote music and released several solo albums. In the late seventies, however, Moran became bored playing his guitar and singing the same songs night after night. Moreover, he felt he was at a dead end, career-wise, because "When the band came on stage they quickly forgot about me." Not surprisingly, Moran directed his artistic talents at storytelling, which was logical because, "I did enjoy talking between the songs."

'Penny Whistle,' Maran's first production, was written in 1977. The play was adopted for television, and when it was shown on the BBC two years later, Maran's new career was off and running—Maran and his team have produced at least one new musical every year since. The productions are unique theatre—combining narrative and images with music. In addition to being entertaining, his plays all make important moral points.

In the early nineties, Mike Maran had an epiphany. He started to seriously focus on his Italian heritage and decided to use some of his shows to explore his Italian roots. "I wish I had the epiphany earlier when my grandparents were alive," he stated later. Teaming up with another talented Italian, Philip Contini, in 1993 Maran wrote 'Italia n'Caledonia,' which told the story of his grandparents and the influx of Italians into Scotland between 1890 and 1900. The show was the surprise smash hit of the Edinburg Festival's Fringe that year. 'Surely You're Joking, Mr. Feynman,' and 'Did You Used to be RD Laing?' followed and were also exceptionally successful productions. In 1999, Maran continued his Italian motif by presenting 'Captain Corelli's Mandolin' at the Fringe. The Maran production preceded the American motion picture and differs in approach, tone and spirit. More focused than the movie, Mike Maran's adoptation of the Louis de Bernieres novel features two musicians and Maran as a storyteller. Unlike the movie (which surprisingly lacked heart), Maran's version has been highly regarded, critically acclaimed and financially successful. In his 2001 production of 'Private Angelo,' another tale of wartime Italy, Maran continues to explore Italian life and psyche. Mike Maran says his work reflects his love of Scottish literature, his love of Italy, and his enthusiasm for some of the most interesting characters who have touched his life.

Nick J. Mileti

BRUCE SPRINGSTEEN

(Born September 23, 1949 in Freehold, New Jersey)

One of the most popular rock musicians of all time, Bruce Springsteen has created fanatically loyal fans by combining his rebellious, small-town outsider persona with his sympathy for the working class, and all things American.

Bruce, the oldest of three children, was very close with his Italian mother, whose maiden name was Adele Zirelli. His Irish/Dutch father, on the other hand, was always at odds with Bruce, and visa-versa. In fact, his father was often unemployed, so the family relied on the mother—who was a secretary—for support.

A natural musician, Bruce taught himself to play the guitar. A songwriter and lyricist, Bruce formed his own rock-and-roll band in high school and was noticed, but not much happened. He experimented with various styles—garage-rock, blues-rock and even folk-rock—but success eluded Bruce. Springsteen's big break came when Columbia Records signed him in 1972. His first two albums were critically acclaimed but went nowhere commercially. Always trying and testing new ideas, Bruce re-juggled his back-up group and named it 'The E Street Band' (Steven Van Zandt was a member). Bruce and the boys toured the country with the group 'Chicago,' and rock fans got an idea of how attractive Springsteen was as a performer.

Finally, in 1974, lightning struck. Bruce released his third album, 'Born To Run.' The title song became a Top-40 hit and the album reached the Top Ten. Bruce

Springsteen was finally a rock-and-roll star. The media called him 'the savior of rock and roll,' and hyped him mercilessly (he was on the cover of Time and Newsweek simultaneously). Rock fans thought Bruce had sold out, and things were dicey for a while. Then, in 1984, incredibly, Bruce became bigger than ever, thanks to the release of 'Born in the U.S.A.' The album, with its upbeat American themes, sold some twenty million copies, threw off seven hit singles, and gave Bruce super-star status and the sobriquet 'The Boss.' In conjunction with the album, Bruce embarked on an extensive two-year tour, selling out the biggest venues around the world. In 1993, Springsteen wrote and recorded 'Streets of Philadelphia' for the movie 'Philadelphia,' starring Tom Hanks. The song was a Top Ten hit, won several Grammy's and an Academy Award for Best Song. In 1999, Bruce re-formed the E Street Band (which he had disbanded earlier) and toured the world.

Then, in response to the September 11, 2001 terrorist attack on America, Springsteen wrote and recorded 'The Rising,' his first song-writing effort in seven years, and his first album of new songs with the E-Street Band since 1984. The album sold over a half-million copies in its first week of release and opened as Number One on Billboards Top 200 album chart. The uplifting message of faith and hope was also the top-seller in Canada and Europe. The album received five Grammy nominations, and received three Grammy Awards.

Rolling Stone Magazine labels Bruce Springsteen "The last true voice of rock and roll."

Nick J. Mileti

NICK TOSCHES

(Born in 1949 in Newark, New Jersey)

Nick Tosches has achieved extraordinary success in three artistic areas—first as a journalist, then as a biographer, and thirdly as a novelist. In all three genres, Tosches' writing is gritty and provocative, and therefore, controversial.

Tosches' father was Italian and his mother was Irish.

He was schooled on the streets and in his father's bar, but Tosches managed to graduate from High School because, he says, his father made him finish. Crossing the river to New York while still in his teens, Tosches became one of the country's first rock critics, writing for irreverent magazines like 'Creem,' 'Fusion,' and 'Rolling Stone.' At the heart (in every way) of the wild late sixties and early seventies, his high energy, no-holds-barred style quickly pushed him to the top rung of rock critics. Tosches, however, decided that he had to transcend the genre and began to write in other forms and about other subjects.

Tosches' second career breakout occurred in 1982 with the publication of 'Hellfire,' a biography of Jerry Lee Lewis. Released to broad critical acclaim (Rolling Stone called it "the best rock and roll biography ever written"), Tosches explained that he wanted to explore the mystery of "How could a person like Jerry Lee Lewis create his own hell." Tosches scored again with another biography, 'Power on Earth,' the story of the disgraced Vatican financier Michele Sindona, which was published in 1986. But it was his third biography, 'Dino: Living High in the

Dirty business of Dreams,' published in 1992, that made the next major splash after 'Hellfire.' Also critically acclaimed, the Dean Martin biography was short-listed for the Esquire-Waterhouse Nonfiction Award, and received the Italian-American Literary Achievement Award for Distinction in Literature, shared with Gay Talese. The year 2000 was another high point for Tosches. The biography, 'The Devil and Sonny Liston' ("How could a person like Sonny Liston even bear to live in such darkness?)" and the nonfiction collection 'The Nick Tosches Reader,' a thirty-year collection of his work, were both released in that year, and were both highly praised.

For most of his career, Tosches' novel writing suffered under the shadow of his powerful biographies. His first novel, 'Cut Numbers' was published in 1988, and his second novel, 'Trinities,' was released in 1994. It was in 2002, however, with the publication of 'In the Hand of Dante,' that Tosches' novel writing approached the stature of his biographies. Prior to publication, Tosches predicted 'Dante' would be his masterpiece, and it was indeed hailed as one by most critics—at least the critics who understood what Nick Tosches was about. Toches has had his poetry published, has written for most major publications, and is presently a Contributing Editor for 'Vanity Fair.' A Damon Runyon character (in the best sense of the term) Nick Tosches is as interesting, and complicated, as his writing.

CHAPTER XII

Illustrious Italians With Non-Italian Names
Born Between 1950-1959

LOUIS J. FREEH

(Born January 6, 1950 in Jersey City, New Jersey)

Louis Freeh has enjoyed a distinguished career in public service and law enforcement, including an eight-year stint as Director of the Federal Bureau of Investigation (FBI) from 1993 to 2001.

Freeh's mother was Italian (Bernice Chinchiola). Addressing the Langley High School class of 2002, Freeh told the graduates about the day a Wall Street firm refused to hire his mother because she was Italian, and used the incident to drive home several obvious, but important, points.

Freeh graduated from Rutgers University, where he received a Batchelor of Art degree (in 1971) and a Juris Doctor degree (in 1974). In 1975, Freeh joined the FBI as a Special Agent, serving in New York City and Washington, D.C. In 1981, he left the FBI and moved up to the United States Attorney's Office for the Southern District of New York as an Assistant United States Attorney—serving in that capacity for six years. From 1987 to 1990, Freeh rose rapidly through the ranks, serving as Chief of the Organized Crime Unit, then Deputy United States Attorney, then Associate United States Attorney. During this period, the dedicated and ambitious attorney studied in the little spare time he had, receiving a L.L.M. degree in criminal law from New York University Law School (in 1984).

In 1990, Freeh was appointed Special Prosecutor for the United States Department of Justice by the Attorney General, and in 1991 he was appointed United States

District Court Judge by then President Bush. In 1993, then President Clinton, a Democrat, appointed Judge Freeh, a Republican, Director of the FBI. This crossover was an obvious nod to Louis Freeh's talent as a crime-fighter—and his integrity.

In his eight years as Head of the Bureau, Freeh took the FBI into the 21st Century. Relating to the globalization of crime and international terror, Freeh doubled the number of FBI branches around the world, focused on cyber crime and DNA technology, and basically changed the FBI's mission when he created the Counter Terrorism Division and the Radical Fundamentalist Unit.

Ironically, Louis Freeh was the first person of Italian blood to head the FBI since another Italian, Charles Joseph Bonaparte, founded the Agency in 1908.

In 2001, after resigning as Director of the FBI, Freeh was appointed Senior Vice Chairman for Administration at the MBNA Corporation, the largest independent credit card lender in the world. In that capacity, Freeh is responsible for personnel, legal affairs, facilities, security, and transportation functions for the company.

Over the years, Louis Freeh has been presented with numerous awards recognizing his many accomplishments in the public sector.

Nick J. Mileti

DINO MENEGHIN

(Born January 18, 1950 in Alano di Piave, Italy)

Dino Meneghin is the finest player in the history of Italian basketball and one of the best International players of all time.

At sixteen years of age, Dino joined the Italian National Team. "When I started playing," he said recently, "I never thought of becoming a professional player. It happened just because I loved to play."

Here's the incredible result of that modest beginning. Dino participated in a record 834 games in Italy's top division while playing for Varese and Milan. For the Italian National Team, Dino played in 271 games over a twenty-year period.

But those numbers only relate to stamina, determination and commitment. The most impressive fact about Dino Meneghin is that he was a winner. For example, Dino holds the individual record for winning more European titles (12) than any other player in history—a record unlikely to be broken.

Dino was a powerful inside player at 6-foot-9, 240 pounds, who always exhibited great hustle. Dino's leadership ability, however, was just as important as his playing ability.

To this day, Dino's fellow players seize every opportunity to praise Meneghin for his unselfishness and commitment to winning, as well as for his leadership.

After joining Varese, Dino led the team to a record ten consecutive Cup of Champions Finals in the seventies. During that period, Varese won numerous titles, including five championships (a record). After Varese, Dino joined the Milan team and in the eighties led them to many more titles, including an additional two championships. Incredibly, Dino's teams captured all four championships—the Playoffs, the Italy Cup, the European Cup and the Intercontinental Cup—in the same year three times (in 1970, 1973 and 1987). As a member of the Italian National Team, Dino led his country's team in four Olympic Games (in 1972, 1976, 1980 [Silver Medal], and 1984) and to numerous titles.

In 1980, Giganti del Basket named Dino Meneghin European Player of the Year, and in 1991 named him Europe's greatest player of all time. In 1983, Dino won 'Euroscar,' the popular Italian newspaper La Gazzetta dello Sport's annual award to the top European basketball player.

In 2003, Dino Meneghin was inducted into the prestigious Basketball Hall of Fame in Springfield, Mass. When inducted, the modest and popular basketball legend said, "Being in the Hall of Fame is like for a painter having his paintings at the Louvre, the Prado or the Guggenheim Museum. The second meaning is: don't forget. Everybody looking into my corner in the Hall of Fame will remember me. I want to say I'm glad to be in the Hall of Fame, but I'll be there joined together with all my teammates, all my coaches and all my club managers (team coaches)."

Nick J. Mileti

FRANCO HARRIS

(Born March 7, 1950 in Fort Dix, New Jersey)

Franco Harris was a record-breaking rusher and one of the greatest running backs in National Football League history.

Franco had an Italian mother, who immigrated to America from Lucca, Italy, and an African-American father. Harris attended Penn State University, and from 1969 to 1971 Franco helped establish a fellow Italian's (Joe Paterno) reputation as one of the greatest college coaches of all time. Nicknamed the 'Italian Stallion' (before Sylvester Stallone appropriated the title for the movie 'Rocky'), Franco Harris's Penn State teams won twenty-nine games and lost only four.

Drafted in the 1st round (13th overall) by the Pittsburgh Steelers football team in 1972, Franco Harris quickly turned the team's fortunes around, almost immediately making the Steelers winners. Within two years, in 1974, Harris led Pittsburgh to its first division title, and most importantly, led his team to an amazing four Super Bowl titles (Super Bowls IX, X, XIII and XIV) in the twelve years he played for Pittsburgh. In the 1975 Super Bowl, Harris gained a record 158 yards against the Minnesota Vikings and was named MVP. In fact, Harris holds, or shares, 29 NFL records, including 25 in postseason play where they count the most.

Franco Harris is also a star in the community, having received numerous awards over the years for his hard work and dedication to his fellow man. He was inducted into the Football Hall of Fame in 1990.

Closet Italians

TED HENDRICKS

(Born November 1, 1947 in Guatemala City, Guatemala)

Ted Hendricks was one of the best linebackers in the history of the National Football League, and one of the most interesting characters to ever play the game.

Ted's mother was named Bonnati; his Italian heritage gave him his well-earned reputation as the premier free spirit in the league (as well as his intellectual approach to the game). John Madden, Ted's Raiders coach from 1975-1978 said, "He (Hendricks) got the reputation as being kind of an eccentric, but once a game started he went like gangbusters. Great players make great plays, and I can't think of any defensive player who made more big plays for us than Ted Hendricks." Ted had one of the best work ethics in football: He never missed a game—playing in 215 straight games for the Colts (helping them win Super Bowl V) and Packers, but hit his stride with the Raiders, where he led his team to three Super bowl victories in his nine seasons. 'The Mad Stork,'—as the unstoppable prototype linebacker was called—confounded as many coaches as opposing players, but was always a winner. Ted Hendricks was enshrined in the NFL Hall of Fame in Canton, Ohio in 1990 with Franco Harris and others.

Nick J. Mileti

STEVEN VAN ZANDT

(Born November 22, 1950 in Winthrop, Mass.)
REAL ITALIAN NAME: STEVEN LENTO

Steven Van Zandt has led a fascinating life. He is a major rock star, a dedicated freedom fighter, a television star on one of the medium's most acclaimed series, and now a radio personality.

Steven Van Zandt is Italian. Steven was given the Dutch name of Van Zandt when his mother remarried and her new husband adopted the youngster.

In his early years as a musician, producer and arranger, Van Zandt helped craft what is now called the 'Asbury Park Sound.' In 1974, Van Zandt's big break came when his friend, Bruce Springsteen—who was looking for his own success as a rock and roller—revised his back-up band. Springsteen named his new group 'The E Street Band,' and a key element of the move was Steven Van Zandt, brought on as singer and second guitarist. Van Zandt helped Springsteen shape his (Springsteen's) breakout album, 'Born to Run,' and the bandana-adorned Steven Van Zandt became a rock-star in his own right. In 1984, after ten years of wildly successful, worldwide, non-stop rock and roll action with Springsteen, Van Zandt decided it was time for a solo career. He co-produced an album named 'Sun City'—a scathing indictment of South African apartheid—and Van Zandt's life turned upside-down. Steven Van Zandt became a human rights activist. In 1985, he established the Solidarity Foundation, whose stated purpose was to support the sovereignty of indigenous people. For the next decade, Van Zandt bounced from musical project to musical project, and from political cause to political cause.

For his efforts, Steven Van Zandt was honored twice by the United Nations for his human rights achievements. While appreciated, awards unfortunately didn't pay the bills, and Van Zandt ran out of money.

Then, like in the movies, good things happen to good people. In the mid-nineties, Bruce Springsteen and David Chase called Steven Van Zandt almost simultaneously. Springsteen reunited his 'E Street Band' (which went on to achieve greater success than ever), and Chase asked Van Zandt to come to Los Angeles for a screen test for a new television series he'd written for HBO, to be called 'The Sopranos.' "They had to make sure that I could act, that I could memorize lines, that I could put three words together in a row," Van Zandt later laughed. "They thought David was crazy for even considering me." Chase stood firm, and Van Zandt was cast as Silvio Dante, one of Tony Soprano's trusted lieutenants, and owner of the Bada Bing Strip Club. The show became a run-away hit and Van Zandt was now a television star as well as a rock star and crusader.

In 2002, Steven Van Zandt spotted the need to preserve the unique phenomenon known as garage bands. Consequently, he launched a show named 'Little Steven's Underground Garage,' and Van Zandt became a successful radio personality. The program, which focuses on the history of garage rock bands, has enjoyed good ratings and critical praise.

Nick J. Mileti

ANJELICA HUSTON

(Born July 8, 1951 in Santa Monica, California)

When Anjelica Huston won an Oscar in 1986 for her movie-stealing portrayal of Mae Rose in 'Prizzi's Honor,' she became the first 3rd generation Oscar winner in motion picture history, exploding out of the shadows of her legendary actor/director father, John Huston, and paternal grandfather, Walter Huston (who not only acted and directed, but also sang in the movies—undoubtedly providing Rex Harrison with sufficient confidence to 'sing/talk' his way through 'My Fair Lady').

Anjelica's mother, Enrica (Ricki) Soma, was a beautiful, vivacious Italian ballerina (Ricki's father, Tony Soma, owned a celebrity restaurant on the then hot, hot, hot 52nd Street in New York City). Although Ricki was John Huston's fourth wife, she was the first to bear his children. When Ricki called her father to tell him she was pregnant, her father is reputed to have bragged, "The man was supposed to be impotent—that (her pregnancy) proves the dominance of the Italian race."

Tragically, Ricki Soma died in 1969 in an automobile accident in France when she was only 39 years old and Anjelica was only 18. Although her parents had been separated for years, Anjelica was extremely close to her worldly mother (with whom she'd lived), who encouraged Anjelica to model and tutored her in the social and cultural aspects of life. When informed of her mother's death, Anjelica was devastated: "My whole world collapsed. It changed my life. It changed my entire consciousness."

Immediately thereafter, John Huston almost literally forced his daughter to be an actor, casting her in two movies in 1969. Even though the experience was less than satisfactory, Anjelica was hooked. The genes kicked in, and Anjelica has become one of Hollywood's premier actors—she has been nominated for seven Golden Globe Awards and three Oscars. Anjelica has appeared in over thirty theatrical features and numerous television films, adamantly refusing to be typecast. For example, Anjelica portrays a desperate mistress in Woody Allen's 'Crimes and Misdemeanors' in 1989, and a worldly, clever writer in 'Manhattan Murder Mystery' in 1993. She plays the hilarious mother Morticia in the spoof 'The Addams Family' in 1991 (and its sequel two years later), but in 'The Grifters' in 1990 and 'The Royal Tennenbaums' in 2001, she plays women in command. In the classic, 'Prizzi's Honor,' which was directed by her father, her award-winning performance of a mobster's daughter brought a startling new dimension to a tired stereotype. Whatever the role, Anjelica Huston remains sophisticated, sensual and, above all, believable.

In 1996, Anjelica Huston made her directorial debut with 'Bastard Out of Carolina,' a hard-hitting made-for-television movie about a young girl who is physically and mentally abused by her stepfather. The picture was both hated (banned by TNT, which ironically had commissioned it) and loved (shown by Showtime, praised at the Cannes Film Festival, and nominated for an Emmy Award for Anjelica's direction).

Nick J. Mileti

MORGAN BRITTANY

(Born December 5, 1951 in Los Angeles, California)
REAL ITALIAN NAME: SUZANNE CUPITO

Morgan Brittany began her showbiz career as a child actress, but will always be remembered as the scheming Katherine Wentworth of the primetime soap 'Dallas.'

Cast in 'Sea Hunt' at the age of five, the pretty youngster performed as Suzanne Cupito in numerous films as a child actor, including 'Gypsy' with Natalie Wood when she was eleven years old. She also appeared in 'The Birds' and 'Marne.' When Suzanne was seventeen years old, in 1968, she made her last movie as a child actor in 'Yours Mine and Ours' with Lucille Ball and Henry Fonda.

A fallow period followed, but when Suzanne Cupito emerged as a beautiful young lady with the new name of Morgan Brittany, her resemblance to Vivian Leigh landed her several rolls portraying that superstar, including 'Gable and Lombard' in 1976.

Then, almost accidentally, lightning struck. Morgan was cast in 'Dallas' as the Queen of Mean, Katherine Wentworth, half-sister of Pamela Ewing. The evil character struck a nerve with the public, and Morgan was one of the cast's most popular members for the three years she appeared on the show.

KAYE STEVENS

(Born July 21, 1935 in Cleveland, Ohio)

Kaye Stevens is a singer, cabaret, stage and television performer.

The personable star has worked steadily since graduating from John Adams High School in Cleveland. She was a regular at Caesars Palace in its early days in the sixties—when Caesars was far and away the Number One venue in Las Vegas—appearing with the big names of the day.

Playing Jeri Clayton on the award-winning soap 'Days Of Our Lives' made Kaye a household name. She has appeared on numerous television shows, including the Carol Burnett Show, and for years was a regular panelist on the wildly popular game show 'Match Game.'

When Kaye toured Vietnam with fellow Clevelander Bob Hope on his USO tour, her life made a U-Turn. "My life was in a shamble because of what I saw," Kaye stated when she received a Doctor of Humane Letters from Brewer Christian College and Graduate School, in recognition of her work in Vietnam with Hope. Since that time, Kaye Stevens has concentrated on spiritual, uplifting, motivational music.

Nick J. Mileti

FRED GARDAPHÉ

(Born c.1953, in Chicago Illinois)
REAL ITALIAN NAME: FRED GUARDAFEDE

Fred Gardaphé is a highly respected literary scholar whose fame lies in his service to Italian-American writers and poets.

Gardaphé grew up in an Italian ghetto in Chicago. He calls them the mean streets, and recently wrote: "If it were not for reading, I would have become a gangster." After Gardaphé received a Masters Degree in English and a Ph.D. in Literature, he taught high school for five years. Subsequently, for twenty years, from 1978 to 1998, he taught English and educational studies at Columbia College in Chicago. At the college, Gardaphé created and taught writing and literature courses. as well as courses in Italian-American film and literature.

Gardaphé became extremely active in bringing the works of Italian-Americans to the general public. In 1989, after he, Paolo A. Giordano, and Anthony Julian Tamburri edited the anthology 'From the Margin: Writings in Italian Americana' (published by The Purdue University Press in 1991 and re-issued twice since), the trio of scholars realized that they had a richness of material but there were no active publishers dedicated to the Italian-American writer. Consequently, they were inspired to co-found Bordighera, Inc. The non-profit, scholarly organization owns The Bordighera Press, which publishes Italian-American literature and poetry, and has an impressive Poetry Award Program. In addition, Bordighera publishes the Journal 'VIA' (Voices in Italian-Americana), a semi-annual literary journal and cultural review dedicated to Italian American studies, which the three founders (Gardaphé, Giordano and Tamburri) co-edit. The trio also publishes and co-edits the annual 'Italiana,' and the book series 'Via Folios' and 'Crossings.' Gardaphé is also Associate Editor of 'Fra Noi,' an Italian-American monthly newspaper. Gardaphé has edited several books, and is the editor of the series in Italian Studies at SUNY Press. He has written two plays and published two books with the fascinating titles, 'Dagoes Read: Tradition and the Italian/American Writer,' in 1996, and in 1998, 'Moustache Pete is Dead!: Italian/American Oral Tradition Preserved in Print.' Gardaphé won the Fondazione Giovanni Agnelli/Italian Ministry of Foreign Affairs Award for 1993 dissertations. Entitled 'Italian Signs, American Streets: The Evolution of Italian American Narrative,' the book was published by Duke University Press in 1996 to highly favorable reviews.

In 1998, Fred Gardaphé was appointed Professor of English and Director of the Italian-American Studies Program at the State University of New York at Stony Brook. Gardaphé was Vice-President of the Italian Cultural Center in Stone Park, Illinois from 1992 to 1998, and President of the American Italian Historical Association from 1996 to 2000. Fred Gardaphé is a much sought after speaker on Italian-American literature and culture.

ANNA QUINDLEN

(Born July 8, 1953, in Kendall Park, New Jersey)

A journalist, novelist, magazine writer and activist, whose accessible style is beautifully summed up by Margaret Gunning, who says, "(Anna Quindlen) has a certain gift for the clear-eyed, unflinching gaze, the ability to look straight at the human condition and report on all its vile atrocities and shining virtues with a passionate accuracy."

Anna's mother was Italian and her father was Irish. While acknowledging her father's support and inspiration, Anna has been most profoundly influenced by her Italian mother, and Anna's writing is laced with references to her. "My mother (who taught me what's important in life) was a humble woman with a great capacity for unconditional love." "My mother taught me that so much of what you take for granted is the bedrock of happiness." "My mother was a sort of a world-class mother." Anna was also greatly influenced in her youth by her Italian grandparents, especially Concetta, her mother's mother. "'To see ourselves as others see us' was the line my grandmother would always throw out when she was crabby and I was full of myself."

In 1974, after graduation from Barnard College, Anna wanted to become a novelist, but since she needed a steady paycheck, she went to work. After a three-year stint as a reporter for the New York Post, she moved on to the New York Times and glory. With dazzling speed, she rose from general assignment reporter, to City Hall reporter, to columnist, to Deputy Metropolitan Editor and creator of a weekly column. In 1990, Anna became the only female columnist on the Times' Op-Ed page, and within two years she won the Pulitzer Prize for Commentary. Anna left the New York Times in 1995 to concentrate on novel writing—she has written four best sellers: 'Object Lessons' (1992), 'One True Thing' (1994), 'Black and Blue' (1998) and 'Blessings' (2002). She has also authored several children's books, coffee table books, non-fiction books and collections.

Anna Quindlen has been a feminist since she was eighteen years old, but there may never be a better statement of the feminist philosophy than she expressed in her Keynote Speech to the Woman's Commission for Refugee Women and Children Voices of Courage awards luncheon, on May 15, 2002: "Many of you in this room are women with power—the power of influence and the power of affluence. Maybe each one of us should walk out of this room today with a shadow at our heels, the shadow of a woman who is really one of us, a woman in Afghanistan, in Bosnia, in Angola—somewhere in the world. Maybe she will remind each of us what we've been given and what we have to give in return. The point was never the corner office. The point was sisterhood, solidarity, freedom and, above all, peace. The point of the whole thing was the whole wide world."

Here is Anna Quindlen's philosophy, in her words: "What could make you happier than to make a better world, a world that is fairer, more egalitarian, that works better for all." Nothing, Anna, nothing.

Nick J. Mileti

LINDA STRACHAN

(Born December 28, 1953 in Edinburgh, Scotland)
REAL ITALIAN NAME: LINDA DONFRANCESCO

Linda Strachan is a renowned writer of children's books. She is also a well-known activist for children and for encouraging children to read.

Linda's father, Gianni Donfrancesco, immigrated to Scotland from Aquino, Italy. He was a successful Edinburgh restaurateur who retired and became the European President of Ciao Italia, the worldwide organization of over 100,000 Italian Restaurants. Linda's mother, Hilda DiRollo, read constantly to her children, but it was when Linda read 'Sleeping Beauty'—the first book she read by herself—that she was hopelessly hooked. At age eleven, Linda was sent to boarding school in Aberdeen, and then attended Kilgraston School in Perthshire. Over the years, her love of reading was joined by a love of writing, and, as they say, the rest is history. To date, Linda has written over thirty children's books, which have been published in the UK, America and Australia, and have sold hundreds of thousands of copies. She has also written graded books for reluctant readers.

Equally important, Linda has been active on numerous fronts to "encourage all children to discover the delights of disappearing into a good book."

For example, the warm and caring Reading Champion worked closely with the Education Minister of Scotland in support of the government's remarkable Home Reading Initiative. Linda not only attended the launch when the grants were announced, she also read from one of her books. One of her most remarkable recent projects was serving as writer in residence for two primary school classes where she conducted a ten-week creative writing workshop. Creative writing workshops are a dime-a-dozen, of course, but Linda had bigger dreams for her children and took the process one step further. Linda had her young students write and illustrate stories and then *had them published* in a book titled 'A Pocket Full of Magic.' Linda is in great demand as a lecturer and seminar member. She also runs the 'buddy system' of the Society of Authors in Scotland and appears regularly at the world famous Edinburgh International Book Festival.

Linda's deep love of children is best illustrated by the letter she (and her colleges) wrote in February, 2003 to The Guardian newspaper: "We are children's writers, illustrators and editors who oppose a war in Iraq. As people whose professional lives are concerned with the well-being of children, we are appalled by the possibility that thousands of children and their carers would be killed or maimed by a war. We are also concerned that the billions of pounds that our governments are already spending is money that could be spent on the education and care of the next generation of people to live on this earth."

Linda Strachan's advice to parents: "Don't force a book on your children." Her advice to children: "Read as wide a variety of books as possible."

Nick J. Mileti

HULK HOGAN

(Born August 11, 1953 in Tampa, Florida)
REAL ITALIAN NAME: TERRENCE GENE BOLLEA

Hulk Hogan is a Professional Wrestling Star who helped make 'wrestling' appeal to mainstream audiences.

Intending to be a rock musician in the early seventies (who didn't?), his 6 foot, 7 inch, 275-pound body suggested otherwise, and Hogan made the not unexpected move to Venice Beach in California. Once there, Hogan joined the other bodybuilders on the sand, and began his training. He debuted as a wrestler in 1978, and was originally cast in the bad boy role. Nothing much happened, career-wise, but Hogan was a working hard and keeping his eyes opened.

Hogan's big breakthrough came in 1982. What happened was, he appeared in 'Rocky III', playing the roll of 'Thunderlips,' the wrestling villain. The response to Hogan was immediate and emotional—people loved Hulk Hogan and wanted to see more of him. This unexpected, but powerful, reaction to Hogan convinced the powers at the World Wrestling Federation (WWF) they should feature him, as a good guy, in the future.

The strategy worked, and due to Hogan—and the growth of cable television—Hulkamania began, and the WWF prospered. Hogan was made Heavyweight Champion and became the spokesman for the WWF, tirelessly working the tube to promote the 'sport,' often appearing on MTV and other popular youth-oriented shows to lure the young audience. In what was called Wrestle Mania I, Hogan and Mister T (the television actor) did their thing, catapulting Pro-Wrestling into the hearts and minds of an ever-growing dedicated mass of fans.

Hulkamania peaked in what was billed as Wrestle Mania III. The Pontiac Silverdome was filled with 93,000 hysterical fans. They'd gone to watch undefeated Andre the Giant (who played the loveable Giant in the movie 'The Princess Bride') try to take away one of the many titles Hulk Hogan held over the years. The fans got their money's worth. When Hogan picked up, and slammed down, the 7 foot 5 inch, 500 pound Andre the Giant, the screaming could be heard as far away as Detroit.

An actor and ham at heart, The Hulkster (as he is called) fit perfectly into the fantasy world of Pro-Wrestling. Hulk Hogan 'won' and 'lost' championship belts like Marcella Hazan changed aprons. He retired and un-retired as many times as Bill Parcells. He changed promoters and roles. But through it all, the kids love him—he is their hero and champion. Hulkamania reigns! Viva the Hulkster!

Underneath his carefully developed and nurtured macho, show biz image, Hulk Hogan has a heart of gold. He loves kids and spends a good deal of time on charity work, particularly for under-privileged children.

Nick J. Mileti

GIORGIO DUBOIN

(Born in 1959 in Turin, Italy)

Giorgio Duboin is one of the best bridge players in the world—he is a World Master and a Grand Master.

Duboin was once a highly regarded computer programmer, but that phase of his life is history. Bridge slowly consumed Duboin, and bowing to the inevitable, he eventually turned professional. Beginning to play bridge when he was thirteen years old, Duboin quickly became one of the best bridge players in Italy. With Guido Ferraro he won the 1980 European Junior Pairs when he was only twenty-one years old. The team won numerous titles in the 1980's, including twice winning the European Union Open Pairs and Teams.

Duboin began partnering with Norberto Bocchi in the early 1990's and most experts now consider Giorgio Doboin and Norberto Bocchi not only the best pair of bridge players in Europe, but also one of the best pairs in the world.

For example, playing with Bocchi and the other Italians, for the Maria Teresa Lavazza Team, Duboin has won four consecutive European Team Championships— in 1997 at Montecatini, in 1999 at Malta, in 2001 at Tenerife, and in 2002 at Salsomaggiore.

The duo of Duboin and Bocchi have also consistently won tournaments on their own all over the world, including the Silver Medal at the European Pairs Championships in Warsaw in 1999. The Lavazza team, staring Duboin and Bocchi, also won the Gold Medal at the World Bridge Team Olympiad in Maastricht in 2000. This was their first World Championship Title.

In 2001, a very good year, in addition to the European Team Championships and the Spingold Cup, the pair won the Austrian Summer NOT and the Forbo Teams. Successful defense of the Spingold Knockout team title has been very rare over the years. Nevertheless, in 2002, a team that included Duboin won the Spingold Knockout Teams at the end of the American Contract Bridge League's Summer Nationals in Washington.

In 2002, in addition to the European Team Championships and Spingold, Duboin and Bocchi spearheaded the winning team in the European Mixed Championships in Ostend, and the World Bridge Championships (the Rosenblum Cup) in Montreal. In 2003, in the Bermuda Bowl (world bridge team championship), the Italian team which included Duboin, won its third world title in Monaco.

Giorgio Duboin and Norberto Bocchi are generally believed to employ a system based on the ideas of the great Italian master, Benito Gorozzo. As in all card games, of course, a system is only as good as the players utilizing it, and Giorgio Duboin is one of the best who ever played the game of bridge.

Chapter XIII

Illustrious Italians With Non-Italian Names
Born Between 1960 And 1969

Nick J. Mileti

STEVE VAI

(Born June 6, 1960, in Carle Place,
Long Island, New York)

Steven Siro Vai (Siro is his grandfather's name) is one of the greatest guitar players to emerge since Les Paul invented the electric guitar. He is also a songwriter, an orchestrator, a producer, and even a guitar designer. To quote the legendary Joe Satriani "Steve Vai is a huge musician. Most people hear him as a guitar player. They don't see all of the different pairs of pants he owns."

Music has been a part of Vai's life since he began playing the organ at six years of age. But when he picked up a guitar seven years later, his life changed forever. Vai quickly realized that if he wanted the instrument to do what he wanted it to do, he needed lessons. Fortunately, he knew a great guitarist in the neighborhood, Joe Satriani, and started taking lessons from him (at $5.00 each). Vai played with local bands and even formed his own groups throughout his school years, and in 1978, the eighteen year-old Vai enrolled in the famous Berklee School of Music in Boston.

Berklee was another milestone for Vai because he was exposed to a broad range of music and musicians, met his future wife (Pia Maiocco), and hooked up with Frank Zappa. Steve Vai—the youngest musician to ever play with Zappa—toured and recorded with Frank Zappa from 1980 through 1983. Now working out of the West Coast, Vai cut some solo albums and then joined the band Alcatrazz. Then, in 1986, when David Lee Roth left Eddie Van Halen, he immediately picked Vai to fill Van Halen's role.

It was during this time that Vai (with Ibanez) helped design and develop a line of seven string guitars called Jem guitars, which have been popular ever since. Leaving Roth to cut some solo albums, Vai was lured to the band Whitesnake in 1989. Vai left Whitesnake two years later and became busier than ever, writing, producing, recording, touring and even singing.

Steve Vai has had four Grammy nominations, one Grammy Award, and has sold some three million albums worldwide as a solo recording artist (if you include his work with other artists, Vai has sold eleven million).

Today, Vai calls his eccentric, dazzling, showy, classically based music "accessible eclectic." Early on, Frank Zappa called Steve Vai "my little Italian virtuoso." Considering the fact that the term virtuoso is normally reserved for the most brilliant musicians who innovate and change the course of musical history, and considering the fact that Zappa is a rock legend in his own right, the compliment is doubly impressive and significant.

Steve Vai has never stopped growing as a musician and as a man, and nobody expects him to. After all, if he stopped growing, Steve Vai wouldn't be a virtuoso.

Nick J. Mileti

DANA REEVE

(Born in 1961 in New York, New York)
REAL ITALIAN NAME: DANA MOROSINI

Dana Reeve is an actress and singer, but she is most well known for being the wife of actor husband Christopher Reeve (Superman). Her loyalty, love and common sense saved Reeve's life—literally—following his tragic horse-riding accident in 1995, which completely paralyzed the handsome, athletic superstar.

Dana's family hails from Venice, Italy. She attended Middlebury College and studied drama in England. She has appeared on Broadway, off-Broadway, in regional theater, on television and in various cabaret venues. Dana met Reeve in 1987, while performing in Williamstown, Massachusetts. The high-profile couple dated for five years before marrying in 1992. "I wanted to be careful, to be certain," Dana explains. They had a child and led the good life, devoted to each other's happiness. "Dana is the one who sees all the positive sides in me," Reeve said later, "because she has gotten me to lighten up, she is my life force."

Their storybook life came to a crashing end three years after they were married. On May 27, 1995 when Reeve was competing in a riding event in Virginia, in a routine jump his horse stopped in mid-jump, too late for Reeve to adjust. He flew over the horse's head and smashed into the ground. The stunned crowd held their collective breath for Reeve, the star they had come to see perform, but everyone's worse fears were soon confirmed. Christopher Reeve had injured his spinal cord in the first and second vertebrae. Close to death, he was left totally paralyzed and could only breath with the help of a respirator.

"Dana came into the room, Reeve later wrote. "She stood beside me and we made eye contact. I mouthed my first lucid words to her. 'Maybe we should let me go.' Dana started crying. She said 'I am only going to say this once: I will support whatever you want to do, because this is your life and your decision. But I want you to know that I'll be with you for the long haul, no matter what.' Then she added the words that saved my life: 'You're still you. And I love you.'" Dana has stayed at her husband's side ever since that tragic day, and they have become tireless and visible advocates for funding and awareness of spinal cord injuries. The couple established the Christopher and Dana Reeve Paralysis Resource Center to help people (and their families) living with paralysis.

In 2002/3, Christopher Reeve experienced slight movement in his fingers and toes, began to feel hugs from his loved ones, started to breath on his own (off the ventilator, for 90 minutes at a time) and started to speak. The doctors were astonished and mystified. The popular wisdom is that after two years, cases like Reeve's are hopeless; any degree of recovery after seven years is unheard of.

"Severed nerves in your spinal cord can't be repaired by a positive attitude," Reeve says, "but Dana is my medication."

Nick J. Mileti

NICOLAS CAGE

(Born January 7, 1964, in Long Beach, California)
REAL ITALIAN NAME: NICOLAS COPPOLA

Nicolas Cage is a major movie star.

The nephew of famed director Francis Ford Coppola (of Godfather fame)—Cage's father is the director's brother. In fact, Cage was struck with the acting bug while visiting his uncle in Northern California, who, knowing a good thing when he saw it, cast him in his first movie role.

Intense in life as well as in his profession, Cage has always resisting the temptation to play it safe—a disease prevalent in show business. His gambles have paid off handsomely. In 'Birdy,' Nicolas Cage, made his move, and in his break out role as the brooding baker opposite Cher in 'Moonstruck,' he put Hollywood on notice that he could make it on his own and didn't need his family's connections to build a career (he even changed his name to prove it).

The most challenging part Cage has undertaken—out of the forty movies he's made—was making a man sympathetic who wants to drink himself to death. Forsaking his usual high fee for the opportunity to try it, incredibly, in 1995, Cage accomplished exactly that, and more, in the award-winning movie 'Leaving Las Vegas. Cage won an Oscar for Best Actor, a Golden Globe Award, a Chicago Film Critic's Award and a National Society of Film Critics Award for his electrifying performance. The multi-talented Nicolas Cage has reached the top of his profession as an actor, and has begun reaching out as a producer and director.

TALIA SHIRE

(Born April 25, 1946 in Lake Success, New York)
REAL ITALIAN NAME: TALIA ROSE COPPOLA

Talia Shire—Francis Ford Coppola's sister and the aunt of Nicolas Cage—is a first-rate actor, best known for her roles in 'The Godfather' and 'Rocky' movies.

Having spent two years at the famous Yale University School of Drama, Talia was also helped by her brother, Coppola, when he cast her in the original 'Godfather' movie in 1972, when she was twenty-six years old. Since then, Talia Shire has also proven that she has more than sufficient talent to make it on her own. Although she has appeared in over forty films, Talia is most remembered for her roles in the three 'Godfathers' (the complex Corleone daughter) and the five 'Rockys' (the shy, waif-like wife). Shire has received Oscar and other nominations for both dramatic roles. Talia Shire has also begun to produce.

Nick J. Mileti

BROOKE SHIELDS

(Born May 31, 1965, in New York, New York)

A model and actor, Brooke Shields has led a public life from her first days on earth.

Brooke Shield's grandmother, Marina Torlonia, was an Italian Princess, and most people trace Brooke's sultry looks and stately manner to her.

Brooke's mother, Teri Shields, has carefully (and brilliantly) steered her daughter's entire life. When Brooke was only eleven months old, she landed her the plum commercial assignment as the Ivory Snow Baby, photographed by the legendary Francesco Scavullo. By the age of three, Brooke was a runway model and for the rest of her life continued to attract prime national clients (Breck, Colgate and Calvin Klein, for example), and the best photographers (Richard Avedon, for example).

When Brooke was twelve years old, in 1977, she had her acting breakthrough when Louis Malle cast her as the young prostitute in the feature film 'Pretty Baby.' The controversial role made Brooke a major movie star, and her performance in that film is considered her best acting. Her performance in the 1979 hit movie, 'The Blue Lagoon,' however, is the roll for which she is most identified and remembered.

In 1978, at thirteen years of age, Brooke was selected by People Magazine as one of the most intriguing people of the year (the honor was repeated two years later), and she was featured on the cover of the then prestigious Life Magazine no less than three times. Brooke's image was everywhere. Between her fifteenth and twentieth years, 1980-1985, she was featured on several hundred magazine covers all over the world, including Time Magazine as the Face of the Eighties.

Although she has since appeared in numerous television and feature films with important co-stars, Brooke never fully made the treacherous transition from child star to adult movie star. She silenced her critics in 1996, however, when she starred in the sitcom 'Suddenly Susan,' for which she received two Golden Globe nominations in the show's four-year run on NBC.

The television series caused another wave of Brooke Shields mania, and in 1996 People Magazine again named her as one of the most intriguing people of the year, this time also adding her to the list of the 50 most beautiful people in the world (which they repeated in 2000).

Brooke's face and celebrity life-style have served her well over the years. She has dated numerous famous men in romances that have been extensively covered by the celebrity-hungry media.

Smart, as well as beautiful, in 1987, Brooke Shields graduated with honors from Princeton University with a degree in French literature.

VIN DIESEL

(Born July 18, 1967 in New York, New York)

Vin Diesel, with his deep sardonic voice, muscular body and shaved head, is a larger-than-life motion picture action hero—superstar—seemingly crafted for today's global era.

Diesel's mother is Italian and his stepfather (the man who raised Diesel and whom he considers his father) is African-American. Diesel readily acknowledges his mother is Italian, but refuses to discuss the nationality of his biological father, carefully cultivating an air of mystery. "There's something cool about this kind of ambiguous chameleon-like ethnicity," Diesel repeatedly states in interviews. "(Besides) the less audiences know about you, the more they can believe in you as a character . . . Right now, people don't have preconceived notions about who I am. That's the way I want it to remain."

Translation. Vin Diesel is an extremely intelligent man, planning his career with meticulous detail. Diesel feels the ambiguity about his father's heritage (and therefore the ambiguity about his own) gives him the freedom to play characters that cut across racial lines and allows every demographic group to claim him as their own. He's right. In Diesel's breakthrough movie, Steven Spielberg's 'Saving Private Ryan,' he played an Italian-American. In 'Pitch Black' he played a Black. In 'Boiler Room' and 'XXX' his characters were of indeterminate heritage.

Vin Diesel was born as Mark Vincent, and was raised in Greenwich Village in New York City. His stepfather, a drama teacher, helped develop Diesel's interest in the theatre and inspired him to take acting classes at New York University. For several years, Diesel worked as a bouncer in trendy clubs (which is where he got the surname Diesel, while Vin was his nickname in the old neighborhood) while trying to break into show biz.

Twenty-seven years old in 1994, and frustrated by the lack of action, Diesel decided to take things in is own hands. He put a few dollars together and made a short film called 'Multi-Facial,' which he wrote, produced, directed and acted in. He managed to get the piece shown at the 1995 Cannes Film Festival, where it caused quite a stir. Eventually, Steven Spielberg saw the 20-minute film, cast Diesel in 'Saving Private Ryan,' and, as they say, the rest is history. But not overnight. Several films followed, but they were largely ignored. Then came 'The Fast and Furious," in 2001. The low-budget film had a huge opening weekend, which it sustained. The monster hit convinced the Hollywood establishment that Vin Diesel could carry a movie. Get out of the way—Vin Diesel's on a roll. 'Knockaround Guys' was released in 2001, 'XXX' in 2002, and 'A Man Apart' in 2003. And there is no end in sight.

It took thirty-four years, but Vin Diesel is now one of the hottest actors in Hollywood and a major force in the action genre.

MATT LE BLANC

(Born July 25, 1967, in Newton Massachusetts)

As Joey Tribbiani on the wildly popular, long-running NBC prime-time ensemble television series, 'Friends,' Matthew LeBlanc was described by Entertainment Weekly as "a rarity—a hunk with a gift for deadpan comedy."

Matt's mother, Pat, hails from Arce, Italy, and Matt is devoted to her. "My mother is the most important thing in my life," he said recently. "I'm a mummy's boy and proud of it. Girlfriends come and go, but she's always there for me. All my drive and inspiration comes from my mum." In fact, Matt's mother shaped his career. What happened was, when Matt was eight years old, he received his first motorcycle, and before long, he was participating in amateur competitions. Matt's dream was to become a professional motorcycle racer. Needless to say, when his Italian mother learned about this, she almost had a heart attack. She dissuaded Matt from the dangerous path and suggested he do something, anything, less threatening to his health—even carpentry might be fine, after all Harrison Ford started out that way. Matt tried his best—he even trained as a carpenter—but his goals were much loftier.

After graduation from Newton North High School, 5' 11" Matt took his Vince Edwards brooding good looks to New York City, determined to succeed at whatever life held in store for him. Matt's obvious first choice was modeling—he had the perfect look—but decided after trying it, modeling wasn't for him. He had too much ambition and energy for the profession. "Modeling's all about the clothes anyway," he said. "I didn't want to stand still all day having my picture taken just to show off a jacket."

Modeling segued into commercials, and before long Matt began to appear in big-budget national spots. He was cast, and noticed, in commercials for Coca-Cola, Doritos and Levi's 501 Jeans. In 1987, at the Cannes Film Festival, a Heinz Ketchup spot in which he appeared was awarded the Gold Lion Award.

Following these modest successes, Matt's mother suggested that if he could act in commercials with no training, imagine what he could accomplish with training. Consequently, in 1988, Matt began formal training with Flo Greenberg to be an actor. A natural, he landed roles in various New York stage plays, and within a year he gained a starring role in the short-lived television series 'TV 101.' He moved to Los Angeles and garnered a string of interesting television roles. But they were merely prologue.

In 1994, lightning struck. Matt was cast as Joey Tribbiani in the long-running monster—hit 'Friends," and his career was made, artistically and financially. Matt has begun making feature films and is gaining recognition in his fourth medium.

In 1999, the National Italian American Foundation honored Matt LeBlanc for his "contribution to the world of entertainment."

JOELY FISHER

(Born October 29, 1967 in Burbank, California)

Joely Fisher is a singer and actor who is best known for her portrayal of the self-indulgent Paige Clark on the television series 'Ellen.'

Joely's mother is Italian, the singer/actor/business woman Connie Stevens (Concetta Ingolia). Her father is singer Eddie Fisher.

"Raised on the road," Joely traveled with her mother and younger sister (Tricia Leigh Fisher, see below) after her parents divorced in 1969—when she was two years old. Joely has only kind words about Connie Stevens, who single handedly raised her, and her sister, while working full time: "My mom is an amazing human being," she says.

Joely enjoined the life on the road, and it wasn't long until she began joining her mother on the stage to sing and dance. Acting in summer stock led to numerous television roles for the red headed beauty. During the Gulf War, she joined Bob Hope and her mother entertaining the troops in the field.

In late 1994, in its second season, Joely landed her signature role. She debuted as a regular on 'Ellen,' playing Paige Clark, Ellen's egotistical, but engaging, best friend. During a 1995 hiatus from 'Ellen,' Joely starred in a three-month Broadway run of 'Grease,' the revival directed by Tommy Tune. Rejoining 'Ellen,' Joely remained with the series until it left the air in 1998, after five seasons. Joely then relived her childhood (so to speak) and went back on the road. After playing the lead in 'Cabaret' for some 230 performances across America and Canada, she then reprised her role in the show on Broadway. Joely has also appeared in several well-regarded theatrical and made-for-TV movies.

TRICIA LEIGH FISHER

(Born December 26, 1968 in Burbank, California)

Tricia Leigh Fisher, Connie Stevens' younger daughter, is also a singer and actor.

In the late seventies, little Tricia Leigh toured the world with her sister and mother in a successful nightclub act that charmed the customers. In later years, Tricia Leigh portrayed less charming characters—Heidi Fleiss and Monica Lewinsky—in TV movies. Tricia Leigh broke into theatrical movies in 1985 with 'The Stick.'

Several years ago, Tricia Leigh, along with her sister and mother, recorded an album named 'Traditions . . . a Family at Christmas." The album enjoyed brisk sales when released, and is popular every year when the Christmas holiday rolls around.

Nick J. Mileti

MARY LOU RETTON

(Born January 24, 1968 in Fairmont, West Virginia)
REAL ITALIAN NAME: MARY LOU RETONI

In the 1984 Olympics, Mary Lou Retton realized her life-long dream to become an Olympic Champion.

Like most grand dreams, Mary Lou's was not easy to achieve. Here's how she did it.

At the age of eight, Mary Lou watched the great Nadia Comaneci's award—winning gymnastics performance in the 1976 Montreal Olympics and decided that she wanted to be a gymnast, too. Mary Lou's supporting family wisely sought-out Bela Karolyi. Almost immediately, Mary Lou began training with Bela Karolyi, who was Nadia Comaneci's coach. Teacher and pupil agreed to target the 1984 Olympics, which were to be held in Los Angeles, even though they had only eight years to prepare.

Every night after school, and all day on weekends, Mary Lou worked at becoming the great gymnast she dreamed she could be. She pushed herself mercilessly and her progress impressed her demanding coach. By 1983, Mary Lou was American Cup Champion, American Classics Champion, and Chunichi Cup Champion. She was ready for the big show. Or so it seemed.

Early in 1984, actually six weeks before the Olympics, disaster struck. In gymnastics, there could be no worse scenario—Mary Lou Retton had broken the cartilage in her knee.

Closet Italians

The sympathetic doctors reluctantly informed Mary Lou that she needed surgery on her knee and that there was no possible way she could participate in the up-coming Olympics. They went on to explain that the rehabilitation period alone was three months, so with the Olympics just six weeks away, her participation was out of the question. The 4 foot 8 ¾ inch, ninety-four pound Mary Lou Retton was having none of it. Utilizing a work ethic instilled in her by her family, she attacked the problem with a vigor that amazed everyone (except herself).

Mary Lou completed her rehabilitation in an extraordinary three weeks instead of three months. The incredulous doctors gave Mary Lou the green light and the rest is history. Mary Lou Retton won five medals, more than any other athlete at the 1984 Olympics. She won two Bronze metals (Uneven Bars and Floor Exercise), two Silver Medals (Team and Vault) and the Gold Medal for the All Around.

It appears that her saga will be fondly remembered forever. In 1985, Mary Lou was inducted into the U S O C Olympic Hall of Fame, and in 1997, she was inducted into the International Gymnastics Hall of Fame. And, incredibly, in 1993 (nine years after her Olympic triumphs), in an Associated Press national survey, Mary Lou Retton was named 'Most Popular Athlete in America.'

Nick J. Mileti

ASHLEY JUDD

(Born April 19, 1968 in Los Angeles, California)
REAL ITALIAN NAME: ASHLEY CIMINELLA

Ashley Judd is a movie star today because, like Nicholas Cage, she wanted to be successful on her own and not ride her family's coattails.

When her mother, Naomi Judd, and her half-sister, Wynonna Judd, became major Country singing stars, everyone naturally assumed that Ashley Judd would follow in her family's footsteps and become a Country singer.

Instead, Ashley decided to get an education. She attended the University of Kentucky, from which she graduated with honors in 1990. Ashley gave serious thought to the Peace Corps, but Wynonna advised her to pursue an acting career. Ashley took her advice and moved to Hollywood, quickly landing a smattering of small roles in television and features.

In 1993, Ashley Judd broke through when she won the New York Film Critics Circle Award and the Sundance Film Festival's Independent Spirit Award for her role in 'Ruby in Paradise.' Ashley quickly became a darling of the hard-boiled critics and industry—who admire her combination of talent, brains and beauty—receiving an Emmy nomination and Golden Globe nomination for her portrayal of the young Marilyn Monroe in the made-for-TV film 'Norma Jean and Marilyn.'

A series of important roles in theatrical features followed (she has made almost twenty to this point), including the major grossing 'A Time to Kill,' in 1996, and 'Double Jeopardy,' in 1999.

In 1996 and 2000, People Magazine named Ashley Judd one of 'The 50 Most Beautiful People in the World,' and in 1999 named her one of 'The 25 Most Intriguing People.'

Ashley has opened a new career window by appearing on the Broadway stage, playing Maggie in 'Cat on a Hot Tin Roof' to favorable reviews.

In 2001, Ashley married the Italian/Scottish racecar driver, Dario Franchitti, a Scot of Italian descent. The highlight of the reception—held in a Scottish castle—was a performance by Naomi and Wynonna Judd. This is significant because in 1991, after selling over twenty million records and at the height of a solid career, Naomi was diagnosed with the usually life-threatening Hepatitis C. After a farewell tour to thank her fans—one critic called Naomi Judd the most fan oriented superstar in Country music history—Naomi retired and devoted herself to good causes while the doctor's waited for her to die. But Naomi Judd didn't die. Many believe Naomi overcame the illness through sheer will power and good works. She wrote about her life, and that of her family, in 'Love Can Build a Bridge,' which was on the New York Times Bestseller List for several months, and the basis for a successful NBC miniseries.

Chapter XIV

Illustrious Italians With Non-Italian Names
Born Between 1970 And 1979

Nick J. Mileti

LIZA HUBER

(Born February 22, 1975 on Long Island, New York)

LINDSAY KORMAN

(Born April 17, 1978 in Rancho Mirage, California)

JESSE EDEN METCALFE

(Born December 9, 1978 in Waterford, Connecticut)

Incredibly, the young actors Liza Huber, Lindsay Korman, and Jesse Metcalfe are all members of the cast of the teen-orientated television soap opera 'Passions.'

Liza Huber's mother is Italian, the daytime legend Susan Lucci.

Liza originated the role of Gwen Winthrop when 'Passions' debuted on NBC in 1999. She played the beautiful and intelligent debutant for one year, then left the series to pursue personal goals, including modeling and studying her acting craft. In 2002, Liza returned to 'Passions' in the same role, Gwen Winthrop. In 1997, Liza graduated from the University of North Carolina at Chapel Hill. In 2000, Liza was named Miss Golden Globe.

L indsay Korman is Italian and Greek.

On 'Passions' she plays the calculating and scheming Theresa Lopez-Fitzgerald who, ironically, fought with our Liza Huber (see above) for the affections of Ethan Winthrop and finally became wife of Julian Crane (stay tuned). Lindsay and her family moved to Las Vegas when she was a child. Lindsay has been singing professionally since she was eleven years old and is a talented singer as well as actor. She has appeared in several stage plays and has won national vocal competitions, including a Los Angeles Philharmonic's Award for Vocal Opera. Lindsay has been nominated by the Soap Opera Digest as Outstanding Female Newcomer in 1999 (for her work on 'Passions') and for Best Younger Actress in 2000.

J esse Metcalfe is Italian, French and Portuguese.

In 'Passions,' Jesse plays Miguel Lopez-Fitzgerald, the brother of Theresa Lopez-Fitzgerald (played by Lindsay Korman, see above). Jesse's hard work at the Tisch School of the Arts at New York University paid off when he won the part of Miguel over several hundred hopefuls at a cattle call for the part. Obviously, his brooding good looks didn't hurt.

CHAPTER XV

Illustrious Italians With Non-Italian Names
Born Between 1980 And 1989

MYA

(Born October 11, 1980 in Washington, D.C.)

Mya Marie Harrison—stage name Mya—is a rising Rhythm and Blues (R&B) singing star whose style is still evolving, but basically combines Soul and Hip-Hop.

Mya's mother, Theresa, is Italian and her father, Sherman, is African-American.

Mya began dancing when she was two years old. She loved all forms of dancing and believed that was where her future lay. At fifteen years of age, however, Mya began studying music and found her true love. By the age of sixteen, Mya had a recording contract with University Music Entertainment/Interscope Records, and two years later her first album was released to strong sales. Mya is also an accomplished songwriter.

Reflecting her multi-racial heritage, Mya says, "It was important that the songs mean something, no bubblegum songs, but songs that relate and reach and bring people together. It's a people thing, not male or female, not one race, but what everyone can relate to."

FRANKIE MUNIZ

(Born December 5, 1985 in Wood Ridge, New Jersey)

Francisco James Muniz IV (stage name Frankie Muniz) is a teen actor who is best known for his on-going starring role as Malcolm in the FOX Network television series 'Malcolm in the Middle.'

Frankie's mother is Italian and Irish, and his father is Puerto Rican.

Acting since he was a child, Frankie's big break came in 1999, when he was cast in the feature film 'My Dog Skip' and as Malcolm, the misunderstood kid genius of 'Malcolm in the Middle.' In addition to his TV role, in 2002, Frankie appeared in several feature films, including 'Big Fat Liar' and 'Deuces Wild.' Muniz appeared as a teen James Bond in 'Agent Cody Banks,' and its sequel. Still in his teens, Frankie has received numerous nominations and awards for his natural acting ability. In 2001 he received a Golden Globe nomination for Best Actor in a Comedy Series, and has also received nominations for an Emmy Award, TV Guide Award, Golden Satellite Award, The Hollywood Reporter Young Star Award, and The Young Artist of Hollywood Award.

Both Mya and Frankie Muniz are presently considered among the Hottest 25 Teen Stars (along with, for example, Christina Aguilera, Freddie Prinze, Jr. and Britney Spears). The odds are good that one, or both, will break the 'teen-star-jinx' and go on to long and prosperous careers in show biz.

Nick J. Mileti

ALICIA KEYS

(Born January 25, 1981 in New York, New York)
REAL NAME: ALICIA AUGELLO COOK

Alicia Keys is a singing star who blends a range of musical styles—urban, R & B, hip-hop and blues—and even combines classical and modern influences.

Alicia's father was African-American and her mother was Italian. Her father left home when Alicia was two years old so her mother raised the child.

Recognized as a true child prodigy by her mother, Alicia started playing the piano at age seven and writing songs at age fourteen. Her mother made her practice the piano at least one hour every day. "You can quit anything else," her mother told Alicia, "but you can never give up your piano lessons." Like most kids, she hated practicing when she was a child, but thanks her mother now.

"My mother has been a great inspiration to me," she says lovingly.

Her mother enrolled Alicia in Manhattan's Professional Performance High School and provided her with vocal coaching. The results of the hard work and dedication are beyond impressive.

Alicia was discovered by legendary Clive Davis, who wisely gave his soon-to-be star considerable artistic freedom. In 2001, at the tender age of twenty, the classically trained Alicia released her debut album, 'Songs in A Minor.' The album contained the best-selling single 'Fallin,' which she wrote and helped produce. Alicia Keys won five Grammys for her touching first effort, including Song of the Year, Best R & B Album and Best New Artist.

In 2003, the beautiful musician released 'The Diary of Alicia Keys.' The album shot to the top of the charts in its first week of release and sold over two million copies.

In 2004, Alicia Keys was one of three co-headliners—with Beyonce and Missy Elliot—on the 'First Ladies Tour.' The tour played twenty-four of the most important cities in America and sold out the largest, most prestigious venues in those cities. Alicia's reviews were uniformly raves. Popular internationally, Alicia Keys has begun performing all over the world—which she has at her feet.

Alicia credits her Italian mother—and the strict, but loving, upbringing she received—for giving her the ability to handle the demands of super-stardom at her young age (which, to the amazement of one and all, she does with ease).

"My mother is everything to me," Alicia Keys has said. "We are very, very close."

READING GROUP GUIDE

Nick J. Mileti

DISCUSSION QUESTIONS:

1. Which of the following statements best describes the book?
   A valuable historical treatise that proves Italians have had a greater influence on history than was previously believed;
   A book that traces the changing role of Italians in America and the world over the last 2000 years;
   A startling expose of the discrimination Italians have had to endure over the centuries;
   An entertaining 'nightstand reading' book;

   All of the above. None of the above. How would you describe the book?

2. What is the main thing you learned from reading the book?

3. Before reading the book, how many of the individuals listed did you know were Italian? How did you happen to know? After reading the book, do you look at people's names more analytically?

4. Do you blame people for changing their names? Would you have done it? Which individual in the book had the most compelling reason to change his/her name? Which person benefited the most from the Non-Italian Name? Who benefited the least? Why?

5. After observing the large number of women in the book who lost their Italian Name when they married, do you believe females (regardless of nationality) should give up their maiden name when they marry? Why?

6. Which Italian with a Non-Italian Name surprised you the most? Which individual was most interesting? Most sympathetic? Most misunderstood? Who do you most admire in the Book? Who was the most influential in history? Why?

7. How do you explain the fact that a few singers were able to transcend the Rock and Roll Revolution, while most were not? Analyze each case individually.

8. Are you surprised there are so many outstanding Italian writers with Non-Italian names? How do you explain this?

9. Why do you think Sonia Gandhi turned down the position of Prime Minister of India? Do you agree with her decision? Discuss her role in the government of India.

10. Why is Napoleon so controversial? How about Columbus? Do you think criticism of them is based on their Italian Heritage?

11. We all know that economic conditions drove many Italians to leave Italy in the late 1800's and into the next Century. Why did so many of them go to America and Scotland? Why do you think Italians have stopped immigrating to these countries? What is the most significant change you have seen in the role of Italians in America and Scotland over the years?

12. Why did the Renaissance start in Italy? Do you think Italy has lost the pre-eminence in philosophy and medicine it had between 500 and 1000 years ago?

13. How significant was Mussolini's Anti-Semitism Law of 1938 in Italy's subsequent history? Which country benefited the most from the ensuing exodus of brainpower? Compare the ramifications of the Italian Law with the actions of Spain, Portugal and France expelling Jews in previous centuries. Which of these four countries suffered the most? Why? Discuss the different rationalizations each country gave for its actions.

14. What motivates countries to co-opt people? Are their actions usually malicious or innocent? Why do you think the French have been so aggressive in this regard? Is it easier or harder for countries to co-opt people today than it used to be? Why?

15. How many individual entries in the book was it comfortable to read at one sitting? Why?

16. Has the book inspired you to read about any of the individuals in depth? If so, which ones?

17. Were you surprised that there are so many Illustrious Italians with Non-Italian Names? Can you think of any who are not included in the book?

18. Would you recommend the book to a friend? Why?